34.50

GOLD OF AFRICA

Timothy F. Garrard

GOLD OF AFRICA

Jewellery and Ornaments
from Ghana, Côte d'Ivoire, Mali and Senegal
in the Collection of the Barbier-Mueller Museum

Photographs by Pierre-Alain Ferrazzini

Prestel

Copyright © 1989 by the Barbier-Mueller Museum, Geneva, and
Prestel-Verlag
Mandlstrasse 26, D-8000 Munich 40
Federal Republic of Germany

Distributed in continental Europe and Japan by
Prestel-Verlag, Verlegerdienst München GMBH & Co KG, Gutenbergstrasse 1, D-8031 Gilching,
Federal Republic of Germany

Distributed in the USA and Canada by
te Neues Publishing Company, 15 East 76th Street, New York, NY 10021, USA

Distributed in the United Kingdom, Ireland and all other countries by
Thames and Hudson Limited, 30–34 Bloomsbury Street, London WC1B 3QP, England

Cover:
Human head, Côte d'Ivoire/Ghana border region: perhaps Anyi or Abron
(Plate 57, page 203, Cat. 214)

Frontispiece:
The Adiukru of southern Cóte d'Ivoire display their family wealth on the occasion of a "fête de
génération". Most of this jewellery is acquired from neighbouring peoples or imported
from Ghana.
Village of Toupah, sub-prefecture of Dabou. Photo: Jean Paul Barbier, December 1988

Typesetting by typo data gmbh, Munich
Maps by Astrid Fischer
Offset lithography by Gebr. Czech & Partner Ges. für Reprotechnik mbH, Munich
Printed by Karl Wenschow-Franzis Druck GmbH, Munich
Bound by Conzella, Pfarrkirchen

Printed in the Federal Republic of Germany

ISBN 3-7913-0914-5 (English edition)
ISBN 3-7913-0913-7 (German edition)

Contents

417
739.27

Acknowledgments

The American Federation of Arts is proud to have had the opportunity to prepare the American tour of this unique exhibition of African gold jewelry. *Gold of Africa* marks the first such collaboration between the AFA and the Barbier-Mueller Museum in Geneva. Our gratitude extends, above all, to Jean Paul Barbier, president of the Barbier-Mueller Museum.

This catalogue and the exhibition it accompanies represent the culmination of work begun in 1981 by Mr. Barbier and his staff, notably Ingeborg Weber, director of the exhibitions and publications program. We are grateful to Mr. Barbier for engaging the talents of Dr. Timothy Garrard, an authority on the gold trade in Africa. Dr. Garrard is guest curator of the exhibition, and has written a text that is at once lively and informative. The exceptional quality of the color plates is a tribute to the photographic skills of the artist Pierre-Alain Ferrazzini.

I wish to acknowledge those staff members of the AFA who worked on the national tour of this exhibition: Robert M. Murdock, director of exhibitions; Harold B. Nelson, chief administrator for exhibitions; Marie-Thérèse Brincard, exhibition coordinator; and Michaelyn Mitchell, publications coordinator.

The AFA extends its thanks to the museums presenting this exhibition: the National Museum of African Art, Smithsonian Institution, the Metro-politan Museum of Art, the Dallas Museum of Art, the Birmingham Museum of Art, the Tampa Museum of Art, the Art Institute of Chicago, the Detroit Institute of Arts, the Indianapolis Museum of Art, and the J. B. Speed Art Museum, Louisville.

Myrna Smoot
Director, The American Federation of Arts

Foreword

But gold shines like fire blazing in the night, supreme of lordly wealth.

Pindar (c. 518 - c. 438 B.C.),
Olympian Odes

Gold. Mere mention of the word has driven poets to rhapsodical phrases and men to search for Priam's Treasure, the legendary gold of Eldorado, and King Solomon's mines. Fascination with this most precious metal has seized men's minds throughout the ages. It has been skillfully fashioned into objects of beauty by people from the ancient Mediterranean world, Africa, western Europe, eastern and south-eastern Asia, and the Americas. Of these, perhaps the least well known is the art of the West African goldsmith, the subject of this exhibition organized by the Barbier-Mueller Museum, Geneva, and circulated by the American Federation of Arts.

Gold objects from North Africa and Egypt have been studied by art historians and archaeologists, but the regions south of the Sahara have been only cursorily examined. This exhibition, with its focus on West Africa, is therefore of special interest and importance. As Timothy Garrard states in the accompanying catalogue, *Gold of Africa*, the Barbier-Mueller collection of more than 300 objects assembled during the past fifty years is "unique in its size and scope". Most of the objects in the collection date to the nineteenth and twentieth centuries. This, as Dr. Garrard explains, is because very little ancient

West African gold survives. Although the late date for these objects is the reality, some interesting historical hypotheses are proposed in this first extensive exhibition.

"Gold of Africa" is a major undertaking that includes objects from two regions: the arid Sahel and the central West African forest. It enables us to begin to lift the veil of mystery that has surrounded the fabled wealth of once glorious kingdoms and courts. As we examine the objects, our questions multiply. How did the art of goldsmithing originate in West Africa? What were the sources of the precious metal? How was it worked? Who worked it? Why has so little survived? How were ornaments used? What are some of the dominant forms? Not all of our questions can be answered. In some cases, one can only conjecture from the evidence at hand. It is clear, however, that this exhibition increases our ability to understand the beauty, meaning, and technical achievements of West African goldwork.

On behalf of all who will be able to enjoy these treasured works of art, I extend special thanks to Jean Paul and Monique Barbier-Mueller. Through their initiative, the extraordinary accomplishments of West African goldsmiths are magnificently revealed.

Sylvia H. Williams
Director, National Museum of African Art,
Washington, D.C.

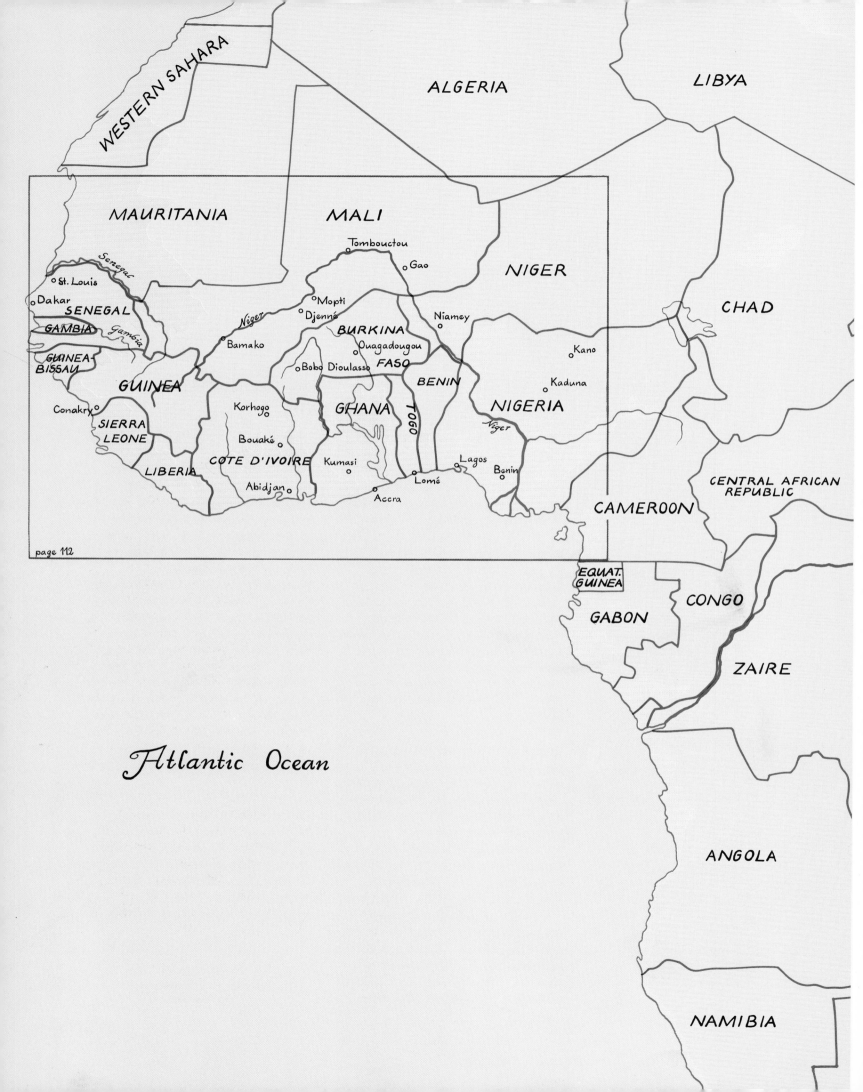

Preface

The collection of jewellery and ornaments presented here by Timothy Garrard has been brought together over a long period extending from the 1920s to the present day. Our most recent acquisitions arrived shortly before this catalogue was printed.

In 1918, at the end of the First World War, my father-in-law Josef Müller began to travel frequently. He usually travelled to Paris and Germany to acquire the paintings that were to make his collection famous, but in 1922 his curiosity led him to make a six-month trip to Africa. He went down the Ubangi by canoe and walked to Brazzaville with a small caravan of porters. From this, his sole visit to the dark continent, he brought back only a few sketches and watercolours, although he had announced in all the villages he visited that he was willing to acquire whatever sculptures and ethnographic objects the people would let him have.

Such an experience hardly encouraged him to acquire on a large scale the statuettes and masks that filled his house at the time of his death in 1977. Here and there he would buy a piece that attracted him, and often a jewel for the lady who was to become the mother of my wife. It was not until the 1930s, when he became friendly with Ernest Ascher and Charles Ratton, that his collection of "art nègre" (a term that included anything exotic) began to expand rapidly.

At that time African gold was attracting enormous prices in comparison with sculpture. A page from Josef Müller's notebook reveals that in the space of a few days he paid 14,000 French francs for a gold ring from Côte d'Ivoire (cat. no. 248) but only 1,600 French francs for a very fine and large Fang statue from the Cameroons.

Owing to this state of affairs Josef Müller devoted only a small part of his resources to buying jewellery, for despite the undoubted excellence of its design such jewellery cannot, from the European point of view, be considered as works of art comparable to the great masterpieces of African statuary.

Well before my father-in-law's death, my wife and I had begun to buy these ornaments. To me their originality and splendour appeared limitless, and their price no longer rose so swiftly — collectors having perhaps realized that "fetish gold" was often less than ten carats.

The painstaking care with which Timothy Garrard has studied this collection over the last two years has truly brought it to life. For many months in Ghana, Côte d'Ivoire, Mali and Senegal, he lingered wherever he could find someone to tell him about these jewels. From time to time he was able to establish friendships with the goldsmiths, such as Diby Koffi, a Baule caster at Bouake, who I had the pleasure to see at work, using a centuries-old technique to make objects destined not only for commerce but also for traditional use by wealthy Baule.

Without more ado, I would like to express my gratitude not only to Tim Garrard, who has become a very good friend, but also to all those who have interested themselves in our project since its inception, and whose support has enabled us to achieve this book and the exhibition. First of all, I thank M. Alain Belkiri, Secretary General of the Government of Côte d'Ivoire (Ivory Coast), and M. Yves Piaget, honorary consul of that country in Geneva, who have facilitated many a journey and shown inexhaustible patience. Next M. Claudio Caratsch, the Swiss ambassador in Côte d'Ivoire, whose sense of curiosity is equalled only by his liking for African traditions. Then Diby Koffi of Bouake, together with Akesse Raphael of Anna. Finally Sylvia Williams, director of the National Museum of African Art in Washington, Cynthia Polsky and Philippe de Montebello, as well as Douglas Newton, whose wish it was that the Metropolitan Museum in New York show these pieces for a period of six months as from September 1989; Myrna Smoot and Marie-Thérèse Brincard, respectively director and exhibition co-ordinator of the American Federation of Arts, who arranged for the exhibition to tour the United States; without forgetting those who have enabled us to assemble a wealth of photographic documentation. And of course I thank my wife Monique, who not only shared every moment of excitement when building this collection, but also prepared the French translation of Tim Garrard's text.

But my last word will be for Josef Müller, who changed the course and meaning of my life. It is to him, who chose some of the finest pieces reproduced here, that I would like to dedicate the results of our work and of our enthusiasm. For this enthusiasm is none other than his own, which we endeavour to maintain.

Jean Paul Barbier

Chapter One

Gold of Africa

The artists of Africa are famed for their works in bronze, wood, ivory and stone. Less well known are their achievements in gold. Yet the objects created by the goldsmiths have great beauty, and are remarkable for their technical sophistication. This book is intended as an introduction to the splendours of the goldsmith's art south of the Sahara.

Outside Egypt, North Africa and the East African coast, with which this study is not concerned, most of the continent's goldwork comes from sub-Saharan West Africa. Here the conditions existed that enabled the goldsmith's art to flourish. In past centuries the region contained many kingdoms and chiefdoms whose rulers sought to demonstrate their power and prestige by artistic display. The common people too, men as well as women, had a natural love of finery. Gold could readily be obtained; there were a number of major goldfields, some of which have been exploited for fifteen hundred years, and the precious metal was widely traded. In consequence goldsmithing developed from a very early period, as an art serving the needs of royalty and commoners alike.

The gold ornaments and jewellery of West Africa have long been known to the outside world. Medieval Arab geographers and travellers left reports of the splendid gold regalia, weapons and horse-trappings owned by the kings of ancient Ghana and Mali. They also mentioned a trade in small twisted gold rings, said to come from "Wangara", the land of gold. From the fifteenth century onwards Portuguese, Dutch and other European merchants also noted the abundance of gold body ornaments worn by some of the people they encountered on the West African coast. Gold is still commonly worn in some parts of the region, and magnificent displays of the precious metal can be seen on ceremonial occasions (fig. 1).

Together with items of gold regalia intended for public display, the goldsmiths of West Africa created a dazzling array of jewellery forms. They were original and inventive. But while their work is African in spirit, they also drew freely for inspiration on the jewellery of North Africa, the Sahara and Europe. This was perhaps inevitable, for they produced what their clients requested, and in West Africa the novelty of foreign fashions has a strong appeal.

West African craftsmen have absorbed the influence of foreign goldwork since remote times. For many hundreds of years ornaments of gold or imitation gold have been imported to the region. In the eleventh century it was reported that a North African goldsmith named Sakan "used to make copper chains and wash them with gold as is done with bridles and send them to be sold in the land of the Sudan" (i.e. south of the Sahara). By the sixteenth century the Portuguese were selling objects of worked gold to the Wolof of Senegal, and three hundred years later European rings, bracelets and other jewellery were regularly copied by coastal African goldsmiths. Some Europeans remarked that the smiths were willing and able to reproduce any pattern shown to them. As a result, one finds among the

Fig. 1 The noble and dignified bearing of West African kings is often enhanced by the magnificence of their attire. The king of the Abron in Côte d'Ivoire, Nana Kofi Yeboa, wears a sumptuous cloth and a rich display of gold jewellery as he sits in state with his gold-covered stool. Photo: Monique Barbier-Mueller, 1986

enormous variety of West African goldwork clear traces of exotic influence.

From an early date African goldsmiths began to adopt European tools (hammers and files) together with European bellows. It is possible that they also had the occasional direct contact

2

Fig. 2   Monique and Jean Paul Barbier-Mueller with a seller of gold ornaments in the Marché Tilène, Dakar, in 1978. In Senegal much of this older jewellery is destined to be melted down and refashioned into new ornaments by the goldsmith.

Fig. 3   Among the Akan of Ghana gold ornaments such as these were frequently melted and recast. At one time the king of Asante required this to be done each year, in order to gain revenue from a tax which he imposed on the recasting. Photo: Jean Paul Barbier

with European goldsmiths. Michael Hemmersam, a goldsmith from Nuremberg, lived on the Gold Coast from 1639 to 1645. A century later a Dutchman sent out for gold prospecting was reported to be gilding spoons and other small objects. Whether such contacts influenced local goldsmithing techniques we cannot say; yet at least one Akan brass *kuduo* vessel is known that has been gilded. One notes, too, that the specialised technique of casting small animals from nature, known to the Akan, had earlier been practised with superb skill by the sixteenth-century goldsmiths of Nuremberg.

Despite the wealth of West African gold jewellery, relatively little seems to have entered museums or private collections whether in or outside Africa. Not only is a considerable outlay required to assemble even a small collection from a single region, but very little is available for public sale. Families and individuals preserve it as their personal treasure, while chiefs and kings rarely part with their gold regalia. Even modern items of traditional design are hard to obtain in West Africa. They have to be commissioned from the goldsmith, and usually the client has to supply the gold and specify the design. Since most goldsmiths work at a leisurely pace, the client must have endless patience.

The Barbier-Mueller Museum of Geneva is thus fortunate to possess a collection of West African gold almost unique in its size and scope. There are about 300 items (1,000 if the gold necklace beads are counted individually), representing all the major regions of West Africa where goldsmithing was practised. The collection was begun in the 1920s by Josef Müller, who acquired about two dozen items from Paris dealers. Over the last thirty years it has been much enlarged by Monique and Jean Paul Barbier-Mueller, with the aim of including pieces representative of the art of each region (fig. 2).

The gold in this collection dates mostly from the nineteenth and twentieth centuries. There are few older pieces for the simple reason that very little ancient West African gold survives. Although the goldsmiths have worked probably for fifteen hundred years, making vast numbers of objects, all but the most recent of this output has vanished. This is due to a variety of causes, of which four deserve special attention: recycling, trade, warfare and the practice of looting burials.

1. Recycling

Since gold is scarce and expensive it is often reused. In West Africa, as elsewhere, jewellery is a form of wealth, and its owner may draw upon it in case of need. Frequently, too, it is not kept when it has become damaged or unfashionable: the owner takes it to the goldsmith to be melted down and made into new ornaments. This practice is common in Senegal, where so much older jewellery has been converted into new that it is rare to find pieces more than forty or fifty years old. They can occasionally be encountered among piles of goldsmith's scrap awaiting the melting pot, being sold by weight without regard to size or quality. While we may regret this loss of older jewellery, the practice has at least served to keep alive the goldsmith's craft, providing new work for the many goldsmiths of Senegal.

In Ghana too, the recycling of gold ornaments has long been the custom. Indeed, at one time it appears to have been made compulsory. It was reported from the Asante capital of Kumasi in 1817 that, by royal decree, all gold ornaments should be melted down and recast into new designs on the approach of the annual Yam Festival. This was a means devised by the king to raise revenue, for he imposed a tax on the recasting.

It is not known for how long this royal decree was in force, but if seriously applied, even for a short period, it could have led to the loss of much older goldsmith's work (fig. 3). This was not an isolated case. According to one oral tradition, on the formation of the Asante confederation in 1701 it was officially decreed that all objects and symbols reminiscent of the past should be destroyed.

In past centuries the Akan states of Ghana fought many wars among themselves, and it often happened that a king or chief was seized in battle. If not beheaded he was held to ransom for an amount fixed in gold, which was payable either in gold-dust or (as frequently happened) in gold

4

Fig. 4   For more than a thousand years West African jewellery and gold-dust were carried north across the Sahara by camel caravans. In Morocco and Egypt much of this gold was minted into coins, such as these dinars of the Abbasid, Fatimid, Almoravid, Mamluk and Saadian dynasties, struck between A.D. 800 and 1600.

Fig. 5   In 1641 the Dutch artist Albert Eckhout painted a man from the Akan kingdom of Fetu. He wears a gold-decorated sword with a large red shell attached to the hilt. The actual sword that the artist used as his model still exists: it was acquired by the National Museum of Denmark in the late 17th century. Photo: Dept. of Ethnography, National Museum of Denmark

ornaments. Similarly, the more rapacious chiefs sought pretexts to impose heavy fines on their wealthier subjects. To meet such demands the victim might have to give up not only personal jewellery but ancestral heirlooms and regalia. The fate of such ornaments was usually to be melted down and converted into gold-dust or bullion.

The endless recycling of gold objects continues today. Although some pieces are still retained as "family heirlooms", both among the Akan and elsewhere, many of these appear to be no older than the colonial period.

2. Trade

All but a tiny fraction of West Africa's gold, whether in the form of gold-dust, nuggets or jewellery, has eventually been exported. It has disappeared from circulation through the currents of long-distance trade.

For centuries worked gold was sent north with the caravans that plied the Saharan routes, bound for North Africa and Egypt. Often it consisted of the "twisted gold rings of Wangara", ear and nose-rings of a type still common in the Sahel region. Some, however, was in other forms. A report of 1809 mentions that an "immense quantity of the gold trinkets of the manufacture of Jinnie" were exported from Jenne and Timbuktu to the Middle East. Another publication of 1756 illustrates a Kulango gold spirit-figure pendant that turned up in Egypt. In 1929 a buried hoard of gold spirit figures, apparently from the same region of West Africa but of archaic style, was discovered in Libya.

In North Africa this imported goldwork, together with gold-dust of the same origin, enabled the various Arab and Berber dynasties to strike a copious coinage of gold dinars. A selection of these, ranging in date from about A.D. 800 to 1600, is shown in fig. 4. They come from mints as far afield as Marrakesh and Cairo.

One dynasty, the Almoravids of Morocco, even established mints on the northern fringe of the Sahara, at Nul Lamta and Sijilmasa, to coin this incoming gold. The dinars of the Almoravids and Merinids were among the most beautiful produced in the Islamic world, and they became famous for their purity and good weight. Many must have been made from West African gold bullion.

From the fifteenth century onwards the West African coast was opened up to European trade. Portuguese, Flemish, Dutch, English, French and Scandinavian merchants sent out ships, and the records suggest that in addition to gold-dust they obtained much worked gold. This included gold beads, necklaces and chains, hair ornaments, finger-rings, bells and bracelets. West Africans, confronted with a tempting array of European goods, were often willing to give up their jewellery in exchange for prestige items such as muskets, chairs and umbrellas.

Virtually nothing survives of this mass of gold taken in four centuries of European trade. The few pieces known to have been acquired in the precolonial period, and still extant in museum collections, seem to be mainly diplomatic gifts sent by African kings to their counterparts in Europe, or curios obtained by missionaries and travellers (fig. 5).

3. Warfare

Warfare (fig. 7) has been responsible for the destruction of many of West Africa's finest gold treasures. Gold is a natural target in time of war, and over the centuries royal treasuries have been ransacked many times. The loss of the golden regalia of the fourteenth-century kings of Mali, and the "gold sceptres and plates" of the rulers of Timbuktu, is due in all likelihood to the numerous conflicts that have swept the region. In the Akan states too, gold ornaments were a frequent casualty. When the Asante king suffered a disastrous defeat at the battle of Katamanso in 1826, to take but one example, he lost not only his wives and daughters but also, according to Reindorf's account, "all his royal badges, state umbrellas, gold-hilted swords, jewels, and the military

6

Fig. 6   Jawbones cast in gold form part of the regalia of some Akan chiefs. A grim reminder of past wars, they emphasise the power of the chief to vanquish all enemies. Cat. 175

Fig. 7   In time of war the Akan frequently removed the skulls, jaws and leg-bones of enemies killed in battle. These were sometimes attached to the royal drums, as seen in this late 19th-century photograph from the Kwahu district. Photo, probably by F. Ramseyer, c. 1890: Basel Mission Archive

Fig. 8   In 1874, and again in 1896, British forces invaded the Asante kingdom. Among the booty taken from the palace in Kumasi were many gold-decorated helmets, swords, sword ornaments and pectoral discs, such as those displayed by this royal attendant. Photo: courtesy of René and Denise David, Kumasi, 1985

chest containing thousands of gold cartouches filled with gold dust instead of gunpowder".

In the case of wars between African kings, the loot of victory rarely survives in identifiable form. On the other hand, the race for conquest in Africa by European powers in the last quarter of the nineteenth century has, paradoxically, preserved for us several spectacular hoards of gold artifacts. In 1893 the French took control of Segou on the Niger, confiscating a treasure of Sahelian gold jewellery that had belonged to Ahmadou and al-Hajj Oumar. In 1874 and again in 1896 British military expeditions entered

Kumasi, where they seized hundreds of items of Asante goldwork (fig. 8). The British also compelled the Asantehene to pay a crushing war indemnity, the first instalment of which was handed over at Fomena in Adanse on 13th February 1874. Sir J. F. Maurice described this event:

The Government gold taker had been brought up from Cape Coast to be ready for any emergency of the kind. He sat on one side receiving the precious metal; on the opposite sat some six or seven of the Ashantees, round a large white cloth of native manufacture, filled with gold plates and figures, nuggets, bracelets, knobs, masks, bells, jaw-bones [fig. 6] and fragments of skulls, plaques, bosses – all of the metal as pure as it can be, and of an endless variety of shape and size. Almost all of these have through them a fine hole for threading to form necklaces or armlets. Besides these, door ornaments and golden nails were thrown in, and a number of odds and ends that must have been wrenched off in the hurry of escape from the palace, and which now added quaintness to the rich handfuls that were poured into the balance.

Among these last items, according to the Frenchman Bonnat, were "two massive gold birds which surmounted the royal throne."

The scene on this occasion was also described by a journalist, Brackenbury:

The leather bag was opened, and the gold … weighed out by the messengers under our little shelter mess-shed at Fommanah. We had with us the official gold-tester from Cape Coast, and he examined every article as it was produced. With the exception of the gold-dust, all was pure virgin gold. Ornaments of every description, masses of what appeared to be broken-up, necklaces and bracelets, large gold plaques, with bosses in the centre, nuggets and ornaments of all sorts, kinds and shapes .... The envoys watched the weighing with the most eager care, and haggled over the 100th part of a grain in the scales .... At last 1000 ounces of gold were carefully weighed out, and then

7

9

The rarity of such finds is misleading, for gold would seem to have been used relatively often in West African burials, notably among the Akan. In past centuries the burial of an Akan chief or rich man was almost always accompanied by gold ornaments and gold-dust. Daniell, in the mid-nineteenth century, described how the limbs of the corpse were "invested with their usual bracelets and other golden ornaments, and the whole body enshrouded in a number of the richest and most sumptuous dresses that can be chosen. If the deceased has been a person of consequence, gold dust is liberally sprinkled over the face and other uncovered surfaces .... Within the coffins of the more affluent are deposited a great variety of native cloths, gold rings and other valuable trinkets, and occasionally a few bottles filled with gold dust ...."

There must have been thousands of such rich burials in recent centuries but none, owing to public sentiment, has ever been officially excavated.

Gold ornaments, nuggets and gold-dust used in burials were in theory sacrosanct, and it was regarded as a heinous offence to dig them up and reuse them without some compelling reason. Thomas Bowdich, after his visit to Kumasi in 1817, wrote that "the gold buried with members of the royal family, and afterwards deposited with their bones in the fetish house at Bantama, is sacred; and cannot be used, but to redeem the capital from the hands of an enemy, or in extreme national distress; and even then, the King must avoid the sight of it, if he would avoid the fatal vengeance of the fetish or deity".

Despite this, Akan burial sites were frequently violated for their gold. In time of war, an invading Akan army would

Fig. 9   A gold pendant earring, dating from the late first millennium A.D., is the oldest manufactured object of gold so far discovered in West Africa. It was found during excavations at the site of Jenne-Jeno in Mali. Here it is worn by a Peul woman of the region. Photo: Michael and Aubine Kirtley, Agence ANA

Fig. 10   This large gold pectoral, excavated near Rao in Senegal, is the finest example of West African goldwork to be found by archaeologists. It dates probably from about the 17th-18th century, and may have come from the burial of a prince. Photo: Photothèque IFAN, Dakar

the envoys were asked for the rest. They declared it could not be given; but a little pressure extracted from various folds of their garments articles weighing about 40 ounces more.

4. Looted Burials

Unlike Central and South America, where archaeologists and illicit diggers continue to unearth a steady stream of treasures, West Africa has little to show by way of buried gold. The archaeological reports of Ghana and Côte d'Ivoire over the past fifty years mention only five minor gold items recovered through excavation: three beads found at Twifo-Hemang, and a small bead and a ring obtained at Efutu, near Cape Coast. Reports from the Sahelian zone are equally meagre. Here the few gold pieces of note so far recovered include an earring of hammered gold from the site of Jenne-Jeno in Mali (dating to the late first millennium A.D.), and an astonishingly beautiful gold pectoral from Rao in Senegal (figs. 9, 10).

dig up the burial places of its opponents in search of gold. In 1718 the graves of the Asante were looted for gold by an invading army from Aowin. In 1807, when the Asante entered Anomabu during their invasion of the Fanti coast, "all the floors of the houses of respectable people, in which it is a custom to bury the dead, were dug up in search of treasure".

While grave robberies by an enemy in war achieved much publicity, less is known of similar events in peacetime; such acts were carried out in great secrecy and the spoils often went straight into the melting pot. But occasionally such events came to light and there was a public outcry, as happened in Accra in 1881 when a number of looters quarrelled among themselves about divisions of the proceeds. In 1874 the Asantehene Kofi Karikari was accused of having removed gold ornaments from the coffins of his predecessors, and subsequently destooled. But the most notorious case involved the famous Golden Stool of Asante (fig. 11). In 1896, when the British seized and deported the Asantehene Prempeh, his followers buried the stool in a secret place to avoid it falling into British hands. In 1920 it was accidentally rediscovered by a group of men who proceeded to strip it of many of its gold ornaments. These were sold or melted down, but the case came to light when one of the ornaments was recognized. The event plunged the Asante into a state of national mourning, and in the subsequent trial the offenders were heavily punished.

To conclude this introductory survey, some idea may be given of the regions of West Africa where gold jewellery is found. It was not used everywhere; over more than half the region the gold-

smith's art did not exist. There were (with possible minor exceptions) no indigenous schools of goldsmithing in Burkina Faso, Liberia, western and northern Côte d'Ivoire, northern and eastern Ghana, Togo, Benin, Nigeria or Cameroon. Indeed, in terms of population the great majority of West Africans did not wear gold in the past, nor at the present day.

Among the reasons for this is the fact that gold was never universally available. In past centuries it was exported along well-defined channels, and many regions did not participate in the gold trade. The precious metal was absent from several of the richest and most powerful West African kingdoms which as a result did not develop a tradition of gold jewellery – there was no goldsmith's art at the courts of the Mossi kings, nor those of Dahomey, Yorubaland or Benin.

Taken as a whole the gold jewellery of West Africa may be considered as coming from two broad zones:

(1) The arid Sahel (which borders the Sahara desert, extending from Senegal eastwards to Mali and Niger), together with parts of the western savanna and forest region of Guinea and Sierra Leone;

(2) the central West African forest of Ghana and Côte d'Ivoire, a region occupied by the Akan and Akan-related peoples.

In the following chapters these peoples and their gold jewellery will be described.

Fig. 11   The Golden Stool of Asante was hidden in 1896 to avoid it falling into British hands. When accidentally rediscovered in 1920, some of its gold ornaments were stolen and melted down. Today it is sometimes displayed on great public occasions, such as the Yam Festival of Kumasi. Photo: courtesy of René and Denise David, Kumasi, 1986

Chapter Two

Sahara, Sahel and Senegambia

The passionate love of jewellery shown by the women of North Africa is shared by their sisters to the south – in the Sahara desert, the Sahel, and the region of the Senegal and Gambia rivers. Here, until very recently, copious quantities of traditional ornaments were worn. Many are of silver, a metal preferred by peoples such as the Tuareg, but gold jewels were also common and eagerly sought by all who could afford them, notably in southern Mali and Senegal. Today, unfortunately, gilded silver has ousted true gold almost everywhere, and the fine older jewels have all but disappeared.

The items of gold jewellery most often seen are small rings, which may be plain, or decorated with a cross-hatched design, or twisted into a torque-like shape (cat. no. 12). These are mentioned in medieval Islamic texts as an important item of commerce in the trans-Saharan gold trade. Al-Bakri, for instance, noted around 1067–68 that they were exported from the Saharan town of Audaghust. Such rings may be worn either singly or in a row along the edge of each ear, or in the nose, or sometimes as a forehead ornament.

One of Africa's most magnificent jewellery forms is found among the Peul women of southern Mali. Here, in the Mopti, Jenne and Macina regions, twisted gold earrings achieve their finest development (fig. 12). They are hammered into a four-lobed shape of great elegance, often embellished with engraved designs. Some attain an enormous size, weighing up to 300 grams each. They were noted by Mungo Park during his travels in 1797–98; he described them as "massy and inconvenient", adding that they were "commonly so heavy as to pull down and lacerate the lobe of the ear; to avoid which, they are supported by a thong of red leather, which passes over the crown of the head from one ear to the other".

In recent times a kind of elongated ear-clip has become popular, especially in Senegal. A number of small rings are set along its length, making unnecessary the piercing of multiple holes along the edge of each ear (fig. 20).

One of the most graceful gold jewels, found in all the Sahelian countries, is an ornament worn at the throat on a very short chain (fig. 22). It occurs in two main forms. One is a swirling motif somewhat resembling a swastika, known in several local languages as the "claws of the lion" (fig. 21). The other is a quatrefoil surmounted by a stylized flower.

Everywhere lavish quantities of beads are worn, of all shapes, sizes and materials. Some are highly prized. The gold beads are of openwork filigree, or constructed from sheet metal adorned with tiny applied spheres of gold (granulation), arranged in patterns with immense skill. Spherical and ovoid shapes predominate, but tubular and bicone beads also exist in different sizes.

Fig. 12 Among the finest gold ornaments of the Sahel are the Peul earrings worn in the Mopti, Jenne and Macina regions of Mali. These attain an astonishing size, and they can weigh up to 300 grams each. To prevent injury to the wearer they are sometimes supported by a cord passing over the head. Cat. 18-20

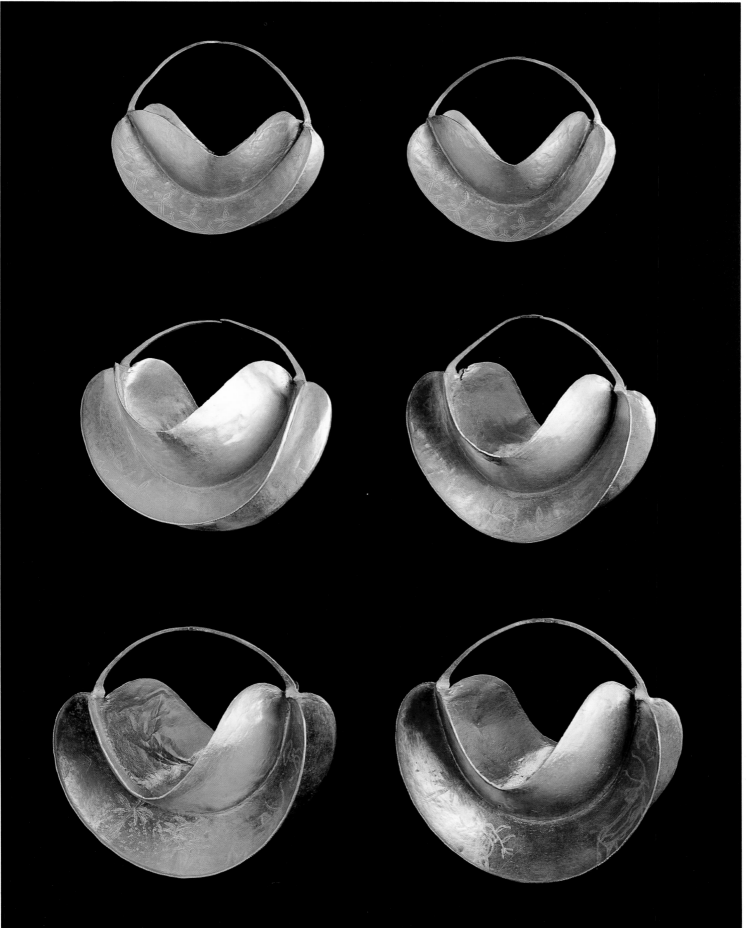

Fig. 13   The gold jewellery of the Sahel was
strongly influenced by that of the Islamic world.
These 11th century gold beads of the Fatimid
period, found in Israel, bear a striking resemblance
to those that can still be seen in Senegal and Mali.
Photo: courtesy of Israel Museum, Jerusalem

Fig. 14   A large gold bicone bead from Mali. Such
beads are often profusely adorned with
granulation, a technique in which tiny granules of
gold are attached to produce a rich, shimmering
effect. Cat. 31

Fig. 15   In the riverside town of Mopti, on the
Niger, Peul women can be seen wearing superb
bicone pendants of gold, together with other
traditional jewellery such as four-lobed earrings
and amber beads. Photo: M. Renaudeau, Agence
Hoa-Qui

13

Gold bicone beads (fig. 13) are widely
distributed in Mali, Guinée and Senegal,
the largest and most splendid coming
from towns along the Middle Niger
(fig. 15).

Similar gold bead shapes have existed
for centuries in the Islamic world. They
occur throughout North Africa, Egypt
and the Middle East, as well as in Spain,
much of which was once under Muslim
rule. A hoard of eleventh-century
Fatimid gold jewellery, found in a pot at
Caesarea in Israel, includes forms that
bear a striking resemblance to those
from the West African Sahel (fig. 14).

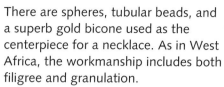

14

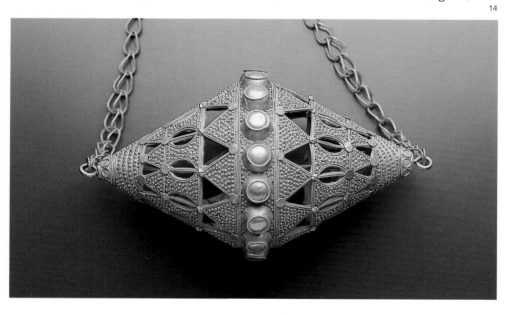

There are spheres, tubular beads, and
a superb gold bicone used as the
centerpiece for a necklace. As in West
Africa, the workmanship includes both
filigree and granulation.

Gold pendants of many shapes are used
as jewels for the hair, or suspended over
the forehead. These include small jingles,
amulets, teardrop or pear-shaped balls,
cruciform and hemispherical pendants,
and a variety of small, ornate hollow
ornaments. The Tukulor make small
trefoil pendants of great delicacy (cat.
nos. 36, 37), usually worn as a series on
forehead or neck. The exceptionally fine
granulations on these ornaments
produce a shimmering effect.

On festive occasions the Wolof women
of Senegal adorn their elaborate
coiffures with gold jewels. Among these
are two popular forms, a pear-shaped
globe and a kind of compressed sphere
surmounted by a stylized flower, both of
considerable size and weight. Several of
these are worn in a cluster on one or
both sides of the head (fig. 26). Similar
though smaller ornaments are found in
Guinée and Mali. According to a Peul
goldsmith of Jenne (who claimed
to have heard it from his grandfather),
these forms were introduced to the
Sahel by the Moroccans.

Up to the nineteenth century gold coins
were commonly pierced for use as
pendants, being worn in a row on the
forehead. They are called *mutukal* (Peul,
Sonrai, Tukulor), *mɛnkɛl dɛ* (Tukulor) or
mɛnkalɛ (Sarakole), names that derive
from the Arabic *mithqal*, a synonym for
the gold dinar (fig. 4). Today most of
these have disappeared, but silver coins
are still worn in the same way.

Other kinds of gold pendant were
displayed on a necklace or chain. One, a
hollow cylinder with openwork designs

Fig. 16   In the Middle Niger towns, women too poor to afford gold may wear imitation jewellery of baked clay (above) or golden-coloured straw (below). The latter, known as "Timbuktu gold", is so realistic that it may be mistaken for the precious metal at first sight. Archives Barbier-Mueller

Fig. 17   Twisted gold earrings have been worn in the Sahelian countries probably since the first millennium A.D. They are often imitated in yellow silk (above) or painted clay (below). Archives Barbier-Mueller

Fig. 18   The Maures were reported to be wearing gold in Roman times, and although most of their women now wear silver, some gold jewellery can still be seen in the desert towns of Walata and Timbuktu. Richly ornamented pendants of gilded silver sometimes form the centrepiece for a necklace of silver, ebony and carnelian beads. Cat. 29

16

17

and granulation (perhaps a kind of amulet case), is known as a "weaver's shuttle" in Sonrai. It is of Moroccan origin, according to some goldsmiths of Senegal. Other Senegalese forms were inspired by European jewellery: they include butterflies, stars, hearts and a variety of fantastic shapes. Elaborately wrought baskets of flowers, some of massive proportions, have long been popular among the Wolof (fig. 29). Other items of gold jewellery include a variety of elaborate chains, bracelets, finger and toe-rings and small bells.

The jewellery so far described is today worn only by women, but in the more

distant past it was not uncommon for men in some parts of the region to adorn themselves with gold hair-ornaments, earrings, bracelets and finger-rings. Similar customs were reported by early visitors to the Gold Coast and south-eastern Côte d'Ivoire. The more important kings of the Sahel wore gold jewellery, and some used gold to adorn the weapons of their attendants.

Little is known of the gold jewellery made for men. It has vanished virtually without trace – although the famous gold pectoral disc and associated jewellery found at Rao in Senegal may have been from the burial of a prince (fig. 10). The use of gold jewellery by men lingered in Senegal until the nineteenth century; its disappearance there and elsewhere in the Sahel was due to the advance of Islam, which discouraged such practices.

In the Sahelian countries gold jewellery is not exclusively for the rich. Poor families, notably among the Peul, struggle to provide their womenfolk with earrings and other essential ornaments of gold. But where even this is beyond their means, they buy imitation jewellery of baked and painted clay (figs. 16, 17). At Timbuktu the very poor (and the tourist) can purchase realistic imitations of goldwork made from beeswax and golden-coloured straw: these are called "Timbuktu gold" (figs. 16, 28).

This brief survey concludes with an account of the peoples most noted for their fine jewellery in the Sahara, Sahel and Senegambia.

1. The Maures

Numbering perhaps three quarters of a million, the Maures occupy an enormous

Fig. 19   The jewellery of the Maures, in the western Sahara, is related to that found in North Africa. Gold ornaments have become rare, but those of silver or silver-gilt remain popular. Photo: M. Renaudeau, Agence Hoa-Qui

Fig. 20   The Sarakole women of Senegal wear a rich assortment of traditional jewellery, including filigree gold spheres and ear-clips with multiple gold rings. Photo: Labitte, Photothèque IFAN, Dakar

territory. They are scattered throughout the vast expanse of the western Sahara, as far north as Morocco, and in the towns and villages of Senegal and southern Mali.

19

The Maures speak a language called Hassania, an Arab dialect strongly influenced by Berber. They call themselves *Bidani*, plural *Bidan* or *Biwan*, meaning "white man". In reality, like all Saharan peoples, they are of very mixed origins, descended in part from the nomadic Sanhaja Berbers who roamed the deserts in the first millennium A.D., and in part from the waves of Arab invaders who swept through North Africa during the same period. Their ancestors also included the former black population of the southern Sahara, and the large numbers of black slaves drawn from West Africa over many centuries. This last segment of the Maure population is still physically distinct.

The Maures formed a vital link between North and West Africa. Berbers from southern Morocco are thought to have made contact with the lands south of the Sahara by the first centuries A.D. Their possession of camels enabled a regular trans-Saharan trade to develop. They came to control not only the desert routes for the gold trade but also, by the eleventh century, the gold-rich kingdom of ancient Ghana; under the Almoravid dynasty their empire extended from Spain to Senegal.

The Maures and Berbers have long been noted for their elaborate jewellery. In the first century A.D. the Roman author Strabo wrote that they wore gold ornaments. Today, as strict Muslims, the men have abandoned this practice and wear only silver. The women, however, still have some ornaments of gold in addition to a profusion of silver. In certain regions, notably around Walata, rich parents continue to deck their girls in fine jewellery of gold or gilded silver (fig. 18).

Walata, described by Ibn Khaldun as the furthest outpost of Mali, has long been associated with gold. In the mid-fourteenth century al-Umari wrote that it was situated in "a land of desolate regions and unknown roads; those who journey through it are impelled to risk its dangers only by the great profits which they make out of the Sudan, for they set out with valueless articles and return with bullion as their camels' burden". The gold trade of this town attracted metalworkers, and even today several families of goldsmiths remain.

Maure society has a prominent caste of artisans (*ma'alem*, plural *ma'almin*), who include many metalworkers. They work in all metals: iron, brass, copper, gold, silver and aluminium. In the past goldsmithing was an important aspect of their craft; its decline may be due more to the scarcity and high cost of gold than the fact that the Maures are today exclusively Muslim.

2. The Tuareg

For centuries the Tuareg have lived in the eastern Sahara, and they frequent all the towns along the Middle Niger. Like the Maures they are of mixed ancestry, being descended partly from old Saharan peoples, partly from Berber pastoralists and partly from black slaves. They speak a form of Berber.

In late Roman and Byzantine times their ancestors the Garamantes played some part in North African trade, and may have been an important link between Carthage on the Mediterranean coast and Jenne-Jeno on the Middle Niger.

The Tuareg claim to be descended from a Berber queen named Tin Hinan, whose reputed tomb, dating to about the fourth century, was opened some years ago. It was found to contain a skeleton with bracelets and other jewellery both of gold and silver. This suggests that the ancestors of the Tuareg may once have worn gold. Today their jewels are of silver, with a little brass or copper.

There is a caste of artisans (*enhad*, plural *inadan* or *enaden*) who include many metalworkers. These are at the same time blacksmiths and silversmiths.

3. The Sarakole

The name Sarakole, although said to mean "white man", is applied to a black population also known as Soninke or Marka. Like the Maures and Tuareg they are of mixed origins, being descendants of Sanhaja Berbers as well as various West African peoples. They are widely scattered in the Sahel, and form an enterprising group of merchants and artisans.

21

court. Al-Bakri, in the eleventh century, mentioned the use of gold for personal ornaments and regalia, from which it is clear that the goldsmith's art was highly developed:

The king adorns himself like a woman, wearing necklaces round his neck and bracelets on his forearms, and he puts on a high cap decorated with gold and wrapped in a turban of fine cotton. He sits in audience ... in a domed pavilion around which stand ten horses covered with gold-embroidered cloth. Behind the king stand ten pages holding shields and swords decorated with gold, and on his right are the sons of the vassal kings of his country ... their hair plaited with gold .... At the door of the pavilion are dogs of excellent pedigree who hardly ever leave the place where the king is, guarding him. Round their necks they wear collars of gold and silver studded with a number of balls of the same metals.

Fig. 21   A golden throat ornament worn by a woman from Niger, forming the central element of a neck-chain. Photo: Labitte, Photothèque IFAN, Dakar

Fig. 22   Gold throat ornaments are popular in Senegal, Mali and Niger. This distinctive form is known as the "claws of the lion" in several languages of the region. Cat. 26

Fig. 23   Peul women are noted for their rich assemblages of jewellery and beads, often worn in conjunction with an elaborate coiffure. The large twisted earrings for which they are famous may be of hammered silver or gold. Archives Barbier-Mueller

22

The wealth of ancient Ghana was drawn from the goldfields of Bambuk and Bure, further south in present-day Senegal and Guinée. In an attempt to control this wealth the Berber Almoravids invaded the kingdom around 1076–77, imposed a tribute on its people and tried to convert them to Islam. These events caused many Sarakole to flee, among them, very probably, goldsmiths and gold-traders. Some migrated to Mali and Senegal.

To this day Sarakole women retain their fondness for traditional gold jewellery, which includes twisted earrings, cruciform pendants, globular jewels for the hair, swastika-shaped throat ornaments, and many pendants and beads of other kinds. One graceful pendant, a filigree sphere, is known as *kangoubo*, "golden calabash". Silver and gold bracelets are also worn.

At some time in the first millennium A.D. their Soninke ancestors founded the kingdom of Ghana or Wagadu, which had a legendary reputation among Arab writers for its wealth of gold. Many caravans came to its capital, a city close to the present border between Mali and Mauritania. Its presumed site is today known as Kumbi-Saleh, which was not the original name of the capital but simply means "tumulus cemetery" in modern Bamana.

North African visitors were impressed by the quantity of gold used at the king's

The Sarakole metalsmith is called *tage*, plural *tagon*. He works in all metals. In some towns a worker in precious metals is distinguished by the name *garanke* or *sawaare*.

4. The Tukulor

Living mainly in Senegal and Guinée, the Tukulor are of part Peul, part Sarakole ancestry. They speak a western dialect of Peul. Their name derives from Takrur, a kingdom that they established in the first millennium A.D. in the vicinity of the Senegal river. Takrur was known to early Arab writers, and drew its wealth in part from the trans-Saharan gold trade. Cuprous metal and other North African imports were reaching it by the late first millennium, probably in exchange for the gold-dust of Bambuk. This gold may have been traded principally to Morocco along the caravan routes of the western Sahara.

Tukulor women share with their neighbours a love of abundant personal jewellery, which bears some stylistic resemblance to that of the Maures. Goldwork (or today gilded silver) is, however, more common than among the Maures, probably because the Tukulor had ready access to the precious metal.

The many Tukulor metalsmiths are known as *bahilo*, plural *wahilbe*. They work in silver and gold. Many of their jewels are constructed from double sheets of hammered metal which gives them a solid, massive look, though in fact they are hollow. The surfaces of these jewels are often profusely adorned with granulation (cat. nos. 36–40).

In addition to the universal twisted gold rings, worn in both nose and ear, Tukulor women have a liking for heavy gold chains and necklace pendants, hair and throat ornaments, and gold beads of various sizes.

5. The Peul

The Peul (also known as Fulbe, Fulani, etc.) are a large, heterogeneous group numbering almost ten million. An amalgam of various peoples, they are scattered throughout the Sahel and northern savanna from Senegal to Chad and Cameroon. Many are nomadic cattle-keepers, others sedentary traders. Historically they made a late conversion to Islam but then became some of its most zealous adherents, fighting a series of "holy wars". In the eighteenth and

Fig. 24 Ancient sites in the Jenne region have yielded numerous items of jewellery in cuprous metal, such as the assortment of bracelets shown here. But despite the wealth reported by Arab chroniclers, the only gold so far discovered is a small earring (fig. 9). Archives Barbier-Mueller

24

nineteenth centuries they founded feudal Muslim kingdoms in Guinée and Mali, conquered the Hausa states of northern Nigeria and came to wield considerable power.

Peul women make lavish use of traditional jewellery, which includes rich necklaces of amber, glass and carnelian beads (fig. 23). Silver Maria Theresa dollars and other coins are pierced and worn in a row on the forehead, while wrists and ankles are adorned with heavy bangles of silver or brass. Gold ornaments are also common. Many Peul

women wear a series of small twisted gold rings along the edge of each ear, in the septum of the nose and suspended from the forehead (fig. 15). These are not reserved for special occasions but worn daily; Peul women can often be seen magnificently decked in jewels while trading in the market, selling milk or going about daily domestic tasks.

The best known Peul ornaments are the large gold earrings hammered into four lobes (fig. 12). These are made by Peul goldsmiths in the Mopti, Jenne and Macina region, and also, according to some, by the Bamana and Sarakole.

Peul metalworkers are called *bahilɔ*, plural *wahilɔbe* or *wahilbe*. This name applies particularly to blacksmiths; the goldsmiths are distinguished by the name *bahilɔ kange* or *tafowo*, plural *tafoobe*. According to one Peul goldsmith working near Jenne, his people first learnt the art of goldsmithing from the Sonrai.

6. The Malinke, Khassonke, Bamana and Diula

The various Mande peoples are a dominant presence in Mali and Guinée, where for centuries they have been active as gold-traders and goldsmiths. They exploited the goldfields of Bambuk and Bure, and developed the commerce of the Middle Niger region. Of special importance were the Mande Diula, a class of professional traders who set up a commercial network spanning enormous distances. Their donkey caravans plied routes through half of West Africa, and journeys often took a year or more. Mande caravans travelled from Sierra Leone to Jenne and from Jenne to the Akan forest zone. As middlemen the Mande came to control much of the gold trade. Their language, notably the dialect of the Diula, has become a widespread lingua franca.

In the course of the first millennium A.D. a number of major commercial centres grew up in the Middle Niger region. Among these were Jenne and Timbuktu, towns that for centuries played a prominent role in the trans-Saharan gold trade. Jenne (whose original site is today known as Jenne-Jeno, "ancient Jenne") was flourishing by the fourth century A.D., importing cuprous metals (fig. 24) through long-distance trade and, presumably, exporting gold.

In the thirteenth century the old kingdom of Ghana fell to Malinke conquerors, who established in its place the empire of Mali. Spanning not only the entire Middle Niger region but also the goldfields of Bambuk and Bure, Mali had access to an extraordinary wealth of gold. Caravans from North Africa and Egypt came frequently to the rich Middle Niger towns, ambassadors were exchanged, and the fame of Mali reached medieval Europe.

One of the kings of Mali, Mansa Musa, made a famous pilgrimage to Mecca in 1324. He passed through Egypt where his fabulous wealth of gold deeply impressed contemporary chroniclers. A generation later a North African visitor to the Malian court described the lavish use of gold, both for personal jewellery and as an adornment for regalia, musical instruments and weapons of war.

The prosperity of Mali lasted several hundred years, and gave rise to a rich tradition of goldsmithing that survives until the present day. The jewellery types common throughout the region are similar to those worn by the Sarakole. Metalworkers are known generally as *numu*, but the term applies more particularly to blacksmiths. In some

25

Fig. 25 The older jewellery of the Wolof was much influenced by that of their neighbours, the Maures and Tukulor. Here beads and pendants of various forms are worn across the forehead, and suspended from the hair. Photo: Labitte, Photothèque IFAN, Dakar

regions the goldsmiths are distinguished by the name *lorhon* or *sanu fagala* ("killer of gold").

7. The Sonrai

The Sonrai are a people of highly mixed ancestry who can be found in all the towns along the Middle Niger, from Jenne and Timbuktu eastwards to Gao. They share with the other peoples of the region a love for rich jewellery, and Sonrai smiths have for centuries worked

26

Fig. 26   Ornate pear-shaped jewels of considerable size and weight are popular among the Wolof of Senegal. They are worn in clusters of three attached to each side of the head. Photo: M. Renaudeau, Agence Hoa-Qui

Fig. 27   Traditional Wolof jewellery is noted for its rich variety of forms. Women sometimes wear a set of ornaments weighing up to half a kilogram. Cat. 1, 3-5, 7

gold, silver, brass and iron. As a group they are called *djam*, plural *djamyo*. Blacksmiths are known as *guru djam* and goldsmiths as *wura djam*.

The Sonrai town of Gao, on the eastern bend of the Niger, had become the capital of a small kingdom by the late first millennium. It was wealthy and of great importance in the trans-Saharan trade. In the second half of the fifteenth century its ruler Sonni Ali attacked

Mali, seizing Timbuktu and Jenne and transforming his kingdom into a far-flung empire. Under his successor Askia Mohammed the Sonrai empire enjoyed a period of great prosperity. In 1591, however, it fell to the Moroccans, whose armies invaded the Middle Niger region and installed their own rulers in the major towns. In succeeding centuries the region became politically unstable, with a rapid succession of weak and ineffective rulers, and the gold trade eventually declined.

8. The Wolof

The Wolof are the largest ethnic group in Senegal, numbering 1.5 million. About the fourteenth century they established the kingdom of Jolof, which appears to have been a successor state to Takrur.

This broke up two centuries later into the smaller rival kingdoms of Jolof, Walo, Baol and Cayor. These kingdoms drew wealth from trade, having contact not only with their Maure and Tukulor neighbours but also with the kingdom of Mali. Small quantities of gold were traded, much of it from the goldfields of Galam and Bambuk which lay to the east.

As a coastal people the Wolof were among the first West Africans to make contact with Portuguese explorers and merchants in the fifteenth century. The trader Andre Alvares de Almada noted in the 1590s that they had a liking for both gold and silver jewellery. They bought silver coins from the Portuguese, melting them down to make rings and chains. They also purchased objects of worked gold, apparently from the Portuguese, which implies that even at this early date they were becoming familiar with European jewellery.

28

Fig. 28   North African influence is evident in some jewellery from the Sahel. These Malian pendants are of straw, plaited to imitate filigree goldwork. Archives Barbier-Mueller

Fig. 29   Much jewellery from Senegal is of European inspiration. This basket of flowers has been a popular design among the Wolof throughout this century. Cat. 43

Among the Wolof, gold ornaments have long been popular (fig. 27). They were formerly worn (as on the Gold Coast) by both men and women. With the spread of Islam from the late eighteenth century onwards men abandoned the wearing of gold, but women continue to regard it as an essential sign of wealth and prestige, and sometimes possess a set of ornaments weighing up to half a kilogram. Jewels for the hair are displayed to maximum effect in conjunction with large and elaborate coiffures. Earrings, necklaces, throat ornaments, chains, pendants, brooches and bangles, together with finger and toe-rings, are considered an important part of the ensemble.

Wolof metalworkers are known as *teug* or *teugu*, irrespective of the metal they work. In practice, however, a distinction has grown up between the black-smiths, who make tools and agricultural implements, and the jewellers, who specialise in working gold and silver.

The name *teug* or *teugu* is of considerable interest, for it closely resembles the Sarakole term *tage*. This similarity suggests that metalworking may have been introduced to the Wolof

by Sarakole smiths, perhaps from the old kingdoms of Ghana and Takrur. One can scarcely doubt that the more traditional forms of Wolof goldwork were influenced in the distant past by their neighbours to the north and east.

The gold jewellery of the sub-Saharan region exhibits an astonishing complexity and variety. It is not truly homogeneous in style, but rather belongs to a spectrum of related styles extending from the Atlantic coast to Lake Chad. It is far from easy, and sometimes impossible, to assign a precise ethnic or geographical provenance to a given item. There are no neat stylistic divisions. Forms and motifs were widely copied, often with only slight variation. Goldsmiths often travelled and worked far from their homeland. And jewellery itself some-times strayed far from its place of origin (cat. nos. 27, 28).

This traditional goldwork is the product of multiple influences, some local and others exotic. Older pieces are often reminiscent of the mixed Berber/Islamic/ Jewish styles of North Africa, and call to mind Moroccan or Egyptian work. But while close to the North African genre, they are at the same time distinctively West African.

Less obvious, but present to a greater or lesser degree, is the influence of European jewellery styles. In the Sahara and inland Sahel this is a recent phenomenon, but in Senegalese goldwork the influence of Portugal and France has long been apparent (fig. 29). Probably by the seventeenth or eighteenth century Wolof goldsmiths were beginning to imitate European forms. The goldsmiths of St. Louis, at the mouth of the Senegal river, have for generations made jewellery to order for

European clients. At the same time they have followed and improved on European jewellery fashions for the elegant ladies of the coast (fig. 142).

During the last hundred years European influence on Wolof jewellery styles has become especially marked. Machinery, tools, chemicals, techniques and pattern books have been imported wholesale, notably from France, and throughout

It is notable that Wolof jewellery makes extensive use of the filigree technique. This knowledge of filigree, and the use of drawn wire and of iron or steel drawplates, may reflect links with North Africa via the Maures. In Wolof hands, however, the technique was further developed and put to new ends. Goldsmiths began to use filigree to imitate mass-produced European jewellery, often with great success. As an example of this, the gilded wirework brooches in the form of a butterfly (fig. 30), popular in Europe early in this century, were admirably copied by Wolof smiths, and remained fashionable among the ladies of Senegal until about the time of independence (fig. 31).

The study of Saharan and Sahelian jewellery is still in its infancy, and this chapter is no more than a general introduction to a complex and fascinating subject. It is clear, however, that the highly accomplished goldsmiths of the region actively developed their craft under the stimulus of new ideas, a process in which the jewellery of North Africa and Europe played a significant part. These external influences are much less evident further south, among the Akan and Akan-related peoples of Ghana and the Côte d'Ivoire, whose goldwork is considered in the following two chapters.

30

Fig. 30   Wolof goldsmiths were often inspired by the European filigree jewellery produced earlier in this century. Models, such as this silver butterfly brooch of European manufacture, were closely copied in Dakar and Saint Louis. Archives Barbier-Mueller

Fig. 31   A Wolof butterfly brooch of silver-gilt filigree can be seen among the rich jewellery worn by this lady of Dakar half a century ago. Photo: Dakar, 1942, Photothèque IFAN, Dakar

the colonial period Wolof goldsmiths made the voyage to Europe for the many colonial exhibitions. There they obtained highly prized certificates and diplomas, and learnt European techniques of jewellery manufacture. Returning home, they put this knowledge into practice, and as a result much Wolof jewellery, though superbly crafted, is today highly Europeanised. It is now difficult to discern any truly indigenous style of Wolof goldsmithing. The more traditional jewellery draws heavily for its inspiration on Maure and Tukulor forms, and on those popular in Mali and Guinée, while the greater part of recent output would not look inappropriate in a Parisian boutique.

31

Chapter Three

The Akan of Ghana

More than any other West African people the Akan have achieved lasting fame not only for their wealth of gold but for the beauty and abundance of their goldsmiths' work. They first came to the notice of Europeans in 1471, when Portuguese vessels appeared off the fishing village of Shama. The discovery was soon made that gold was available in the form of gold-dust, nuggets and worked jewellery. For the next four hundred years ships crowded the coastal waters trading for gold. Several dozen European forts and castles sprang up on shore, and the region proved so rich that it became known as the Gold Coast, a name that survived until the independence of Ghana in 1957.

The term "Akan", as used today, denotes a large group of related peoples in central and southern Ghana. They number six or seven million, share a broadly similar culture, and speak dialects of one language. The name Akan has not always been used in this sense, however. Five centuries ago Europeans visiting the coast found that it was divided up into numerous political units: small states that typically consisted of a town ruled by a king, who received the allegiance of the heads of nearby villages. Many of these "town-states" were more or less independent. There was much warfare between them, and periodically, by agreement or through conquest, groups of them coalesced into larger confederations of towns, whose kings in turn owed allegiance to a paramount king. In this kaleidoscopic scene of warfare and shifting allegiances there was no common, generally accepted term for the ethnic group as a whole nor even for its language.

It was not until the late nineteenth century that the term "Akan" came into use to denote the ethnic group as a whole, and the name "Twi" to denote its language. Today these names are firmly established. It remains unclear why they should have been selected in preference to other possible choices, but their origin is not in doubt. "Akan" derives from Akanni, the name given from the fifteenth to the eighteenth century to the gold-rich kingdoms situated around the confluence of the Pra, Ofin and Birim rivers. The people of Akanni, famous as gold-traders, were called Okanni, plural Akanfo ("the Akan people"). The name "Twi" derives from Twifo, another early kingdom situated between Akanni and the coast.

Akan territory extends almost three hundred miles along the West African coast, and for about the same distance inland. Until recently much of this land was thick tropical forest. It is watered by several important rivers, the Tano, Ankobra, Pra, Ofin and Birim. Scattered gold deposits occur over much of the region, and in places, notably at Obuasi and Tarkwa, they proved incredibly rich. In past centuries there was intensive gold-mining activity, virtually all the significant deposits being discovered in precolonial times. Panning for gold took place around streams and rivers and even on the sea shore, while shallow pits and deep mines were dug in many parts of the forest.

To the north the Akan extend into the savanna grasslands of the Brong region,

Fig. 32   Great public occasions such as Yam Festivals and other traditional events provide the setting for some of the most magnificent displays of Akan gold. Photo: courtesy of René and Denise David

and it was here, from about the fourteenth century, that the earliest Akan townships and states began to emerge. Among them were Begho, Bono-Manso, Techiman and Wenchi. Situated along the northern edge of the forest, these towns served as a natural focus for trade between forest and savanna. They attracted merchants from afar, and as their markets grew many of these foreign traders took up permanent residence. As was the custom in the savanna, the new arrivals established their own separate quarters in each town.

The early history of these northern Akan towns is closely associated with the presence of the Mande. Originating in Mali and Guinée, the Mande seem to have made contact with the northern Akan around the fourteenth century, and soon became an indispensable element of the local commercial scene. One of their subgroups, the Diula, excelled in organising long-distance and local market trade; they also included many artisans and craftsmen. Another group, the Numu, were professional blacksmiths.

The Mande were keenly active in the gold trade, often purchasing the precious metal in exchange for brass and copper. They introduced the concept of using gold-dust as currency, and of weighing it with brass goldweights and scales. The earliest Akan weights, like those of the Mande, were based on the old Islamic weight-standards used in the Western Sudan.

While gold was available locally, brass and copper had to be imported, and it was the Mande who supplied the first cuprous metal for Akan casting work. They also introduced a wide range of exotic brassware, some of it from as far afield as North Africa, Egypt and the

32

Middle East. The earliest forms of Akan gold jewellery and regalia, ritual brass vessels, goldweights and the like were often derived, via the Mande, from forms then current in the Islamic world.

In matters of technology the Mande had considerable influence. Their metalsmiths imparted to the Akan knowledge of the various techniques of working gold and brass, including lost wax casting. Their many cloth-workers introduced the technology of spinning,

33

Fig. 33   Akan queen-mothers possess their own gold jewellery and regalia, differing little in design from that of male chiefs. Photo: Historisches Museum Berne

Fig. 34   European travellers brought back reports of the splendid jewellery worn by Akan chiefs. This 18th century engraving depicts a coastal dignitary with a gold pendant and chain necklaces. Archives Barbier-Mueller

weaving, dyeing and tailoring. This was not all. Some Mande were literate Muslims, skilled not only as scribes but as purveyors of magical talismans and amulets. Through such men the Akan were introduced to the mystery of the written word, and they were deeply impressed. While never themselves achieving literacy in Arabic, they remained ever afterwards convinced of the potency of written symbols, signs and letters.

In these and other ways contact with the Mande had a profound effect on Akan

society. The emergence of a gold trade led to increased mining activity, the growth of new markets, and the accumulation of wealth on a scale never known before. Akan chiefs and kings were now able to appear attired in woven cloths and resplendent with golden jewellery and regalia. All this occurred a century or more before the coming of the Europeans. By 1482, when a Portuguese expedition arrived to build a trade fort at Elmina, they were met by an Akan chief whose arms, legs and neck were "covered with chains and trinkets of gold in many shapes, and countless bells and large beads of gold were hanging from the hair of his beard and his head".

The Portuguese established a flourishing trade with the Akan, bartering a wide range of European goods for gold-dust. They were also successful in persuading the Akan to trade their gold jewellery, apparently in quite large quantities. In 1502, according to the contemporary historian Joao de Barros, a Portuguese ship sailed from Elmina carrying 250 marks or 2,000 ounces of gold, "all in manillas and jewels, which the negroes are accustomed to wear". He claimed that twelve or fifteen ships brought a similar amount each year. None of this early Akan goldwork survives; all went into the melting pot, valued solely for its bullion content.

The arrival of Portuguese, English and later Dutch merchants may have led to the destruction of much Akan gold-work, but at the same time it served as a stimulus to the Akan goldsmithing industry. The smiths were encouraged to increase their output, and they eagerly sought brass and silver from the Europeans to adulterate gold.

In the sixteenth and seventeenth centuries the work of the Akan goldsmiths was much admired. Brief descriptions were left by several European visitors to the coast. In 1554 an Englishman, John Lok, recorded that the Akan women of the coast were "laden with collars, bracelets, hoops, and chains, either of gold, copper or ivory .... Some of their women wear on their bare arms certain foresleeves made of the plates of beaten gold, and on their fingers, rings made of golden wires, with a knot or wreath."

At Elmina his crew acquired in trade "certain dog-chains and collars" made of gold.

The Dutchman Pieter de Marees lived on the Gold Coast for eleven months in 1601. He found the Akan "very ingenious in making things, especially in working gold, for they make amazingly beautiful chains and other ornaments such as rings". He described one of the coastal Akan kings as "beautifully adorned in accordance with their custom, his beard strung with golden beads and other finery, and gold bracelets around his arms and legs". Referring to the king's treasurer, or *sannaahene*, he remarked that "these men are next after the king, and usually go about with even more golden ornaments covering their arms, legs, feet and neck than the king himself".

In the 1660s the coastal kingdom of Fetu was ruled by king Aduaffo, a white-haired old man. He was described as rich in gold; his hair was adorned with gold beads and other gold ornaments, and he wore a profusion of gold bracelets and rings on his fingers, arms and legs. His attendants carried regalia of fine beaten gold.

Gold ornaments were not restricted to kings and important officials. They were commonly worn by women, notably

Gentilhomme de la côte d'or.

34

Fig. 35   Asante was the most powerful Akan state, and its ruler, the Asantehene, came to be recognised as the most important of the Akan kings. In this photograph, dating from the 1930s, the Asantehene Prempeh II is seen with the Governor of the Gold Coast. Photo: Basel Mission Archive

Fig. 36   A royal headband of velvet adorned with gold-leafed ornaments in the form of flowers, snakes and protective amulets. Cat. 57

Fig. 37   A queen-mother of the coastal Fanti, attired in a richly woven *kente* cloth and golden chains. Photo: Doran H. Ross

among the Fanti, the largest Akan coastal group. A Dutchman stationed in one of the coastal forts recorded in his journal in 1654 that "the Braffo of Fanti's three wives came to dance here in the afternoon, well dressed up in their fashion, each having a peruque on her head, hung full of gold, a gold ring (of the thickness of an arm) round the neck, three gold rings on the arms and also on the legs".

35

The Frenchman Villault de Bellefond was impressed by the skill of the Akan goldsmiths; he declared that they much surpassed those of Europe. Their lost wax castings were as delicate as filigree and all kinds of objects were made, including hat-bands (apparently for European clients) of the finest gold thread.

The most detailed description of seventeenth-century Akan goldwork was left by a French Huguenot slave trader, Jean Barbot, who visited the Gold Coast twice, in 1679 and 1682. He too

had great praise for the goldsmiths, and provided a detailed list of their output:

They can make many sorts of small utensils and ornaments of gold; especially buttons plain, or in filigreen, rings plain, or in chains, toothpickers, curious hat-bands, and sword-hilts, besides many other sorts of curiosities: amongst which I have very often admired their ability in casting gold in filigreen, so as to represent very exactly the forms of large sea perwinkles, and all other species of snail or shell-fish etc.... [They] now make of fine gold, breast-plates, helmets, bracelets, idols, hunting horns, pattins, plates, ornaments for the neck, hat-bands, chain and plain rings, buttons, and shell-fish; they also cast very curiously all sorts of wild and tame beasts; the heads and skeletons of lions, tygers, leopards, oxen, deer, monkey and goats etc., which serve them by way of idols either plain work or filigreen all cast in moulds; of which sort I brought over several pieces of figures, but particularly that of a perwinkle, as big as an ordinary goose-egg; which were all much admired at Rochel and Paris, and even by the best goldsmiths.

His lack of extensive knowledge of Akan culture may have led Barbot to misidentify some of these objects. The "buttons", for instance, are more likely to have been disc-shaped gold beads. The so-called "skeletons" of animals may simply have been animals modelled in wax threads with openwork designs; such castings are still made in south-eastern Côte d'Ivoire (cat. nos. 201–203). Lastly, his "breast-plates" were perhaps the large disc-shaped or triangular pectorals made for chiefs and their entourage.

Barbot not only formed a collection of Akan gold but left a unique record of his purchases. His manuscript journal of 1678–79 contains careful and accurate drawings of eighteen gold beads acquired on his first voyage, as well as a large gold bracelet and a ring. In another manuscript dated 1688 a further selection of about twenty-five gold beads are illustrated, together with gold bracelets, necklaces, animal skulls and a sword-hilt; these were perhaps objects acquired on his second voyage. An engraving in the published version of his work (1732) shows more beads, bracelets, skulls and a large filigree gold snail-shell, presumably the one that he showed to goldsmiths in France. Taken together, Barbot's drawings illustrate seventy or more items of Akan goldwork (figs. 54, 55).

Europeans in the sixteenth and seventeenth centuries found that Akan territory was divided into dozens of independent kingdoms, many of them small, but some large and powerful. Among these, along the coast, were Axim, Ahanta, Eguafo, Fetu, Asebu, Agona and Gomoa; further inland Egwira, Inkasa, Wassa, Twifo, Ati, Assin, Adanse, Akyem, Denkyira and Akwamu. In the central forest and the far north bordering on the savanna there were yet more Akan kingdoms of which Europeans could learn very little, among them Tafo, Kaase, Wenchi and Bono. In most of these kingdoms gold-dust was the regular currency, and their rulers had a wealth of gold regalia and other ornaments.

Among the most powerful of these states was Denkyira, which through conquests had come to control the major trade routes to the coast as well as some of the richest gold mines. The wealth of its ruler was proverbial, and he was even reputed to have a golden stool. In the summer of 1701, however, Denkyira suffered a sudden and crushing defeat at the hands of a relatively unknown Akan people – the Asante.

Asante was in origin a confederation of small central forest states which united to throw off the yoke of Denkyira. It consisted of Kumasi, Mampong, Juaben, Kokofu, Nsuta, Kumawu, Esumigya and

36

37

Bekwai. These states gave allegiance to Osei Tutu, their paramount king, who was styled the Asantehene, king of the Asante. After the victory against Denkyira he produced his own golden stool, which according to tradition descended from the skies, summoned by a famous fetish priest named Okomfo Anokye. The Golden Stool of Asante was to become the most sacred item of Akan regalia. On rare occasions, at the most important state ceremonies, it is brought out for public display in the Asante capital of Kumasi (fig. 11). It is regarded with deep veneration by all Asante.

38

In the first half of the eighteenth century Asante embarked on a ruthless policy of expansion under its first two rulers, Osei Tutu and Opoku Ware I. Enriched by the spoils of Denkyira, these kings launched a series of attacks against Aowin, Wassa, Bono, Akyem and other Akan states, which fell to Asante one by one. In tribute to their invincibility the victorious Asante armies took to calling themselves *Asante kɔtɔkɔ*, "the Asante porcupine" (fig. 38).

In consequence of these campaigns increasing quantities of wealth, reckoned in gold and slaves, now flowed through Kumasi. As the Asante empire swallowed its neighbours, Kumasi became increasingly the centre of the Akan world. With each major victory, goldsmiths from the defeated states

were captured and brought back to Kumasi to work for the Asantehene and his court. By the mid-eighteenth century the best goldsmiths from Denkyira, Techiman and Akyem were at work in Kumasi, producing ever more splendid jewellery. The result was a mingling of artistic influences from north and south, and an elaboration of art forms.

In 1817 the British envoy Thomas Bowdich spent three turbulent months in Kumasi, where he received a state reception and witnessed the annual Yam Festival. He left a vivid description of the Asantehene Osei Bonsu and his attendants. The king wore

a necklace of gold cockspur shells strung by their largest ends, and over his right shoulder a red silk cord, suspending three saphies cased in gold; his bracelets were the richest mixtures of beads and gold, and his fingers covered with rings; his cloth was of a dark green silk .... His ancle strings of gold ornaments of the most delicate workmanship, small drums, sankos [harp-lutes], stools, swords, guns, and birds, clustered together; his sandals, of a soft white leather, were embossed across the instep band with small gold and silver cases of saphies; he was seated in a low chair, richly ornamented with gold; he wore a pair of gold castanets on his finger and thumb, which he clapped to enforce silence.

The royal attendants were a no less splendid sight:

The belts of the guards behind his chair were cased in gold, and covered in small jaw bones of the same metal; the elephant tails, waving like a small cloud before him, were spangled with gold, and large plumes of feathers were flourished amid them. His eunuch presided over these attendants, wearing only one massy piece of gold about his neck; the royal stool, entirely cased in gold, was displayed under a splendid umbrella, with drums, sankos, horns, and various musical instruments, cased in gold, about the thickness of cartridge paper; large circles of gold hung by scarlet cloth from the swords of state, the sheaths as well as the

Fig. 38   The porcupine, noted for its valour, became the symbol of the Asante nation. Depicted here as a golden sword-ornament, it alludes to the invincibility of the Asante army. Photo: Doran H. Ross

Fig. 39   In a famous account of 1817, Thomas Bowdich described the magnificence of the Asantehene and his principal chiefs. Scenes no less splendid can still be witnessed today, at the annual Yam Festivals and other great public occasions. Photo: courtesy of René and Denise David

handles of which were also cased; hatchets of the same were intermixed with them; the breasts of the Ocrahs ["soul-washers"], and various attendants, were adorned with large stars, stools, crescents, and gossamer wings of solid gold.

There were royal messengers wearing gold pectorals, and war chiefs resplendent in eagle-feather head-dresses with a pair of gold ram's horns projecting in front. The executioner wore "a massy gold hatchet" on his

40

chest, while the four royal linguists carried gold canes. Bowdich observed that the Sannaahene or keeper of the royal treasury "added to his own magnificence by the ostentatious display of his service; the blow pan, boxes, scales and weights, were of solid gold".

A large number of Asante chiefs were present to greet the British visitor, attired in their most magnificent *kente* cloths and with a rich variety of beads and gold jewellery:

a small silk fillet generally encircled their temples, and massy gold necklaces, intricately wrought; suspended Moorish charms, dearly purchased, and enclosed in small square cases of gold, silver, and curious embroidery. Some wore necklaces reaching to the navel entirely of aggry beads; a band of gold and beads encircled the knee, from which several strings of the same depended; small circles of gold like guineas, rings, and casts of animals, were strung round their ancles; their sandals were of green, red, and delicate white leather; manillas, and rude lumps of rock gold, hung from their left wrists, which were so heavily laden as to be supported on the head of one of their handsomest boys. Gold and silver pipes, and canes dazzled the eye in every direction. Wolves and rams heads as large as life, cast in gold, were suspended from their gold handled swords, which were held around them in great numbers ... the horns (the teeth of young elephants) were ornamented at the mouth-piece with gold, and the jaw bones of human victims ... large fans, of the wing feathers of the ostrich, played around the dignitaries; immediately behind their chairs (which were of a black wood, almost covered by inlays of ivory and gold embossment) stood their handsomest youths, with corslets of leopard's skin covered with gold cockle shells, and stuck full of small knives, sheathed in gold and silver, and the handles of blue agate; cartouch boxes of elephant's hide hung below, ornamented in the same manner; a large gold handled sword was fixed behind the left shoulder.

At the close of this magnificent reception, attended by more than thirty thousand people, the king "stopped to enquire our names a second time, and to wish us good night; his address was mild and deliberate; he was followed by his aunts, sisters, and others of his family, with rows of fine gold chains around their necks".

Displays of finery were by no means restricted to sumptuous state occasions. At weddings, for instance, the bride and

Fig. 40   A young *okra* or "soul" of the Akuapemhene Akuffo, photographed about 1900. He bears the full insignia of his office, including a large gold pectoral, a sword, protective talismans, and an eagle-feather head-dress incorporating two golden horns. Photo: Basel Mission Archive

Fig. 41   The lion is not native to the Akan forest region, but in the nineteenth century it became a popular symbol of royal power. The Akan took as their model the European heraldic lion, known to them through contacts with the British and Dutch. This gold sword-ornament comes from Berekum. Cat. 171

her attendants would be decked out in their richest cloths and finest gold jewellery. The following description of a Fanti bride, also in 1817, was recorded by Mrs Bowdich at Cape Coast as she waited for her husband to return from Kumasi:

[The girl's hair] was combed in the form of a cone to the top of her head, and profusely decorated with golden butterflies and devices; her shirt was fastened in front with four brooches, and a large golden button at the collar and each wrist; manillas encircled her arms half-way up to the elbow, and the most splendid chains were hung across her shoulders; every finger was covered with rings as far as the first joint; her cloth was girt round her hips, and on this girdle hung golden lions and other ornaments; her ankles were also laden, and every toe was decorated like her fingers. The two slaves who followed her into the room were also richly dressed, and each had a bandeau of English guineas round their heads, fastened together with pieces of gold wire. The workmanship of many of these ornaments is exquisite, and they sometimes represent musical instruments, bells, stools, etc., and many are imitated from European patterns.

42

Fig. 42   The Asantehene Agyeman Prempeh II sitting in state. The two gold birds surmounting the royal chair are replacements for those surrendered to the British in 1874, after Sir Garnet Wolseley entered and burnt Kumasi. Photo: courtesy of Eva Meyerowitz

Fig. 43   Gold-ornamented helmets, caps and sandals are owned by every Akan chief. Some of the finest known examples were removed from the palace of Asantehene Kofi Karikari during the British invasion of 1874. Cat. 49, 58, 165

Until this time little Akan gold had been seen in Europe. Bowdich brought back a few examples which he presented to the British Museum; these are marvellously delicate small castings. A few other items were acquired by missionaries, finding their way into European museums. In 1841, for instance, the missionary T. B. Freeman obtained an openwork gold ring of fine workmanship (now in Basel) while visiting Kumasi. But it was not until 1874 that a spectacular treasure of Akan gold reached England. In that year, following repeated Asante threats to invade the coast, a British expeditionary force under Sir Garnet Wolseley marched into Kumasi. The king fled, saving the Golden Stool but leaving behind much other precious regalia. The British ransacked the palace and imposed an indemnity of 50,000 ounces of gold, part of which the Asante managed to pay by handing over a great quantity of gold beads and other worked jewellery. Deplorable though the looting of cultural objects may be, this act did save for future generations a collection of superb Akan goldwork much of which would otherwise have been melted down, recast and remodelled over the years. Some of the finest objects are now in the Museum of Mankind, London. The remainder were dispersed among private buyers.

In the last quarter of the nineteenth century more examples of Asante gold reached Britain. In 1883 the Asantehene presented to Queen Victoria the famous *Sika Akuma* or Golden Axe of Asante, which is now in Windsor Castle. Though intended as a symbol of peace and reconciliation (the "axe which cuts through all difficulties"), many Englishmen at the time misinterpreted it as a threat of warlike intentions on the part of the Asante. In 1896 another consignment of Asante gold reached London after the British had found

further pretexts to invade the Asante kingdom. On this occasion they not only entered Kumasi but seized and subsequently deported the young Asantehene, Prempeh I. His palace was again ransacked for gold and regalia. On this occasion the objects seized included a horned cap and a variety of royal swords, including the *Mponponsuo* sword, adorned with a large coiled snake of gold. This sword had been used by

Fig. 44   Royal attendants display swords, muskets, drums, stools and a tobacco pipe in this late nineteenth-century photograph, taken in the Kwahu district east of Kumasi. Several of them wear gold "soul discs" and two of the gun-bearers have bandoliers ornamented with golden shells. Photo, probably by F. Ramseyer: Basel Mission Archive

Fig. 45   The mudfish is a popular motif in Akan goldwork, often represented among sword-ornaments and finger-rings. It can be interpreted in various ways, but sometimes refers to a person who has a sense of responsibility towards the society in which he lives. Cat. 157, 168, 207

the Asantehene Opoku Ware I (1720–50) in dedicating his life to his people in war; ever since, senior chiefs had used it to swear allegiance to the Asantehene.

A photograph of these last objects appeared in the *Illustrated London News* on 14th March 1896, together with a brief description:

King Prempeh's crown is made of thin hide, lined with silk, and surmounted by two golden horns. All round the side are affixed models in solid gold of lions' heads, together with human heads and jaw-bones .... Another peculiar curiosity is a cup made of solid gold, after exactly the same pattern as

those used for incense in the Roman Catholic ritual. This and sundry other trinkets are chiefly of interest for the close imitation of European models shown in their workmanship .... The sheath of the chief sacrifical sword is the most notable item among the spoils. This bears embossed designs in gold of the trunks of beheaded men. Smaller articles of jewellery, which are supposed to have belonged to the Queen, are of quaint design, but few of them are of solid gold.

In this way the Asante nation came to suffer great losses of its golden treasures between 1874 and 1896 (replacements for some of these objects have been made in the present century). The full extent of the loss is difficult to assess. Observers in the 1870s suggested that the weight of the Asantehene's gold regalia was about 12,500 ounces (800 pounds), an extraordinary amount but much less than some Europeans had supposed. According to the *Illustrated London News*, the objects seized in 1896 were worth some £2,000 sterling in actual bullion, which indicates a weight of about 500 ounces. The exact total seized by the British is not known, but it would certainly have amounted to several thousand ounces.

These losses were confined almost entirely to Asante. The other Akan states did not suffer from British punitive raids, and most managed to preserve intact their assemblages of royal goldwork. In consequence little gold from these areas was represented in European collections. Officially, objects of state regalia and other gold ornaments could not be sold, except in very particular circumstances and with the consent of all the elders. From the beginning of this century, however, cases repeatedly occurred in which a chief hard-pressed for cash would sell or pledge an ornament belonging to his stool. This was a source of much friction and sometimes led to the destoolment of the chief concerned.

The transactions often took place, not with Europeans, but with other Akan chiefs, goldsmiths and astute Lebanese traders.

A typical instance is recorded in papers now in the National Archives of Ghana (file no. 1082, Jamasi Native Affairs, NAG Kumasi). In 1934 it was alleged that the Ohene (king) of Jamasi, Nana Adu Akyampong, had "pledged a *Petre* [a casting of a mudfish, *pitire*] made into gold to a certain Syrian called Kamel, and if he has got it back I cannot tell. One Syrian called Nazer also bought some *Adam* [gold castings of cockle shells] from the Chief; and further one Chief called Kojo Adiyia who wants the betterment of his stool has purchased one gold Lion from this chief Adu Akyampong."

After stating that the regalia had included twelve gold *adam* shells attached to a cartridge belt, the complainant accused the chief of misappropriating nine of these, together with two small gold bells and a golden jawbone (*abogye*). When these losses came to light, he said, Adu Akyampong went to the chief of Asoromaso, Kwasi Gyabaa, who was a goldsmith, and asked him to make replacements. This chief made wax models of five *adam* shells, a bell and a jawbone, and completed the casting of two small *adam* worth £ 4. The other wax models were produced as evidence in court.

The papers in this case are of particular interest for they list in detail the regalia and other property owned by the stool. Among them are almost seventy gold objects:

- 4 hats decorated with gold
- 1 *nsenɛ* hat decorated with gold
- 1 head-band decorated with 39 gold ornaments

Fig. 46   Some of the greatest Akan kings possessed stools of gold. The most famous is that of Asante, but others have been made at various times by the rulers of Denkyira and Akyem (in Ghana) and Abron, Gyaman and Sakassou (in Côte d'Ivoire). This delicate gold pendant of the 18th or 19th century depicts a royal stool. Cat. 91

Fig. 47   On great occasions Akan kings appear publicly in their most splendid jewellery: massive gold chains, bracelets and finger-rings, a profusion of gold beads strung around the wrist and forearm, gold talismans, and sandals and crowns ornamented with gold. Photo: courtesy of René and Denise David, Kumasi, 1985

  2   pairs of sandals decorated with gold
  1   gold lock and 1 silver lock
 19   large gold *adam* shells
 11   small gold *adam* shells
  2   gold bells
  2   gold clapper-bells (*dawa*)
  2   gold jawbones (*mmogye*)
  1   large gold lion *abosodeε* attached to a sword
  1   large gold mudfish *abosodeε* attached to a sword
  2   old swords decorated with gold
  2   gold umbrella heads
 14   gold knives
  2   gold finger-rings
  1   large gold bangle.

46

According to evidence given by the state treasurer of Jamasi, Sannaahene Kojo Subunu, virtually all this goldwork except the knives, ring and bangle had been commissioned by the previous Jamasihene, Panin Kwaku Tufuor, prior to his destoolment in 1927.

The foregoing list represents the gold used by the chief of a single Asante town of medium importance in the 1930s. It is probably fairly representative (though no mention is made of the necklaces and bracelets of gold beads possessed by most chiefs, nor of the queen-mother's gold ornaments).

It is difficult to visualize the quantity of gold regalia existing in the entire Akan region, but there are several hundred town-chiefs or "kings" (*ɔhene*, plural *ahene*) and paramount chiefs (*ɔmanhene*, plural *amanhene*), together with innumerable village heads (*adikrofo*). There are also the queen-mothers (*ahemmaa*). Not all town chieftaincies were as richly endowed as Jamasi, but some were richer. We can be fairly certain that there were, and still are, tens of thousands of items of gold regalia in the Akan region as a whole.

The wealth and magnificence of the Akan state was reflected not only in gold but in a variety of other property belonging to the stool. Much of this was displayed on public occasions together with the gold regalia, giving Akan public ceremonies their unique and splendid character. The list compiled at Jamasi in 1934 gives a good idea of the nature of this other property:

  4   rich *kente* cloths (named as *adwinasa*, *manman*, *kubi* and *akyεmpim*)
  2   *adinkra* cloths
  9   European cloths (*ntama*)
  1   gown with talismans (*batakari*)
  1   large blanket (*tabankro*)
  1   European blanket (*nasuor*)
  1   northern blanket (*kasa*)
  1   other blanket (*nsaa*)
  1   European carpet
  2   European table-cloths
  9   wooden swords
  1   single-barrelled gun
  2   flintlock guns
  1   linguist staff (*abanpoma*)
  1   state umbrella for the Stool
  4   other state umbrellas
  2   small umbrellas
  2   elephant teeth (*sonsii*)
  3   elephant tails (*bodua*)
  4   bundles of ostrich feathers (*sohori ntakara*)
  1   *sesia* (basket?)
  1   brass pot (*kuduo*)
  1   large brass pot for water
  1   sword-bearer's hat (*krɔbɔnkyε*)
  3   European chairs
  2   Akan chairs (*asipim*)
  2   Akan white stools (*nkondwafufuo*)
  6   drums (*dɔnnɔ*)

2 drums (*mpintinowa*)
3 skin purses (*nkotokua*) to hold the bag
   containing the treasury weights and
   weighing equipment (*futuo*)
1 bundle containing the treasury weights
   and weighing equipment (*futuo*)
6 empty boxes (*nnaka*) [probably to hold
   gold-dust and other valuables]
1 typewriter.
   (List in file no. 1082, Jamasi Native Affairs,
   National Archives of Ghana, Kumasi).

The remainder of this chapter will
consider some of the major types of
goldwork used by the Akan.

48

Fig. 48   Akan rings of the nineteenth century were
smaller than those made today. This photograph
taken about 1880 shows one of the more
prominent Akan kings, the Okyenhene Amoako
Atta, wearing small gold rings on each finger of
both hands. Photo: Basel Mission Archive

Fig. 49   Goldsmiths of the 18th and 19th centuries
made finger-rings bearing a great variety of motifs.
Some of these allude to an Akan proverb or wise
saying. Others, particularly those made in the
coastal towns, were inspired by European rings.
Cat. 120, 121, 129, 131, 148

1. Rings

Among the Akan of Ghana gold rings
became a sophisticated art form.
Some were worn by chiefs, others
adorned the fingers, thumbs and toes
of wealthy men and women. Gold
and silver rings were also made to
decorate the long bamboo stems of
chiefs' tobacco-pipes (fig. 44).

Most Akan rings have an inner
diameter between 1.5 and 2.3 cm.
These were for fingers or toes. The
few examples with a diameter

exceeding 2.3 cm were most likely
intended to be worn on the thumb or
big toe; those smaller than 1.5 cm
may have been made for tobacco-
pipe stems.

Like the savanna peoples living to the
north, many Akan wear small simple
rings of base metal (iron, copper or
brass). This has probably been the
custom for centuries. Iron rings are
often worn for their supposed magical
protective powers, the particular
power of each ring being known only
to its owner. Gold rings, on the other
hand, do not appear to have been
worn for such purposes by the Akan;
they were not regarded as "fetish"
(*suman*), but were purely for
ostentation and display.

The earliest Akan gold rings were
probably simple forms. John Lok, in
1554, had referred to them as "made
of golden wires, with a knot or
wreath", while Barbot in the late
seventeenth century mentioned
"chain and plain rings". The single
ring that he illustrates is without
decoration of any kind. In the
eighteenth and nineteenth centuries, however, finger-rings
became increasingly ornate and
assumed an astonishing variety of
forms.

The most striking feature of Akan gold
rings is their wealth of proverbial
imagery (fig. 51). Most depict some
object (animal, bird, fish, insect, fruit,
seed, man-made artifact, etc.) that is
associated with an Akan proverb or
aphorism. In this way the rings convey
a message to the beholder. Frequently
the message may emphasize the
power, wealth, bravery or invincibility
of the chief, or serve as a warning to
his enemies and detractors. Other ring
motifs are social in content, conveying

50

A number of Akan gold rings entered European collections in the nineteenth century, and these attest the beauty and delicacy of Akan workmanship at that time. They are relatively small (fig. 48), and few weigh more than 20 grams. The gold usually appears to be of good quality, or at least has little visible alloy. Some of these rings show European influence (cat. nos. 115–124). They imitate signet rings, or take the form of hearts and other European devices, and sometimes they bear the initials of the owner, either stamped into the wax prior to casting or punched into the gold afterwards. A very popular ring form, often made for sale to visiting Europeans, has a broad band carrying the signs of the zodiac. Not all these European-style rings were intended for Europeans, however; many were worn by the Akan themselves. Most of these probably came from workshops along the coast, in Fanti country and also at Accra, where there was a thriving colony of goldsmiths.

In this century the casting of gold rings has continued and even increased. These recent productions tend to be extravagantly large and heavy, often weighing between 30 and 50 grams. While traditional designs are still followed, the standard of workmanship is uneven. The best of them are fine castings, but others are crude and unpleasing, reflecting a gradual decline in artistic skills. The fabric is often poor, heavily alloyed with copper or silver. Such rings are often made in pairs, particularly when commissioned by a chief.

Fig. 50   The fingers of great chiefs are laden with gold rings of every kind, while their forearms are covered with beads and bracelets. While walking in procession the chief sometimes supports this weight on the heads of young attendants. Archives Barbier-Mueller

Fig. 51   Like much Akan royal art, many finger-rings were designed to convey a moral message to the beholder. Often they emphasise the power, wisdom and patience of the chief as well as his valour and the futility of opposing him. Cat. 144, 145

some moral message applicable to individuals in society. This use of proverbial motifs on Akan rings is exactly paralleled among Akan goldweights.

Ross has suggested that there are more than a hundred ring motifs. Many of these may have originated in the eighteenth century, though some may be older. The fairly common twisted knot motif (perhaps inspired by the form of certain iron rings) could be the design referred to by John Lok in 1554.

2. Beads and Pendants

Jean Barbot's drawings from the 1670s and 1680s show that gold bead forms were then purely abstract and geometric, often of openwork design

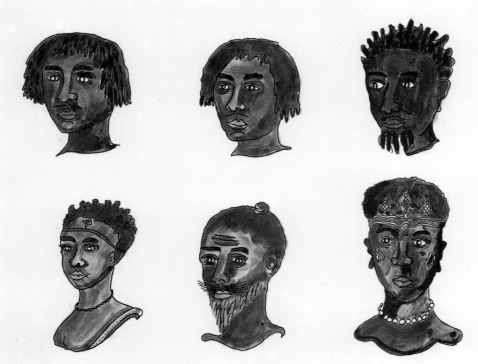

52

Fig. 52   The French merchant Jean Barbot kept a journal of his visit to the coast in 1678–79, which he illustrated with many small sketches. These six Akan heads include women wearing necklaces of gold beads and gold forehead ornaments. Photo: Photothèque IFAN, Dakar

Fig. 53   Gold beads of the 18th–19th centuries are notable for their fine workmanship. They are small, delicate, and of fine metal. Those made in this century tend to be larger and more coarsely executed, and the quality of the alloy is often poor. Cat. 83-85

Figs. 54, 55 (overleaf)   In the late 17th century Jean Barbot purchased many gold beads, pendants and other ornaments from the Akan. He left a unique series of drawings, which are here brought together and rearranged from three sources: his manuscripts of 1679 and 1688, and his published work of 1732.

(figs. 54, 55). Discs and spirals predominate, but there were also rectangular, diamond-shaped, tubular and conical beads. In most cases the form seems to have been built up from wax threads, a technique that Barbot particularly admired. He called this kind of work filigree, inaccurately perhaps since the beads were true lost wax castings and not made from drawn gold wire.

Barbot drew his beads with such close attention to detail that Asante goldsmiths of the present day have no difficulty identifying them as Akan. These forms have survived for centuries. Comparable examples can still be found

on necklaces and bracelets of Akan gold beads (fig. 53), and also among the Baule of Côte d'Ivoire, where types such as discs and rectangles are particularly common (fig. 88).

A number of these seventeenth-century Akan bead types also have a close resemblance to certain gold beads from Mali. Dupuis-Yakouba, in a monograph on the crafts and occupations of Timbuktu (1921), illustrates three types of local gold ornament that are very similar to Akan work. These are spiral and openwork disc forms, named as *kumna*, *betu* and *sorrofune*.

Barbot's journal of 1678–79 contains a unique drawing of the heads of six Akan, four men and two women (fig. 52). Both women wear pendants on their forehead identical to one of his gold bead forms: a diamond shape with a small ball at each corner. One of these heads is said to represent women at Cape Coast and Accra, while the other appears from his text (28th December 1678) to be a lady from Assini on the Côte d'Ivoire. Although the Akan no longer use ornaments of this type, close parallels still exist in Senegal and Mali – notably the cruciform pendants of the Tukulor, Maure and Tuareg (fig. 18). The custom of wearing gold forehead ornaments also survives in the lagoons region of Côte d'Ivoire, although here they have ceased to be abstract forms (figs. 98, 99).

These strands of evidence suggest that some early Akan goldwork – beads and pendants – may have been derived from Sahelian prototypes. The gold jewellery of the Sahel has a long history and its forms recur over immense distances. Given the known pattern of cultural borrowing by the Akan, it would be logical to expect that Akan goldsmiths of the fifteenth century

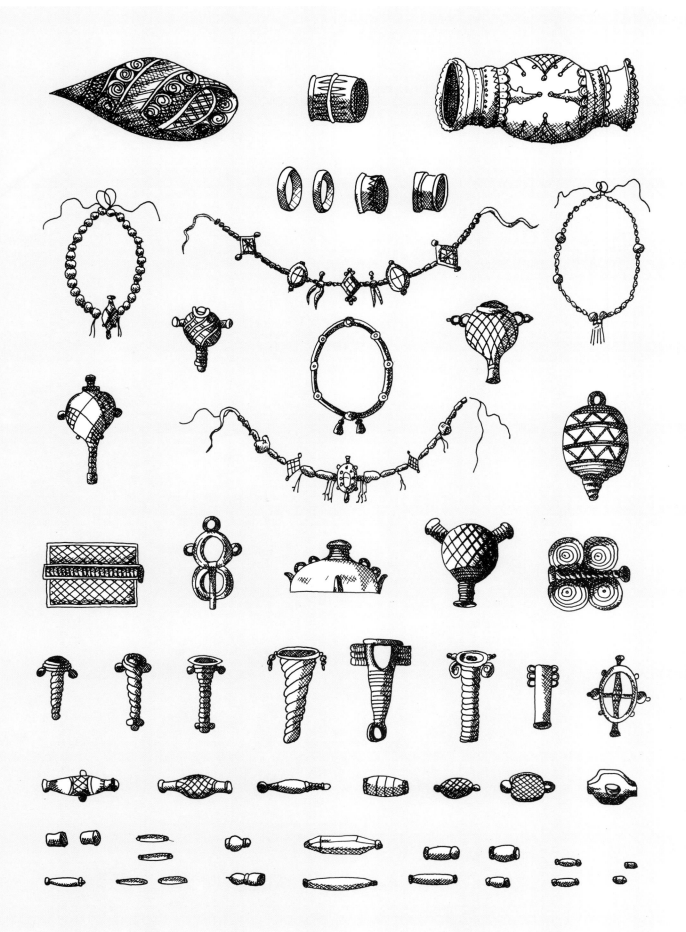

adapted some jewellery forms from elsewhere. Such a hypothesis is not improbable. Since the earliest forms of Akan weights, scales, spoons and ritual brass vessels were with little doubt inspired by exotic imports that reached them through the Mande, probably from Mali, it would not be surprising if some early Akan jewellery forms had the same origin.

There was much elaboration of Akan art forms in the eighteenth century, with

are at least thirty-five distinct forms (see cat. no. 83), representing objects as diverse as small seeds, kola nuts, silk-cotton husks, corn cobs, snails, cowry shells, palm grubs, crab claws, human molar and canine teeth, weaver-birds' nests, stars, knots, gold nuggets, padlocks, keys, drums, barrels, gunpowder flasks, open bells, pellet bells, amulets and talismans. There are also more abstract types with fanciful names: "the chicken's eye", "the back of the tortoise", "crossroads", "things sewn together", "Mankata". The last of these was named after Sir Charles McCarthy, a Governor of the Gold Coast, who in 1824 suffered a disastrous defeat at the hands of the Asante and met an ignominious death. The Asante celebrated by attaching a gold effigy of him to the Golden Stool, while his name passed into common usage to designate a popular form of bead.

Like finger-rings, Akan gold beads of the nineteenth century or earlier are characteristically small and modelled with great skill. Often a rich mixture of types was strung together on the same necklace or bracelet. Such an assemblage is called *suman* ("talisman" or "amulet"), indicating that they are, or once were, regarded as a kind of magical protective charm (fig. 57). This was confirmed by Barbot, who referred to Akan beads and pendants as "gold toys worn as spells, or things sacred" (English edition, 1752, p. 264).

In this century the art of casting gold beads has declined. As in the case of finger-rings, an increase in size is accompanied by a degeneration of technique. Castings lack the delicacy of former times, and are often of poor alloy. Some are merely brass-castings washed in gold. There are today very few Akan goldsmiths with the skill and experience to make such beads. Most

56

Fig. 56 Akan gold beads followed the same line of evolution as finger-rings and goldweights. To the original abstract forms were added, in the 18th and 19th centuries, an astonishing range of objects depicting fruits and seeds, small animals and man-made artifacts. These often had proverbial significance. Archives Barbier-Mueller

Fig. 57 Assemblages of gold beads worn by the chiefs are called *asuman*, literally "amulets" or "talismans", indicating that they are intended to provide magical protection for the wearer.

the rise of the Asante empire. The marked tendency towards figurative and proverbial representation (seen in Akan brass weights, clay tobacco-pipes, and gold rings) also seems to have affected gold beads. In addition to the abstract, linear designs depicted by Barbot, many beads were now cast in figurative form. When Bowdich met the Asantehene in 1817, he described his gold ankle ornaments as "of the most delicate workmanship, small drums, sankos, stools, swords, guns, and birds". The gold beads in the Barbier-Mueller collection are more modest, yet there

modern castings come from a few workshops in and around Kumasi.

3. Pectoral Discs

Among the most beautiful examples of Akan goldwork are the pectoral discs often named in the literature as "soul discs", "soul washer's badges" or *akrafokɔnmu* (figs. 59, 61, 63). These were worn as badges of rank by the *ɔkra*,

an official whose duty it was to "wash" or purify the chief's soul (fig. 40). They were also used in other contexts. Some, in the past, formed part of the insignia of a royal messenger. They might also be worn by linguists, heralds, subchiefs and war-leaders (i. e. the Benkumhene and Nifahene, leaders of the left and right wings of the army). In certain chieftaincies they were worn by junior officials; in others by the chief himself. Nor was their usage restricted to the court. Young women formerly displayed them at puberty ceremonies, while today they sometimes indicate the principal mourner at a funeral.

These discs were not, therefore, restricted to a single narrow purpose in the royal panoply. They were multi-functional objects that could be worn in many situations, and usage probably varied, in accordance with local custom, from one region to another. Usually they are displayed on the chest, suspended round the neck by a white cord of pineapple fibre, but this was not invariably the case. The late Omanhene of Enchi wore one of these golden discs on his ankle.

Of the many persons interviewed in Asante in 1986–87, only a few referred to this kind of pectoral as *akrafokɔnmu*. It was more commonly called *awisiado* or *ewisiado*, and spoken of in a funeral context. As the Chief Goldsmith of Kumasi explained:

In olden days akrafokɔnmu *was not for funerals. Before the king sent a messenger to another place he gave him this together with a sword to show his rank. This was the original use. But today it is often used at funerals, and we call it* ewisiado. *If someone dies the surviving spouse wears it on the neck. Anyone can wear it.*

In reality these so-called "soul-discs" form part of a whole complex of disc-shaped devices made by the Akan

Fig. 58   Gold pectoral discs are usually worn by royal servants, suspended round the neck on a cord of white pineapple fibres. Photo: Doran H. Ross, Cape Coast, 1978

Fig. 59   An Asante pectoral disc of cast gold. This finely cast ornament may date from the late 19th or early 20th century. Cat. 65

Fig. 60   A few gold pectorals depart from the traditional disc form. This unusual example is worn by a sword-bearer at a ceremony in Kumasi. A smaller disc is attached to the hilt of his state sword. Photo: courtesy of René and Denise David

Fig. 61   An Asante pectoral of cast gold. This style of casting is typical of workshops in and around Kumasi. Cat. 72

58

59

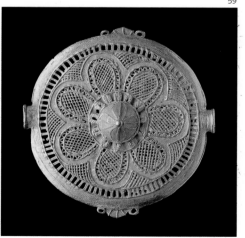

goldsmith. There are the flat disc-shaped beads of various sizes, some with spiral openwork decoration (known as *akyekyedeɛ akyi*, "the back of the tortoise"). Disc-like ornaments of silver or gold also appear on sacred and ceremonial stools, chairs, treasury boxes, royal coffins and swords: these are sometimes called *tadeɛ* (a pool of water) or *nnɛm*. Bowdich mentioned "large circles of gold" that hung by scarlet cloth from state swords (figs. 8, 60).

What was the source of inspiration for these disc and rosette-shaped motifs that abound in Akan goldwork? One finds parallels in goldwork from the Sahelian region. Disc-shaped jewels were worn by women until recently in the Middle Niger region of Mali, and as far west as Senegal. Most appear to have been fairly small, but the large and magnificent pectoral excavated at Rao in Senegal (fig. 10) instantly calls to mind the pectoral discs of the Akan (fig. 63). It requires no great imagination to suppose that the Akan disc-forms derive from the Sahel. Their ultimate origins, however, may lie in North Africa and Egypt; in Cairo, for instance, large and ornate disc-shaped jewels of gold were worn by rich women up to the nineteenth century.

For some at least of these Akan gold discs, a further possible source of inspiration may be suggested. The early gold dinars or "mithqals" struck by the Almoravids, Merinids and other North African Muslim dynasties (fig. 4) were widely used as jewellery both north and south of the Sahara; many surviving examples have been pierced. The fame of these coins reached the Akan. Joseph Dupuis, who visited Kumasi in 1820, found that these coins were not only used by the Mande but eagerly sought for and worn by the Akan:

60

61

Fig. 62   Royal musicians and attendants, some wearing gold pectoral discs, from a late 19th century photograph. Photo, probably by F. Ramseyer, Kwahu district: Museum für Volkskunde, Basel

Fig. 63   The disc-shaped form of Akan pectorals was perhaps inspired by Sahelian goldwork such as the famous pectoral of Rao. Smaller discs may have been intended to imitate North African gold dinars, which were once known to the Akan and highly prized by them. Cat. 69

62

Such of them as are esteemed by the Moslems for antiquity and the epoch of a celebrated prince are highly prized by the heathens, who, when they are procured, give a great price for them, for the purpose of dedicating to their patron gods and wearing on days appropriate to religious ceremony. In fact, some of these mitskals are the fetische of the sovreign and nobles (i. e. the Asantehene and his court).

The fact that the Akan knew these coins, and even wore them as "fetish" jewellery, suggests that some of the disc-shapes found in their goldwork may be Akan imitations of North African dinars.

The Akan sought protective and spiritual power from whatever source; their use of Muslim amulets is well known. This need for protection and power may account for the popularity of gold discs among them. In the world of North Africa, the Sahara and the Sahel, all bright, shiny objects – and especially gold – were regarded as an effective means of protection against the "evil eye". Many jewellery items were worn for this purpose, and rosette designs with a similar function are known on North African leatherwork. It is not difficult to conceive that the Akan heard of such protection from Muslim advisers, merchants or goldsmiths. Since they lacked a specific belief in the evil eye it seems likely, as Cole and Ross suggest, that among them these golden discs became a generalised charm against all evils.

Fig. 64   Akan kings and queen-mothers wear cast gold bracelets of impressive size. This splendid example is displayed by the Omanhene of Ejisu, ruler of an Akan state lying east of Kumasi. Photo: Doran H. Ross, 1974

Fig. 65   Five royal bracelets of cast gold. The largest were worn by male chiefs; the two smaller examples belonged to queen-mothers. Cat. 106–110

4. Royal Bracelets

Unlike their savanna neighbours to the north, who until recently wore a rich profusion of bracelets, anklets and arm-rings, the Akan people as a whole have little use for metal bangles. To this statement there is, however, one significant exception. Among Akan chiefs, both male and female, ornate bracelets of gold or silver have become an important art form (fig. 65).

Akan kings and queen-mothers sometimes possess hollow-cast gold bracelets of remarkable size, known as *benfra, benfena* or *berenfena* (fig. 64).

64

These are usually worn on the left wrist or forearm (being then known as *benkum benfra*), but where the owner has more than one he may wear them on both arms. Occasionally a large twisted gold bracelet would also be worn on the left ankle.

Some of the finest of these bracelets have a complex spiky design, which may be further elaborated by incised patterns. Another group of royal gold bracelets have scrolling designs reminiscent of (and possibly derived from) European rococo.

Queen-mothers sometimes wear other kinds of bracelets, less massive but of equally fine workmanship. Typical of these is a knobbed angular design, of which there are many variations, commonly known as *babadua*. This name is taken from the *babadua* plant, a tall straggling shrub with angular joints that is extensively used in house-building and thatching. It is often tied into the framework of a house. The shrub spreads very rapidly and is thus an appropriate symbol of female fertility, giving rise to the following Akan proverb:
Babadua ko ase ntu da.
A plantation of babadua never stops spreading.
(A large clan can never be exhausted.)

The babadua plant also connotes toughness and resilience, and is thus used as an emblem on the tops of state umbrellas, where it indicates the toughness of the chief.

These royal bracelets were often cast in two halves, which are secured by a pin. They exist in silver as well as gold, and some are of wood covered with gold leaf. It seems that they are worn purely for ostentation; magical or protective powers are not attributed to them.

5. Swords and Sword Ornaments

Among the Akan people there is a long history of ceremonial swords (fig. 67). They were noted by seventeenth-century observers, who added that they were similar to those of the Moors. It was customary to adorn the pommels with sheets of beaten gold, and they were further embellished with an emblem or trophy attached at the

66

Fig. 66   In their eagle-feathered head-dresses the chief sword-bearers are an imposing sight. A sword-bearer of the Ohene of Abetifi poses beside a drum decorated with human skulls in this photograph of 1888. Photo: F. Ramseyer, Basel Mission Archive

Fig. 67   Akan swords decorated with gold leaf have been made at least since the 17th century. They appear to be purely ceremonial; no record exists of their use in warfare, and they lack a cutting edge. Cat. 176–179

junction of blade and pommel. Popular ornaments were the highly valued red cockle shells, *adam*, imported from the Canary Islands in exchange for gold, and also the skulls of wild animals such as monkeys and leopards. An Akan sword ornament in the form of a shell appears in a Dutch painting of 1641 by Albert Eckhout (fig. 5).

Eventually it became the custom for wealthy chiefs to have these objects cast in gold. When this practice began is uncertain, but Barbot mentioned the casting of animal heads in gold. In 1701 a French priest, Godefroy Loyer, found that the king of Assini (on the Côte d'Ivoire) had gold-hilted swords each with a gold sheep's skull hanging from it, and with a large gold shell on the scabbard.

Gold sword-ornaments became more common from the eighteenth century. Animal heads remained a popular subject, and when Bowdich visited Kumasi in 1817 he saw many gold-handled state swords adorned with "wolves and rams heads as large as life, cast in gold". A fine example of a ram's head ornament in gold was taken from Kumasi in 1874 and is now in the Royal Artillery Mess at Woolwich.

Around 1765 the Asantehene Osei Kwadwo defeated and killed an enemy chief, Worosa of Banda, after a fierce campaign. To commemorate the victory he is said to have had a gold sword ornament made in the form of Worosa's head. Later other heads were cast to depict enemy kings slain in war; this occurred, for instance, after the killing of Adinkra, king of Gyaman, in 1818. Among the spoils of war taken from Kumasi by the British in 1874 was a large gold head, now in the Wallace Collection, London, that represents either Worosa of Banda or Adinkra of Gyaman. In the literature it has often been described, with total inaccuracy, as a "mask" of the Asantehene Kofi Karikari.

In the nineteenth century sword ornaments became more varied and numerous, often representing a proverbial theme. Further proliferation occurred in this century, and more specifically after 1924, when the Asantehene Prempeh I returned from his long exile in the Seychelles Islands.

Between about 1925 and 1940 many of the Akan chieftaincies tried to add to their gold regalia and restore the splendours of the past. Most existing gold sword ornaments were probably cast about that time. This was no mean achievement, for many weigh between 400 and 800 grams, and although they were often much alloyed with silver, the cost of making them was considerable. Chiefs who could not afford such a commission sometimes contented themselves with sword ornaments of gilded brass, or even of wood covered with gold leaf. Gold sword ornaments fall into the broad class of objects known as *abosodeɛ*, "things of the fetish", a name that indicates their spiritual significance. Some of the finest come from the Asante paramount chieftaincies. In a survey of ten paramountcies in 1977, Doran Ross documented 67 cast gold sword ornaments which between them represented 32 motifs.

Fig. 68   A large double crocodile in gold adorns this Asante royal sword. Many such ornaments were cast earlier in this century to enhance the prestige of the chiefs, notably after 1924 when the Asantehene returned from exile. Photo: courtesy of René and Denise David

Fig. 69   Sword ornaments include some of the largest gold castings made by the Akan, weighing up to 800 grams. These two examples represent a monitor lizard or skink (above) and a crocodile (below). Cat. 169, 170

68

6. Umbrella Finials and Linguist Staffs

Umbrellas or parasols have been used by Akan kings at least since the seventeenth century, when they are first mentioned in written sources. Some were gifts from Europeans but others appear to have been made locally. Even at this time they were topped by an emblematic finial. In 1707, to encourage trade, the English planned to send to the Asantehene some fringed umbrellas of scarlet cloth with "a bird or beast on the top of the stick". Just over a century later Bowdich observed that the umbrellas in Kumasi were "crowned on the top with crescents, pelicans, elephants, barrels, and arms and swords of gold".

Umbrella finials (*kyinie akyi*) are of carved wood covered with gold leaf. They are symbols of the chief's wisdom and power, and often allude to an Akan proverb (fig. 70). On great public occasions these glittering symbols convey their message to the multitude; they are visible from afar, twirling and dancing above a majestic canopy of silk.

Fig. 70 The carved wooden tops of umbrellas and linguist staffs have symbolic meaning. This gold-leafed finial for a royal umbrella represents a hand holding an egg, indicating that authority must be exercised with care. If not held firmly the egg will fall and break; if held too tightly it will be crushed. The chief, therefore, must be neither too lenient nor too severe. Cat. 180

Fig. 71 This linguist staff top depicts a chief seated on a stool and holding an egg. The symbolism is the same as for the umbrella finial shown in Fig. 70: a chief must govern responsibly. Cat. 181

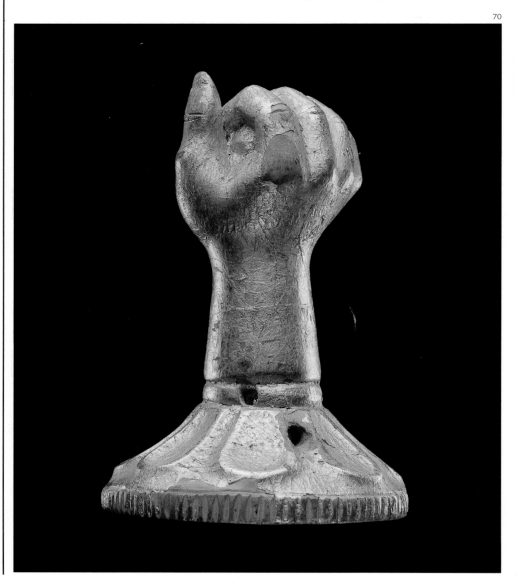

70

Fig. 72   The motif of an elephant carrying a palm tree, shown here on a linguist staff from the Fanti region, became popular during the period of British colonial rule. Photo: Doran H. Ross, Mankesim, 1976

Fig. 73   The range of proverbial themes depicted by linguist staffs is very great. Shown here are an elephant standing beside a cow; woodpeckers on a tree; and a hungry man standing in front of another man who eats a dish of soup. Each of these was intended to convey some moral message to the beholder. Cat. 183, 186, 187

It is not known for certain how or when umbrellas with golden finials came to be used among the Akan, but there are some tantalising clues. The use of umbrellas in tropical Africa is thought to have spread from Egypt, where they were present, topped with golden symbols, at the courts of the Fatimid and Mamluk sultans. In 1324 the Malian king, Mansa Musa, made his famous pilgrimage to Mecca, passing through

72

Egypt where he was given a splendid reception; shortly afterwards Arab travellers to Mali reported that at the king's court there were umbrellas "made of silk, and surmounted by a bird in gold about the size of a falcon". Golden umbrella finials were thus present in West Africa by the fourteenth century, and between then and the seventeenth they may have been introduced to the

Akan through the medium of Sudanic trade.

Linguist staffs (ɔkyeame poma) have a different history. They trace their origin to the silver-topped canes that European merchants brought to the Gold Coast in the seventeenth century. It became the custom that when a messenger was despatched, for instance to a chief, he carried one of these canes to show that he came by authority. In time some of these "messenger-sticks" were given to coastal kings and other dignitaries, who used them in the same way. Wilhelm Mueller noted that on the Fanti coast, in the 1660s, "when they go out for a walk, they carry in their hand a long stick, coloured white, red or yellow and mounted with silver. This stick is generally given to them as a present by the Christians trading here. On it the names of the donor and the recipient are engraved. This stick is used as a token of truthfulness, if they send someone a message."

At that time a coastal king who possessed such a cane would hold it in his hand like a European. Mueller noted that king Aduaffo of Fetu had one: "Instead of a royal sceptre he has in his hand a long staff, mounted with the finest silver, on which his name is engraved." In the eighteenth or nineteenth century this practice changed. Akan kings were now too great to hold the cane themselves, and this function was delegated to their linguist or spokesman (ɔkyeame). The earlier practice survived only in south-eastern Côte d'Ivoire and among the Baule, where, to this day, the cane is sometimes held by the king or other principal dignitary.

Among the Akan of Ghana, therefore, the cane became increasingly associated with the linguist, until it is today his

74

carried a wide range of proverbial and symbolic messages (figs. 71–75).

These staff tops were a relatively late development. They had come into use by the 1890s in the coastal Akan states (and perhaps also in the lagoons region of Côte d'Ivoire). Further inland they spread more slowly. In Asante, it appears, they were not made until after 1924, for the Asantehene was still in exile and it was only after his return that he gave permission for their use.

On the earliest gilded staffs, dating from about the 1890s to the 1920s, the sheets of hammered gold leaf were usually secured to the wood by tiny gold staples. This technique was abandoned in favour of glueing, probably around the 1920s.

Once the idea of ornate gilded linguist-staff tops had become prevalent, this art form was rapidly developed in the hands of such master carvers as Osei Bonsu of Kumasi (1900–1977). The staffs achieved enormous popularity and added much to the grandeur of state occasions. Today they are an integral part of Akan ceremonial, and their influence is seen even beyond the Akan region: chiefs among the Ewe to the east and the Baule to the west now buy linguist staffs from Kumasi or commission their own from local carvers.

Fig. 74 Linguist staffs with elaborate gold-leafed finials were almost unknown a hundred years ago. Today they play a prominent role in Akan ceremonial. This linguist carries a recently carved staff at the Akropong Yam Festival. Photo: Doran H. Ross, Akropong, 1976

Fig. 75 The *sankofa* bird with its head turned backwards is a popular symbol that signifies: "Learn from past experience". Cat. 182

badge of office. Such canes were originally silver-topped, but as regalia became more splendid, golden tops began to appear. These carved and gilded linguist staff tops would seem to have been inspired directly by the umbrella finials (which were carved by the same craftsmen), and like them they

7. Caps, Helmets and Crowns

For centuries the Akan have been fascinated by exotic headgear. This interest is reflected in the variety of forms worn by the chief and his entourage. Hats, caps, helmets and crowns (*ɛkyɛ*), together with velvet headbands (*abotire*), were made from costly materials and often embellished by the goldsmith. Ornaments of gold leaf or thick hammered gold created a spectacular effect, enhancing the royal prestige while at the same time conveying a symbolic message.

Perhaps the most widely used chiefs' hats today are headbands of rich velvet (usually red or black) with a profusion of gold-leafed ornaments (fig. 36). The designs of these ornaments are carefully chosen to represent a maxim or proverb. Stars, crescent moons, Maltese crosses, snakes, flowers, cowry shells and talismans are among the many designs, usually carved in a light wood and covered with gold leaf.

Crowns based on English and other European models became popular in the colonial period (fig. 76), doubtless because Akan chiefs had learned that for the white man crowns were synonymous with royalty. This is a striking instance of the Akan predilection for copying foreign forms. The Akan

Fig. 76   While Akan crowns were inspired by those of Europe, the goldsmiths showed much inventive skill. This gold crown was made for the paramount chief of Akwapim, Frederick William Kwasi Akuffo. It is adorned with eagles set among sprays of foliage and flowers, and bears the inscription: "KING. F.W. KWASI AKUFFO AKROPONG JAN.1.1896". Photo: Basel Mission Archive

Fig. 77   This gold-leafed crown is based on a British imperial model, but in place of the Christian cross it is surmounted by three pods of the *okra* plant. Cat. 50

76

Fig. 78   A royal official at the Asantehene's court in Kumasi wears on his head a large rectangular amulet covered with a sheet of richly embossed gold. Photo: E. Elisofon, 1971

Fig. 79   The large amulets encased in gold, worn on the head by certain officials, probably contain powders or other substances reputed to have magical protective powers, or sheets of paper covered with Arabic script. Cat. 51, 53, 54

78

product is artistically carved, and often features crosses, stars and fleurs-de-lys, the whole being gilded.

Helmets known as *krɔbɔnkyɛ* (fig. 43) were made from blackened antelope skin, sometimes with openwork designs. The more splendid examples are edged and divided into panels by ribbons of embossed sheet gold, with symbolic gold finials and ornaments in each panel. A few, including some that the British seized from Kumasi in 1874, have alternate gold and silver ornaments.

They seem to have been made in pairs or sets.

These caps are usually worn by young attendants of the chief, notably sword and gun-bearers, but they may also be worn by the chief himself. As their shape suggests, they may have been inspired by some form of European military hat, perhaps of the eighteenth or early nineteenth century. In effect they appear to identify members of the royal guard, with the chief as its commander.

Chapter Four

The Akan-related Peoples of Côte d'Ivoire

The republic of Côte d'Ivoire (Ivory Coast), with a population approaching ten million, lies west of Ghana and south of Mali. Its many ethnic groups may be divided broadly into Mande and Voltaic peoples in the open savanna grasslands of the north, Kru peoples in the mountains and forests to the west, and Akan and Akan-related peoples in the central and south-eastern regions. There are scattered deposits of gold in parts of the country, but these are not as rich as those of Ghana. Most occur in the south-east as an extension of the Ghanaian goldfields. Here the precious metal was exploited in the past, and although output was not spectacular, its presence led to a development of goldsmithing in the region.

Little use was made of gold jewellery over much of the Côte d'Ivoire. The Voltaic and Kru groups produced none, and the output of the Mande was inconspicuous. In the south-eastern quadrant of the country, however, where the auriferous zones lay, the goldsmith's art was able to flourish.

The gold resources of the south-east lie in the territories of a complex cluster of ethnic groups who, for want of a better name, may be termed Akan-related. These are peoples who share a common (though sometimes remote) linguistic ancestry with the Akan of Ghana. Some have argued that they should be

termed Akan, citing a number of shared cultural traits. But while they had some historical contact with the Akan, the Ivoirian groups never used this name to describe themselves, and such cultural similarities as exist are outweighed by other marked divergences of language, material culture and social organisation.

The Akan-related peoples of the south-east may be divided into two broad categories:

(a) *The Anyi-Baule-Nzima cluster.* This includes three peoples speaking closely related languages or dialects: the Anyi, living mainly between the Comoe river and the Ghana-Côte d'Ivoire border; the Baule to the west of them; and the Nzima, who occupy the extreme south-eastern corner of Côte d'Ivoire and the neighbouring territory in Ghana.

(b) *The so-called "Lagoons Peoples".* These are a dozen or more distinct ethnic groups, some numbering only a few thousand but each speaking a separate language. They include the true lagoons peoples, the Avikam, Adiukru, Aizi, Alladian, Ebrie (Kyaman), Mbato, Abure, Esuma and Eotile, who as their name indicates live around the coastal lagoons. Well to the north of them, away from the lagoons, live the remainder of this group: the Ega, Abidji, Krobu, Abe and Atie (Akie), the last of whom are neighbours of the Baule.

In addition there are the Abron and Dormaa living in the Bonduku region. These are true Akan, linguistically and culturally part of the Akan of Ghana but today divided by a modern international boundary.

There were formerly many goldsmiths both in villages around the lagoons and further inland. Owing to changes of fashion and the rising cost and scarcity

Fig. 80 The Anyi king of Indenye, Nana Osei Bonzou II, holds court in his palace at Abengourou. Photo: Jean Paul Barbier, 1988

of gold, traditional goldsmithing has declined drastically in recent years; most goldsmiths have disappeared from the lagoons villages within the last generation, and among the Baule very few remain.

Until the end of the nineteenth century gold-dust circulated as a form of general currency throughout south-eastern Côte d'Ivoire. All the ethnic groups of this region used gold jewellery. The older goldwork consists almost entirely of lost wax castings, but in this century less costly objects of wood covered with gold leaf have become popular.
Gold used in casting work is frequently very impure, being mixed with a high percentage of silver or copper.

The cast goldwork of south-eastern Côte d'Ivoire consists mainly of personal ornaments, with a profusion of bead and pendant forms. There is little by way of cast gold chieftaincy regalia, unlike in Ghana. This difference of emphasis may be due to the fact that the highly organized system of chieftaincy evolved by the Akan of Ghana had no counterpart in much of south-eastern Côte d'Ivoire. There were no paramount chiefs among the lagoons peoples, with the exception of the Abure (who trace their origins to Ghana). The Baule too, in precolonial times, had almost no traditional leaders ranking higher than *klɔ kpɛngbɛn*, "village elder". Only in one or two places (notably at Sakassou) did immigrants from Ghana succeed in introducing Akan-style chieftaincies among them, and these were not influential. Consequently there was until recent times little demand for the elaborate forms of regalia found among the Akan.

During the colonial period the French sought to consolidate their authority over the peoples of the south-east by creating district or cantonal chiefs. Though untraditional, these offices have survived, and their occupants have increasingly sought to gain status by adopting Akan-style regalia (as have the few traditional paramount chiefs in the region). Consequently one now sees these persons adorned with bracelets, rings, gold sandals, headgear, chains and other regalia, in some cases not only patterned after the Akan model but actually imported from Ghana (fig. 81). Both among the Baule and in the lagoons region, chiefs and notables today often display regalia purchased from Asante goldsmiths in Kumasi.

In contrast with the south-east, true Akan chieftaincies have long been established among the Abron of the Bonduku region and the Anyi living close to the Ghana border (fig. 80). The Abron kingdom is historically an Akan state, and its ruler, with his seat at Herebo, has a wealth of Akan-style regalia, including a gold-covered stool (fig. 1). Formerly this regalia was made locally, but in recent times much of it has been obtained from Kumasi.

There are thus close historical links between the goldwork of Côte d'Ivoire and Ghana. The direction of influence has generally been from Ghana to Côte d'Ivoire rather than the reverse, i.e. from the central and coastal Akan to the Akan-related peoples of the periphery. But despite this strong Akan influence Ivoirian goldwork has in some respects developed independently. The gold-hilted fly-whisks of the Baule, for instance, have a shape quite unlike those from Ghana; they were used not merely by chiefs but by clan heads and village elders, and might even be held by women.

Gold rings, a fully developed art form among the Akan, are almost absent

Fig. 81 The peoples of the lagoons region have adopted much Akan-style regalia for their own use. Here an Ebrie dignitary is seen with his linguist and elders in the village of Anna near Bingerville. Photo: E. Elisofon, 1971

from the corpus of traditional goldwork from the Baule and lagoons regions. With a few rare exceptions (such as cat. no. 246), the gold rings that one sees among the Baule are either of modern design, sometimes of European inspiration, or Akan imports from Ghana. A very few gold rings were also produced locally by peoples living close to the Ghana border, such as the Anyi and Nzima (cat. no. 247).

Style and Provenance

In the literature on Ivoirian gold jewellery the impression is sometimes given that there are distinctive ethnic styles: one sees a given piece confidently attributed to the Baule, Atie, Ebrie or some other particular group. This idea is not borne out by fieldwork. There is no obvious reason why styles of goldwork should have followed ethnic, linguistic or political divisions, and while Ivoirian goldwork is usually distinguishable from that of Ghana, it is not easy to divide it further into regional styles or substyles.

There were no separate ethnic styles among the lagoons peoples, nor can their work always be distinguished from that of the Baule. It may be equally wrong to suppose that there was a single homogeneous "lagoons style" of goldwork, or even a single "Baule style". The matter is considerably more complex.

Certain object-types, such as gold beads and gold-leafed fly-whisks, tend to have standardised forms and motifs. These may have been made with little variation over a wide area, persisting without great change for generations. Other kinds of object were less standardised. The gold pendant heads, for instance, show an enormous range of variation (figs. 85, 93). These were evidently

produced in a fairly large number of workshops by innovative and individualistic craftsmen, the result being a rich kaleidoscope of varying personal styles and "workshop styles". To divide these along ethnic lines is probably impossible.

In most cases the true provenance of a given object is unknown. There is no record of the town or village from which it came, nor of the name and ethnic identity of its maker. Even where it can be assigned to a particular geographical region, it by no means follows that it was made by the ethnic group inhabiting that region. Some Baule smiths, for example, migrated south, setting up workshops among the Alladian, Ebrie and others. Nzima goldsmiths likewise came west to seek a wider clientele in the various coastal towns. To complicate the matter further, objects themselves often travelled far from their place of origin, and in some cases they were commissioned by strangers from a distant region.

These difficulties are such that it is unwise to attempt attributions in more than the most general terms. For the purposes of this study some items have been classified broadly as "south-eastern Côte d'Ivoire", others more specifically as "Baule", "lagoons area" or "Ghana/Côte d'Ivoire border region". Some of these attributions are tentative. Certain objects may have come from anywhere in the region, others occur in fairly distinctive styles or substyles whose origin is unknown. It should not be forgotten that over much of the region goldwork has never been closely documented.

A cautionary word should be said about the various attributions found in the literature. Often these are valueless. Some are concocted by unscrupulous

Fig. 82   In a few cases gold leaf was used to adorn Baule figural sculpture. This statuette represents a *blolo bian*, that is, the man whom a Baule woman believed to be her spouse in the spirit world. The gold leaf may have been added to emphasise his wealth. Archives Barbier-Mueller

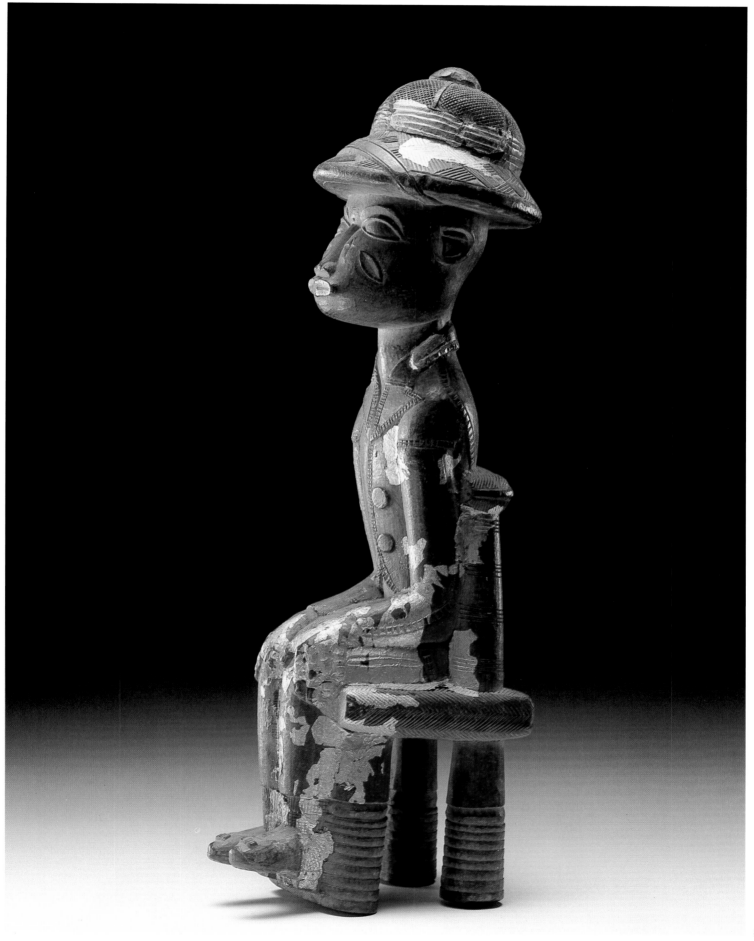

Fig. 83 Making the wax model for a pendant head in the lagoons region, 1971. The goldsmith is an Ebrie from the village of Anna. Photo: E. Elisofon, 1971

Fig. 84 Wax model for a pendant gold head made by the Baule goldsmith Diby Koffi of Bouake, 1986. Photo: Timothy F. Garrard

Fig. 85 Pendant gold heads show great stylistic variation. Openwork forms (above) and those pierced by triangular holes (centre) are characteristic of the lagoons region, while those of more naturalistic appearance (below) were mostly made by the Baule and other inland goldsmiths. Cat. 221, 223–225

83

dealers, others are labels hopefully applied by scholars but amounting to little more than guesswork. There are cases where a genuine "provenance" is supplied, but this usually indicates where an object is known to have been collected, not where and by whom it was made. It is rare to have accurate information about the place of manufacture and the ethnic identity of the goldsmith.

These general statements can be qualified to some extent. Most gold-leafed wooden objects, for instance, seem to have been made by the Baule (sometimes for clients in other regions).

84

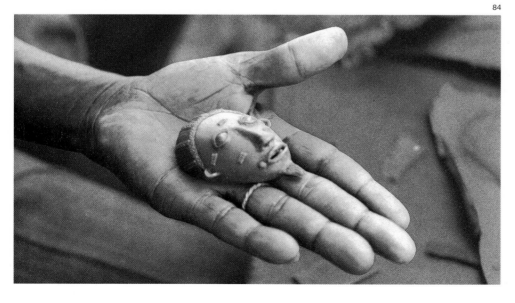

It is possible that centres of goldleafing may once have existed elsewhere, but within living memory this kind of work has been performed exclusively in a few Baule villages, and the style of carving is typical of the Baule (figs. 82, 101).

Gold beads, too, are usually attributed to the Baule, and great numbers were certainly worn by them. They are still made in a few Baule workshops. But some may also come from the Anyi (whose goldwork has never been systematically studied), and according to some accounts they were once made by the Ebrie.

It is beyond doubt that many of the castings with highly ridged surfaces, built up from numerous strands of wax threads, were produced by goldsmiths living around the lagoons, for instance at Grand Bassam and in the Ebrie village of Anna near Bingerville (figs. 95, 98, 100). Often these lagoons products show traces of numerous casting sprues. Some also have crudely cut triangular perforations (figs. 96, 97), which seem to be rare on work from the Baule region. But this is not an infallible guide, for Baule goldsmiths also used the wax thread technique with outstanding success. The quality of the casting may be a more reliable indicator of origin. Baule workmanship tends to be very fine (fig. 93), whereas the lagoons products are sometimes crude and roughly finished (fig. 95).

Gold pendant heads were made throughout the region. They exist in many variations. Experienced Ivoirian goldsmiths tend to attribute those modelled with the greatest neatness and realism to the Baule (figs. 84, 93), and the more schematic forms to the lagoons region (figs. 83, 96). These attributions are doubtless correct, for the first group

is sometimes close in style to Baule wood statuary (masks in particular), while the few remaining Ebrie casters still make heads in a schematised style. But there are no neat dividing lines. The majority of pendant heads fall between these two extremes and cannot readily be assigned to any particular geographic area.

Pendants of other forms come predominantly from the lagoons region, where they were often worn, hoarded or publicly exhibited. Among the Baule they were less common. Baule goldsmiths are rather vague about them, and seem reluctant to accept any but the disc, lozenge and crescent forms as local work.

The Origins of Goldsmithing

The first references to gold jewellery in Côte d'Ivoire date from the seventeenth century. Although earlier evidence is lacking, it seems reasonable to suppose that the goldsmith's art here was a westward extension of that found on the Gold Coast. Goldsmithing in the lagoons region may thus have begun in the fifteenth or sixteenth century.

Further inland, among the Anyi and Baule, almost nothing is known of the early history of goldsmithing. No direct documentary references exist before the late nineteenth century when the French first penetrated the area. Despite this, it is beyond doubt that brass-casters (who were also goldsmiths) have long been active in the region, for ancient brass-castings are found, including Anyi and Baule weights of early style, attributable to the seventeenth century or earlier. We may presume that gold jewellery was made at the same time. Dutch reports of the early eighteenth century mention that the Aowin (eastern Anyi)

were rich in gold, of which some was in the form of "fetish" ornaments.

The Akan goldfields of Ghana were worked from about the fourteenth century, and the major sources of gold were probably soon discovered. With gold fever raging among the Akan, the neighbouring Anyi and Baule deposits may not have escaped notice for long. Their first exploitation (and with it the appearance of goldsmiths) may thus date back to the fifteenth or sixteenth century. If this is correct, the goldsmith's art in south-eastern Côte d'Ivoire may be almost as old as in Ghana.

Some Baule goldsmiths maintain that their ancestors introduced the art of goldsmithing from Ghana in the eighteenth century. Such claims are based on a popular but unhistorical legend according to which the Baule people as a whole came from Ghana at that time. In reality the Baule have been established in their present country much longer. Some groups of immigrants from Ghana undoubtedly settled among them in the eighteenth century, establishing chieftaincies and probably employing goldsmiths at their courts, but the mass of the population was of local origin. The traditions of the immigrant lineages have served to obscure the fact that goldsmithing had existed among the Baule from a very much earlier period. It dates back, in all probability, to the first exploitation of gold deposits in the region.

The remainder of this chapter will consider the main categories of Ivoirian goldwork.

Fig. 86   Some of the finest Akan gold castings were produced in the royal workshops of Kumasi. This superb bracelet, dating from the 19th century, may have belonged to the Asantehene Prempeh I. It was acquired by Sir Cecil Armitage, who entered Kumasi with British troops in 1896. Cat. 105

1. Beads

Among the Baule, and possibly elsewhere, great numbers of beads were cast in gold. They also exist in brass, and a few are of silver. These beads probably represent old Akan forms (such as those illustrated by Jean Barbot) which were adopted by the Anyi and Baule in the seventeenth or eighteenth century. Their forms are basically simple and abstract: discs, rectangles, tubes and bicone forms predominate (figs. 87, 88). A few others represent tusks, horns, claws and leopard's teeth, but these are

uncommon. There is no equivalent to the rich variety of nineteenth-century Akan bead types in the form of seeds, shells, drums, stars, human teeth, stools etc.

The Ivoirian beads were most often worn by women and children (fig. 89), but they were also used in other contexts. It was not unknown for them to be used to adorn items of wood sculpture, such as "spirit spouse" figures and the statuettes used by spirit mediums. Large disc-shaped and rectangular beads were sometimes made

Fig. 87   The work of making gold beads is highly skilled. Among the foremost living exponents of the art are the Baule goldsmith Diby Koffi and his son Koffi Yao Christophe of Bouake. Photo: Jean Paul Barbier, 1988

Fig. 88   Gold beads of exceptional quality can be found on some older Baule necklaces. The variety of shapes and designs creates a rich, aesthetically satisfying effect. Cat. 230

87

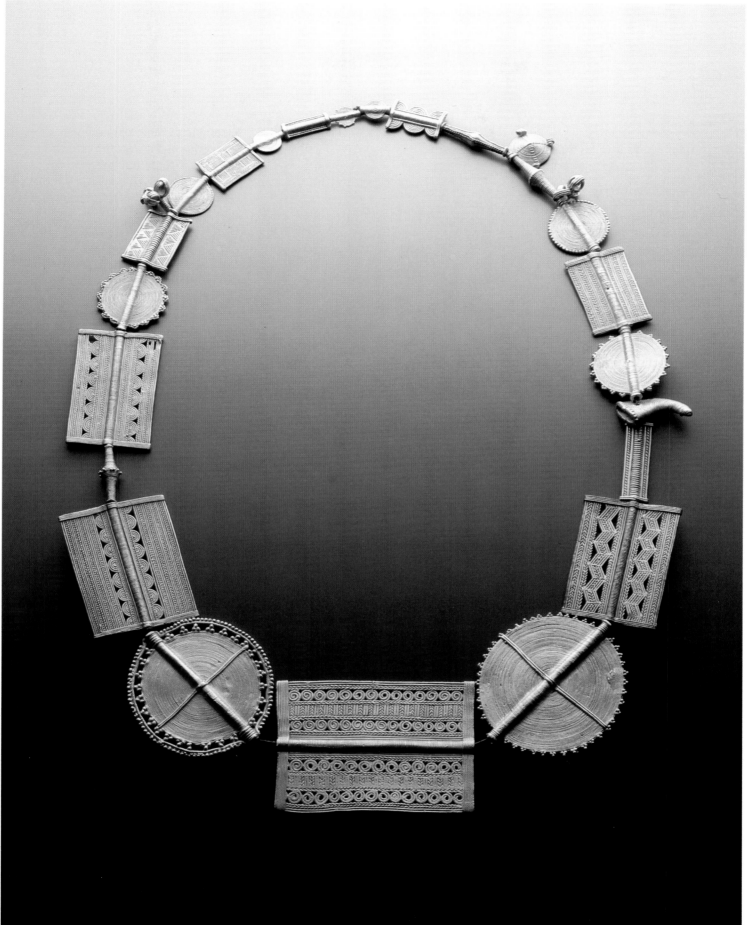

Fig. 89   Baule women wore necklaces of gold beads on festive occasions. Archives Barbier-Mueller

Fig. 90   Strings of large gold beads are sometimes hung in front of a Baule chief on festive occasions. Photo: Timothy F. Garrard, 1985

Fig. 91   The most common Baule bead forms are discs and rectangles. They are named according to their size or the arrangement of the wax threads forming the design: for instance *senze*, "setting sun", and *kwa jamma*, "slave's toe" for large disc beads, and *srala*, "bamboo door" for a rectangular bead.

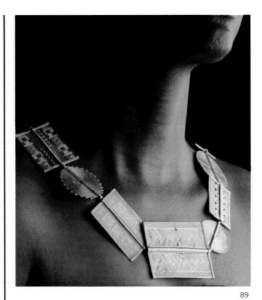

89

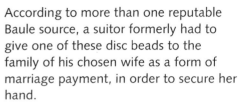

90

for a chief; on public occasions they were hung before him suspended from strings (figs. 90, 91). Whether this was done simply to emphasize his prestige or for some ulterior motive (such as to keep away evil influences) is not known.

Particular virtues were attributed to the spiral disc forms, fine examples of which are highly prized by the Baule.

According to more than one reputable Baule source, a suitor formerly had to give one of these disc beads to the family of his chosen wife as a form of marriage payment, in order to secure her hand.

The workmanship of some of the older beads is exquisite. Most are built up from various arrangements of wax threads, sometimes of exceptional fineness, and some are further decorated with a border of plaited ropework or tiny pellets. Openwork designs are also found. In recent years some Baule goldsmiths have begun to ornament the flat surface of the larger disc beads with depictions of birds, fishes, crocodiles, spiders etc. They frankly admit that such designs have no special significance, being added simply to attract buyers. Embellishments of this kind are rare among older beads, though not entirely unknown (cat. no. 241).

The Baule bestowed many fanciful names on their different bead types. Most of these are unknown to the present generation, but they are still remembered by old ladies and by a few goldsmiths. The disc beads were usually called *aflɛ mma* or *taliɛ*, the latter name probably derived from the Akan *tadeɛ*, "a pool of water". Those of larger size were known as *sɛnzɛ*, "the setting sun," or even *kwa jamma*, "the slave's toe". A goldsmith explained the last name by saying that "the slave walks a lot so his toes become bigger."

Flat beads comprising a central spiral flanked by a bisected spiral at each end were called *jue lua* or *jue che*, "fish tail".

Tubular or tapering beads such as *ayɛkpɛ* and *ndoama* might also be known as *able waka*, "corn stalk", or *adjamiaa*, said to signify "I don't need

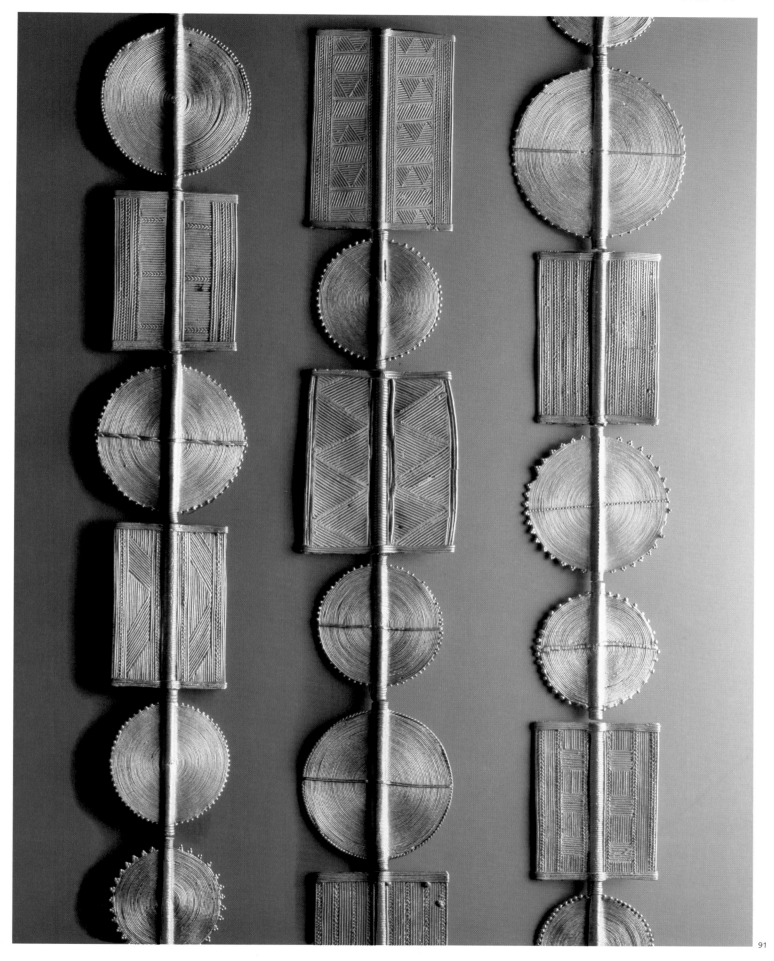

Fig. 92   Depictions of a human face, known as *sran trε*, "a person's head", were worn as pendants on a necklace, or attached to the hair. Sometimes, as here, they were also used to adorn the caps worn by dignitaries. Most are of cast gold, but this example is of carved wood covered in gold leaf. Photo: G. Wocker, Coll. Musée de l'Homme

Fig. 93   Some of the finest pendants of gold heads were made in the Baule region. These two examples are probably the work of the same goldsmith, and may come from the region of Sakassou, the seat of the major Baule chieftaincy. Cat. 216, 217

92

to marry to live". Rectangular beads had a variety of names depending on the pattern formed by the arrangement of wax threads: *srala* ("bamboo door"), *akɔndrε* ("chicken feather"), *alekue* (the cups on the board for the *awale* game), *laliε waka* ("knife handle"), *jomo owie* ("dog's bone"), *besin besin* ("back to back"), *kɔkɔyaka* ("taro roots" or "taro foot") and *akwatika sinbui* ("the back of the tortoise"). Other names, such as *boloa atre*, *ble* and *suesakun*, could no longer be explained.

2. Pendant Heads

Some of the finest Ivoirian gold castings are pendants in the form of a human face or head. These are well known throughout the south-east, and most were probably made in Baule and lagoons workshops. In the literature they are often referred to as "masks", quite wrongly since they have no known association with masks or masking cults. Neither the Baule nor the lagoons peoples identify them as masks, but instead simply call them "heads" or "human heads" in the various local

languages. They might perhaps more accurately be termed "faces", since the face rather than the entire head is usually depicted.

In most cases these castings appear to depict a male face, with beard and small moustaches, and often with elaborate hairstyles and facial scarifications of a kind no longer in use today (fig. 93). Although some local informants claim that such pendants could represent anyone, male or female, it remains uncertain whether any were intended to be specifically female.

Among the Baule these pendants are named as *ngblo* or *sran trε*, "a human head". They are said to have been worn, by both men and women, as ornaments attached to the hair or suspended from a necklace. Occasionally they are still worn on special festive occasions, for beauty and prestige. While most are lost wax castings, they also exist in carved wood covered with gold leaf. A Baule dignitary may sometimes be seen with such a carving attached to his cap (fig. 92).

In the lagoons region these pendants were sometimes put to interesting uses. Niangoran-Bouah relates that among the Abure they could be used to prevent the participants in a quarrel from coming to blows. When a person thought he was about to be struck, he would repeat the ritual words *Ntale ntcha te* or *Ntale ete*, literally "I have a man's head". In doing so he placed himself under the protection of the ancestors, and his opponent, no matter how angry, would not dare to strike him for fear of offending them. When violence threatened between two clans the village chief would take two gold heads from his treasury and give one to the leader of each faction. This indicated that the dispute must be heard before the chief and his elders. The antagonists were then bound to appear on the date fixed and restore the gold heads to the chief, after which the case could be heard.

There was no particular restriction on the ownership of such ornaments. The Baule say that they might be owned by any person rich enough to afford one. Most are today regarded as family heirlooms, forming part of the gold treasure belonging to the whole family and handed down from one generation to the next. Nowadays they are rarely if ever commissioned for traditional use among the Baule, but a few lagoons goldsmiths still make them at the request of local clients.

Asked whom these pendants represent, Ivoirian informants tend to be very vague. Some Baule regard them as "portraits" of friends or lovers, others say they may represent anyone, whether beautiful or ugly. In the lagoons region they are sometimes said to be "portraits" of ancestors or former kings, though no individual is named.

Among these pendants there is a small group that show the head on a circular or oval plaque. They vary greatly in style. Some are in the crude styles probably to be attributed to the Grand Bassam region; others resemble Baule work (cat. no. 226). The feature of a plaque combined with the face seems to be of European inspiration.

In the mid-nineteenth century the French were seeking to extend their influence in the lagoons area by signing treaties of friendship. Towards the end of 1853 Captain Faidherbe, aided by the Abure king of Moussou, Moulo Asamoa, built a small fort at Dabou. It is recorded that "to commemorate this event and to mark her gratitude to the Abure of Moussou, imperial France caused a gold

93

Fig. 94   The pendant gold heads served different uses in Ghana and Côte d'Ivoire. In Ghana they were usually attached to state swords, where they represent the heads of enemies killed in battle. In Côte d'Ivoire, on the other hand, they are used as personal jewellery, and are said to represent friends, lovers or ancestral kings. Photo: courtesy of René and Denise David

Fig. 95   Pendants made in the lagoons region sometimes combine the human face with another form such as a ram's horns, a crescent moon, or an outstretched human hand. This casting is said to represent a ram's horns. Cat. 199

medal to be struck bearing the head of king Moulo Assamoi" (J. A. Able, *Histoire et Tradition Politique du Pays Abouré*, Abidjan, 1978, p. 52). The original French gold medal presumably showed the head of the king, Moulo Asamoa, on a circular plaque. It is likely to have created a profound impression among the kings and chiefs of the coast.

94

In consequence, it would seem, they began to commission their own "medals", showing a face on a plaque, from local goldsmiths. The local castings of a head on a plaque are thus "commemorative medals", directly inspired by the form of the French medallion.

From their contexts of use and the interpretations offered it seems that these gold pendant heads are to be associated with the ancestors. They were possibly once intended to represent specific individuals. However, they are not portraits in the European sense, but rather stereotyped depictions of the human face, produced in multiple examples in the style of a given workshop or craftsman. In some cases, notably in the lagoons region, they have become highly stylised abstractions that merely incorporate a few elements of the human face such as eyes and a nose.

These small gold pendant heads from Côte d'Ivoire have no exact equivalent

in Ghana, but they may be related to the larger gold heads (*abosodeε*) that the Akan of Ghana attached to state swords or hung from royal stools (fig. 94). These were likewise commemorative "portrait" heads, intended to represent actual persons such as Worosa, king of Banda, and Adinkira, king of Gyaman. They are often called "trophy heads" since they represented, in effect, the heads of enemy chiefs killed and decapitated in battle.

While the concept of making gold heads is common to the two countries, their function differs. The Ivoirian heads are items of personal jewellery, representing persons to be remembered with respect (ancestors, kings, friends, lovers). In contrast the Akan heads from Ghana form part of state regalia and depict public enemies. Only one instance seems to be known of an Ivoirian gold head used in this way: a particularly fine and large example (height 9.5 cm) attributed to the Adiukru, which was received by the Musée de l'Homme, Paris, in 1892. According to Noll and N'Diaye, it was a sword ornament.

It should not be forgotten that depictions of the human head or face also occur in brass. They are fairly numerous among goldweights from both Ghana and Côte d'Ivoire, and some of the oldest may date back to the seventeenth century. It is perhaps significant that while many Akan identify them as trophy heads, others say quite simply that they are likenesses or "portraits" of the ancestors. This suggests that the Ghanaian and Ivoirian traditions of making commemorative "portraits", whether in brass or gold, may ultimately derive from a common origin.

Fig. 96   This pendant human head is in a style typical of the lagoons region. It was made in 1988 by an Ebrie goldsmith, Akesse Raphael, who works in the village of Anna near Bingerville. He names the design as *gobieheme*, "female healer". Its highly stylised form is taken from one of the stock models that have been used in his workshop for decades. Archives Barbier-Mueller

Fig. 97   Akesse Raphael displays a gold pendant cast by him in December 1987. It is said to represent a male crab. The triangular holes are a common feature of gold pendants from the lagoons region. Photo: Jean Paul Barbier, 1988

Fig. 98   In the lagoons region gold pendants were sometimes worn attached to the hair on festive occasions. This Ebrie girl was photographed in 1960 at the ceremonies to mark the independence of Côte d'Ivoire. Photo: E. Elisofon, 1960

3. Other Pendant Ornaments

Ivoirian goldsmiths made many other ornamental jewels of pendant form. Prominent among them are subjects drawn from the animal world: a creature resembling a kind of sawfish, together with the crocodile, tortoise, turtle, catfish or mudfish, python, frog, snail,

96

bushcow, elephant, leopard, antelope, pangolin and chicken. A number of highly stylised castings are said to represent male and female crabs (fig. 97). There are also horned ram's heads and representations of a human hand, in addition to more abstract forms

97

based on the disc, lozenge and crescent. Certain pendants from the lagoons region, such as the human hand and the crescent, sometimes incorporate a rather surprising addition – a small human face (fig. 95).

These ornaments exist in a large number of variations, doubtless reflecting the fact that they emanated from many workshops over a wide area. The focus of the tradition is, however, clearly coastal; they are found in profusion among the lagoons peoples, but are apparently quite scarce (and restricted almost entirely to abstract forms) among the Baule and other inland groups.

Early accounts sometimes refer to these jewels as "fetishes," suggesting that they were not intended to be merely decorative but were believed to possess magical protective powers. Some of the abstract forms are still regarded in this way, notably the discs and lozenges. As with other categories of metalwork, it seems likely that these pendants have been elaborated over the centuries, with the castings tending to increase in size and representational forms being added to an original corpus of abstract types.

The lagoons peoples have used such ornaments at least since the seventeenth century, when European visitors noticed that the coastal men and women tied gold jewels in their hair. Such castings were still commonly worn in the nineteenth century, as jewellery for the hair, or on the forehead, or suspended from a necklace. At Grand Bassam, in 1844, Lieutenant Besson found that almost all the men wore four or five pendants, while their wives had many gold jewels around their neck, arms and legs. Such customs have now largely died out, although some coastal notables still keep these ornaments for use by their attendants, and women

Fig. 99   Abrogoua, an Ebrie chief, is seen here with his entourage about 1930. In the past many gold pendants were worn by the family and attendants of coastal dignitiaries. Doc. et cliché Arch. Nat. France (Centre des Archives d'Outre-Mer)

Fig. 100   In the lagoons region there is a spectacular public event known as the "display of gold". A rich man who seeks to consolidate his prestige will display publicly his accumulated treasure of gold ornaments. As many as 60 or 70 pendants may be shown, of many different designs, laid out on tables in the public street. Cat. 197, 198, 200, 209

occasionally still wear the old jewels on festive or ceremonial occasions (figs. 98, 99).

Among the lagoons peoples these gold pendants play a major role in a spectacular public ceremony: the "exhibition of gold". Fleuriot de Langle observed in 1873 that the pride of the "big men" was to expose their wealth to public view on certain days, spread out on tables. This is an old custom known throughout the lagoons region; it appears to have existed for generations. Every man's ambition was to add to the family treasure inherited from his ancestors, and if, through his own efforts, he acquired significant wealth, he could improve his social status and elevate himself to the ranks of the "big men". This he achieved by a public display of his gold (fig. 100).

Such a ceremony was not lightly undertaken. A man would not attempt it until, after making discreet enquiries, he was certain that his self-acquired gold ornaments were sufficient in number and quality to meet with general approval. If they were not, he would risk public scorn and ridicule. He also needed sufficient means to provide a feast for the whole community.

On the appointed day the festivities would begin. Amidst singing, dancing and drumming, punctuated with musket fire, the owner of the gold exposed his wealth to public view. His accumulated treasure of gold pendants was set out on a table in the street, where the whole world could examine them. While the display was in progress, those who had already established their status as "big men" could exhibit their gold in the same way. This increased the interest of the occasion and no doubt provided a standard by which the efforts of the new aspirant could be judged.

There was no fixed requirement as to the amount of gold that had to be displayed. It is said that in the past a dozen or twenty gold pendants were sufficient. Today, thirty is perhaps the bare minimum. The tendency has been to aim for an ever larger quantity, even at the expense of quality; the greater the number, the higher the status of their owner. Sixty or seventy ornaments were shown in 1979 at a ceremony in Petit Cocody, and a hundred and one, reputedly, at Anokoua-Kouté in 1980.

By holding a successful exhibition a man raised his status from that of an ordinary commoner. He now joined the ranks of the respected elders in his community, and might even – according to some – style himself as a "king". By the public demonstration of his personal success he had proved himself worthy of his ancestors, or as the Ebrie say, *ɛn mo yi ka amando laka romɛ*, "he has added something to the family chest".

99

These ceremonies of social ascent occur in various forms among most, if not all, of the lagoons peoples. The Ebrie call them *min di matcha, hon di matcha* or *an di batcha*; the Adiukru know them as *angbandji*. Further inland they are little known; there was no equivalent ceremony, for instance, among the Baule.

4. Gold-leafed Objects

To complete this survey of Ivoirian goldwork, mention should be made of the very numerous objects of carved wood covered with gold leaf (figs. 101, 102). Most, if not all, of these objects appear to originate from the Baule region, where two or three villages still specialise in gold-leafing work.

According to some Baule goldsmiths, the art of gold-leafing is not indigenous, but was introduced from the Akan region of Ghana.

The products of the Baule workshops command a wide sale, and are often found far from their place of origin. They include innumerable fly-whisks, together with linguist staffs, knife hilts, combs, hairpins, amulets and even the occasional statue of a spouse from the spirit world (fig. 82). To these should be added a variety of amusing non-functional objects such as trumpets, rifles, helmets, hats and umbrellas. Such carvings – often inspired by items of European origin – became popular in the colonial period, adding an exotic and humorous element to Baule public festivals.

Fig. 101   Fly-whisks adorned with gold leaf are owned by many chiefs and dignitaries in south-eastern Côte d'Ivoire. Here they are displayed by a group of Baule women at a public ceremony. Photo: M. Huet, Agence Hoa-Qui

Fig. 102   This handle of a Baule fly-whisk depicts a parrot. It is carved in a light wood covered in a thin sheet of hammered gold. According to Baule goldsmiths, the technique of gold-leafing was introduced from the Akan region of Ghana. Cat. 253

101

Chapter Five

The Gold Mines
of West Africa

West African gold comes from many widely scattered localities in the forest and savanna. It occurs naturally in quartz reefs, sands and river gravels. The greater part is in the form of tiny grains and particles, but nuggets are also found (figs. 105, 109). The relentless action of tropical rainstorms and fast-flowing streams over millions of years has had the effect of dispersing great quantities of gold-dust over a huge area. There are extensive alluvial deposits, and in places the tiny grains can be seen sparkling in the soil after rainfall.

The three most important auriferous zones are Bambuk (Bambuhu), lying between the Senegal and Faleme rivers; Bure around the Upper Niger and its tributaries; and the Akan region of Ghana together with the adjacent Anyi and Baule regions of Côte d'Ivoire (fig. 104). While exact production figures are not available, these three goldfields have always accounted for the majority of West African gold output.

There were also a few medium-sized goldfields, some of which have been exploited over long periods of time. Among them were those of the Poura and Lobi regions in Burkina Faso, the Yaure goldfields of central Côte d'Ivoire, and those near Bole and Wasipe in north-western Ghana. Other sources of gold existed in places as far apart as

Sierra Leone and Hausaland. The returns from individual goldfields were unspectacular, but their combined output may not have been insignificant.

Apart from these, dozens if not hundreds of very minor goldfields were worked in the past. These attracted little attention. Their individual output was very small, barely enough to justify the labour involved, and many must have been rapidly exhausted and abandoned. They are rarely mentioned in historical records, though many have been rediscovered in the course of geological surveys in this century.

West Africans have probably been aware of gold since prehistoric times. Nuggets, being conspicuous, could not have escaped notice for long when washed from the ground by heavy rains. They may sometimes have been unearthed by farmers, or picked out of river gravels. But it is doubtful whether this gold was actively sought for its beauty or value, for there is reason to believe that from early times it was positively feared and avoided by many West African peoples.

There was an ancient and widespread belief that this bright, untarnishable metal contained a life of its own – an evil and dangerous spirit that had power to kill or injure the finder, drive him insane, or bring disaster on his family. It was commonly said that gold could grow like a plant, multiply in the earth and even move from one place to another. Arab geographers reported these West African beliefs a thousand years ago, and today they are still very much alive. They recur in similar form in all the major goldfields of Senegal, Guinée, Ghana and Côte d'Ivoire.

This deeply rooted fear of gold may long have deterred the local populations from

Fig. 103   From ancient times gold nuggets have been pierced and worn as ornaments. They were regarded as possessing a spirit that could confer magical protection on the wearer. Such nuggets can still be seen on the bracelets and necklaces of Akan chiefs. Photo: Doran H. Ross, Legu, southern Ghana, 1975

Fig. 104   The gold mines of West Africa. This map shows the principal regions where gold deposits were exploited in the past.

Fig. 105   Gold nuggets were rare and exceptional finds. In the Akan region, chiefs had a customary right to all nuggets over a certain weight. To evade this requirement, the finder of a nugget sometimes broke it into several pieces. Photo: H. M. Berney

exploiting the metal. Occasionally the finder of a gold nugget may have been bold enough to keep it, perhaps piercing it to be worn together with stone or shell beads as a bracelet. But this was probably done for magical, protective purposes rather than beauty or display. The nugget with its potent force may have been regarded as a kind of personal god. To the present day, among the Akan of Ghana, gold nuggets strung on bracelets or necklaces are far from being simple ornaments; they are called *asuman*, "fetishes", i.e.

talismans worn for protection against all kinds of evil and mischief, or as a remedy against diseases and witchcraft (fig. 103).

North Africans did not share the primordial West African fear of gold, but instead had their own superstitions concerning the "evil eye". Their women wore quantities of gold jewellery in the belief that this helped to avert the maleficent influence of the evil eye; it was thought that protection could be obtained from gold or other bright,

104

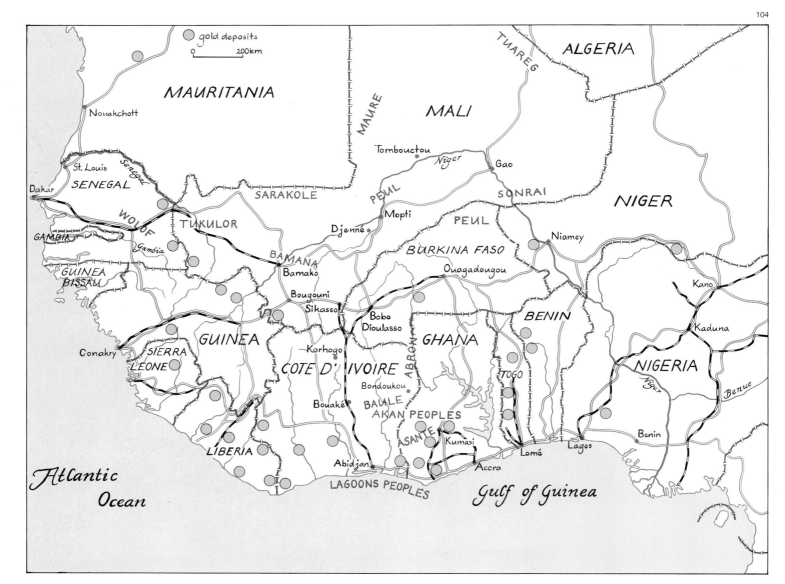

shining metals. As trans-Saharan contacts grew, these beliefs gained currency in the Sahel, whose peoples gradually overcame their fear of touching, using or exploiting the precious metal. When gold jewellery came into use and the benefits of a gold trade were realized, West Africans were induced to take up panning, mining and prospecting. Yet even then the old attitudes persisted; it was still widely believed that gold could not safely be reduced into possession without ritual precautions.

The more accessible goldfields of Bambuk and Bure seem to have been the first to be exploited, perhaps from about the fourth century A.D. For the next thousand years almost all the gold traded to North Africa came from these sources. When the Arabs swept through North Africa in the late seventh century they quickly became aware that there was gold beyond the desert. They hoped to find its source, but apart from gaining some knowledge of the rich Sahelian kingdoms where the metal was traded – ancient Ghana and Takrur – they heard only rumours. The mines of Bambuk and Bure lay further south, and the Sahelian kings took care not to reveal their precise location to strangers.

The even richer Akan goldfields remained unknown to the outside world until about the fourteenth century. This was no doubt due to the relative isolation of the region. Between the dense Akan forest and the commercial centres of the Middle Niger lay a vast expanse of inhospitable savanna where groups of Voltaic hunters and farmers eked out a precarious existence. For centuries these Voltaic peoples were victims of slave-raiding expeditions launched from the Sahel; in Muslim eyes they were infidels who might lawfully be killed or enslaved. Not surprisingly, this

treatment left them suspicious of strangers and bitterly hostile to Islamic penetration. They were not entirely averse to trade contacts, for imported salt and brass ornaments were welcomed, but the heavily armed trade caravans could pass through their territory only at great risk.

In these circumstances Sahelian merchants were slow to establish markets and trade routes in the Voltaic savanna. It was not until about the

106

Fig. 106   In parts of West Africa gold panning is a communal activity at the beginning of the rainy season. The Lobi women of Burkina Faso still practice their centuries-old technique of panning for gold in the region of Gaoua. Photo: Labitte, Photothèque IFAN, Dakar

Fig. 107   A miner extracting gold-bearing ore in the Kenieba region of south-western Mali. Photo: Guy Philippart de Foy (Explorer), 1982

fourteenth century that they were able to extend commercial contacts as far south as the lands of the Akan. When this occurred, however, the discovery of gold seems to have been quickly made. The new mines promised a rich harvest, and attracted caravans from as far afield as Jenne. Early settlements such as Begho, Bono-Manso and Techiman on the borders of Akan territory grew into important gold-trading towns. The Akan, stimulated by the appearance of exotic imports from the north, were now induced to search for gold. Over the next few centuries new goldfields were explored and exploited, some as far afield as the Côte d'Ivoire, and the Akan

region became the focus of some of the most vigorous commercial activity seen in West Africa.

Against this background some account may be given of the basic techniques of prospecting, mining and panning. Prospecting for gold was carried out with such thoroughness that most of the significant deposits were discovered and worked in precolonial times. Sands and river gravels were carefully searched, and in the Akan region prospectors often looked for earth of a blue-black or grey colour which they knew from experience to lie above auriferous gravels. Other less scientific methods were also adopted. A liquid medicine made from magic herbs was sometimes rubbed over the face in the belief that it enabled the prospector to detect gold hidden in the ground. Some persons put their faith in spiral mists or vapours that were thought to indicate the presence of gold. Others sought out certain kinds of trees, ferns and other plants for the same reason.

Gold prospectors were much influenced by omens and dreams. In Bambuk and Bure, it is said, if a person dreamt of fire or red monkeys running towards a certain place, he would go to dig there. Various forms of magical divination were also practised. Some men consulted kola nuts, others invoked the powers of magic squares or verses from the Koran. Both here and in the Akan region village communities sometimes called in a learned Muslim to prospect or use his divining skills on their behalf. For these services he received a handsome fee, sometimes in gold.

Most gold was obtained by the simple panning of sand, river gravels or gold-bearing soil. Many shallow pits were dug. The worker commonly used a set of calabashes or carved wooden bowls of descending sizes. In the largest a quantity of soil and water was carefully swilled round, the heavier gold particles sinking towards the bottom while extraneous earth was eliminated by hand or with the aid of a switch. The residue of gold-bearing soil was then tipped into a smaller bowl (fig. 110) and the process repeated until, in the final bowl, a tiny quantity of visible gold-dust appeared. The work was tedious, but a good panner could process up to 200–250 kg of soil in the course of a full day.

This simple method of gold-winning can still be seen in the Lobi region (fig. 106). Around Gaoua, for instance, after heavy rainfall, women and girls hurry to the fields armed with a calabash or two. At any convenient puddle they scrape a quantity of gravel into the largest calabash and commence panning. One panner can extract from a very ordinary puddle, in less than an hour, enough gold-dust to cover her finger-nail.

In the richer goldfields shafts were dug, often to a depth of between ten or twenty metres or even more (fig. 107). Each shaft was just wide enough to permit the worker to descend, with toeholds cut in the sides. He squatted at the bottom with an iron-tipped digging stick, and a basket or bowl in which to collect gold-bearing soil. This was dangerous work, for no attempt was made to shore up the shaft and all too often miners lost their lives when it collapsed. Sometimes a number of adjacent goldholes were joined up underground by a series of galleries.

In heavily forested regions these shafts presented a great hazard to unwary travellers, as the complaints of nineteenth-century visitors make clear. Holes were dug anywhere, even in the middle of a path, and when abandoned and overgrown they became almost

Fig. 108   On the Ankobra river in southern Ghana men dived for gold, scooping up gravel from the river bed. Large nuggets were sometimes found in this way. This engraving appeared in Olfert Dapper's description of Africa, first published in Amsterdam in 1668. Photo: Olfert Dapper's book (first edition: 1668)

Fig. 109   Gold-dust was the lure that for centuries attracted foreign merchants to West Africa. Some came with camel caravans from north of the Sahara, others with ships from Portugal, England, France, Holland and Denmark. Archives Barbier-Mueller

invisible. On one occasion Lady Hodgson, wife of the Governor of the Gold Coast, narrowly escaped being thrown down an old mine shaft when her hammock-bearers stumbled across it. Apart from the danger to travellers, children and animals sometimes fell in.

In parts of the Akan region a form of strip-mining was practised. The miners opened a large square pit and dug systematically down towards the water table. According to some reports the pits resembled stepped terraces.

Rich quartz reefs were sometimes tenaciously followed into a hillside for a considerable distance. The rock was hacked off and carried away to be broken up and crushed. This involved much arduous manual labour, the quartz being hammered and ground into a fine powder which was then panned. Returns from this activity were relatively small.

A different method of gold-winning was practised on the Ankobra river in

southern Ghana. Here swimmers dived for gold, carrying a pan to scoop up the river gravels (fig. 108). Nuggets of considerable size were found in this way.

The work of gold production was hedged about with ceremonies and restrictions. In the Bambuk and Bure regions the opening of a new mine was a ritual operation. Red kola nuts were distributed, and a learned Muslim would say prayers and recite Koranic verses. A goat, bull or red fowl were then sacrificed. The Akan too would call in a fetish priest before opening a mine. He sacrificed a fowl, poured a libation on the earth, and offered prayers to the earth spirit and to the ancestors.

Further sacrifices had to be offered on making a rich find; in some areas these were intended to kill the spirit of the gold. In Bambuk, according to Mollien (writing in 1820), it was "the opinion current among the people, that certain death awaits the proprietor, who after discovering a new mine fails to sacrifice a black cow to the gold, which is supposed to possess the power of sorcery...." Sacrifices were also made if digging was unsuccessful or if the earth had been desecrated by the violation of some taboo. Custom in many areas required that the miner abstain from sexual contact on the night before work began. He also had to refrain from evil thoughts while digging in the pit. If his lamp went out in the mine it was a bad omen and he had to stop work for that day. Menstruating women were forbidden to approach a mine and could not take part in gold-panning.

Gold nuggets were sometimes ceremonially reburied by the Akan in the hope that they would multiply in the ground. Liquor was also sprinkled on the earth "to make the gold grow". Miners often worked barefoot, for it was

108

thought that if they approached the mine in leather sandals the gold would run away. It was unlucky to use a brass pan in mining for the same reason. Miners went in constant dread that the malevolent gold spirit would appear to them in the form of a golden animal – a dog, a snake, or a hen with chicks. This was a sign of imminent disaster; the terrified miners would scramble out of the pits and flee for their lives, abandoning the mine permanently.

Some persons played on these superstitious fears to frighten rivals away from a mining area. One highly effective trick was to place a "fetish" in a rival's mine. This sometimes happened in time of war. The Asante once perpetrated this trick on the Akyem in the late eighteenth century, successfully halting their enemy's gold production for several years.

Most miners worked as small family groups, a man being helped by his wives and children. Some chiefs and rich men are said to have employed slave labour, but this may not have been widespread. It was, however, the practice in many gold-mining districts for certain days to be set aside for communal mining on behalf of the chief.

Akan chiefs commonly levied small taxes on miners, and strangers to the district were sometimes required to make over a third of their winnings for the right to dig. All nuggets over a certain weight were by custom regarded as the property of the chief irrespective of who had found them. These had to be handed over to him, usually in exchange for token compensation, though to evade this requirement it was not unknown for the finder to break the nugget into several pieces. Since miners naturally tried to conceal or minimize their finds, some chiefs would station an

official close to the gold-diggings to check on output. According to Akan traditions, a miner who attempted to deprive the chief of his due could be punished by summary decapitation.

In most of the West African goldfields it was rare for digging to take place all the year round. There were two very practical reasons for this. In the first place the miners were also farmers, who had to produce enough food to feed themselves and their families. Part of the year was therefore spent in planting, tending their crops, weeding and harvesting. Secondly, gold mining required an ample supply of water for panning operations, and in many places this was not available in the dry season, when rivers and streams tended to dry up. Nor was it practicable to mine at the height of the wet season, when the torrential tropical rains flooded mineshafts and caused them to collapse.

For these reasons the digging season was usually short, often no more than two or three months in the year. Most digging took place at the beginning of the rainy season, around March or April, when the ground had become soft and there was an adequate water supply for panning. Even at this time of year the miners did not work continuously. No digging took place on the various calendar days regarded as "unlucky", nor at the time of festivals and funerals. Work was also prohibited by custom on one fixed day of the week, often a Tuesday or Thursday. Consequently the number of days spent actually mining could be quite small. In most areas, it seems, no more than 75 days of the year would be spent in gold-winning operations.

Traditional methods of extracting gold were arduous and unrewarding, and few individuals made fortunes from this

Fig. 110   Even today new sources of gold are sometimes found. This is the signal for a gold-rush: fortune-seekers converge on the area from all sides. Such an event happened at Bamako, the Malian capital, in 1981, when a small gold nugget was found on the banks of the Niger. Photo: G. Philippart de Foy (Explorer), Bamako, 1981

Fig. 111   The laborious work of gold panning produced small returns. A woman was fortunate to obtain half a gram of gold from a day's work. In the course of an annual mining season (about 75 working days) she could expect to obtain from 25 to 35 grams of gold-dust. Photo: Agence Hoa-Qui

110

work. Many regarded it as only fit for slaves. There is much evidence to show that an average day's work for a West African gold miner generally yielded no more than 0.4–0.5 grams of gold. Sometimes it was less. In the course of the annual digging season he could expect to obtain about 25–35 grams, or approximately one ounce of gold. These were small returns for a hard and sometimes dangerous job. While rich strikes were sometimes made, these

In the nineteenth century it became fashionable to write in glowing terms of West African gold output. This was done with an ulterior motive, that of attracting investment for European mining ventures. The highly inflated estimates given at that time owed more to fertile imagination than sober fact. One such estimate is that of Sir Richard Burton, who in 1883 claimed that the Akan mines had produced gold worth six or seven hundred million pounds sterling over the previous four centuries. Reckoned by weight this is 150–175 million troy ounces, or about 13 tons a year. Modern research has drastically reduced these figures. A recent review of the evidence concludes that between 1400 and 1900 total Akan production was probably in the region of 14–15 million ounces. This is an average of about 28,000 ounces a year (0.8 tons), less than ten per cent of Burton's estimate.

Fig. 112   Among the Akan, Baule and lagoons peoples, an elaborate set of equipment was used for weighing gold. This gold-weigher, with scales suspended over his left thumb, was photographed with his two assistants about 1892, probably in the lagoons region of Côte d'Ivoire. Photo: Marcel Monnier, published in France Noire, Paris, 1894

Fig. 113   Among the Akan and some of their neighbours, the small brass weights used for weighing gold became a highly developed art form. Some were of abstract or geometric form, others depicted an astonishing range of proverbial motifs. Archives Barbier-Mueller

were exceptional, and they were more than offset by the many occasions when digging proved fruitless.

Although many have described the West African goldfields as rich, their output has been exaggerated. They were not the El Dorado many have supposed. By modern standards the output of the mines was not remarkable, and it becomes impressive only when viewed in a historical and cultural perspective – as an achievement of the pre-industrial populations of the past, working with inefficient traditional methods.

Akan gold production fluctuated, reaching its peak in the seventeenth century. At that time gold output averaged around 42,000 ounces or 1.2 tons a year, and in the best years as much as two tons may have been obtained. This indicates a labour force of around forty or fifty thousand persons engaged in gold-winning. In the following century output declined, largely, it is thought, as a result of warfare and the slave trade – less gold was mined because slaves were being used to pay for foreign imports.

The Akan goldfields were the most prolific in West Africa after the fifteenth century. Their output was certainly greater than Bure, and far exceeded that of Bambuk and the lesser goldfields. The yield of these other gold sources is still very uncertain and more research needs to be done. It may not be unrealistic, however, to regard total West African gold output in the period 1400–1900 as somewhere in the region of 1,000 tons (32 million ounces). This is equivalent to an average yearly production of 2 tons.

This quantity of gold, extracted annually, soon found its way into the hands of traders, chiefs and goldsmiths. In regions where gold-dust was a general currency (for instance among the Akan), it circulated among the population as a whole. The tiny quantities required for daily trade were measured out and tied up in small packets or knots of cloth. For weighing this gold (figs. 111, 112) a complex system of weights came into use, not only among the Akan (whose brass weights are famed for their artistry) but also among the Muslims of Senegambia and the Sahel. Fair quantities of newly mined gold must have found their way into the hands of goldsmiths. But more passed sooner or later to the professional gold-traders who were a conspicuous presence at all the goldfields.

Eventually all but a tiny fraction of the gold mined in West Africa was exported – partly as gold-dust, and partly in the form of manufactured ornaments. For a millennium and a half great quantities were traded north to the empires of the Sahel, and thence across the Sahara by camel caravan to North Africa and Egypt. With the arrival of European ships from the mid-fifteenth century onwards the coastal kingdoms also grew in wealth and prominence, while those inland declined. Gold-mining activities were intensified in the heavily forested regions of the south, and goldsmiths proliferated in the new mining districts. They also set up workshops in the coastal towns and villages where the gold trade was carried on, and close to the courts of kings. Thus, as the mines flourished, new schools of goldsmithing emerged, less dependent on influences from the Sahel.

Chapter Six

Goldsmiths and Their Technology

This survey of African goldwork would be incomplete without some account of the goldsmiths and their technology. Art historians and anthropologists have examined goldsmithing techniques and the organisation of the craft in Senegal, Côte d'Ivoire, Ghana and elsewhere, but these studies, though informative, deal with the ethnographic present. It cannot lightly be assumed that the craft has remained unchanged over the generations. In this century there have been significant developments: a decline in artistic standards, the replacement of fine gold by silver-gilt, the rapid assimilation of European designs, the rise of mass-production and, at the same time, an increasing reliance on European tools, materials and technology.

For previous centuries information is sparse. European visitors to West Africa sometimes met goldsmiths, but their descriptions tend to be brief in the extreme. David, who explored the Bambuk goldfields in 1744, left only the following account:

These blacksmiths are likewise the goldsmiths of the country; the only implements they possess are an earthen chafing dish, a pair of bellows and a large and small hammer; with their small hammer they work the gold in a cold state, and make it into trinkets at once delicate and surprising.... All the gold bartered in the country is always in earrings, or in ornaments, like those worn by the negroes.

Writing of the same region in the 1720s, Father Labat provided a little more detail:

Among them the tool-makers are also goldsmiths, cutlers, sword-makers and brass-workers; they combine in a single group all the workmen who use hammer and anvil. They have neither forge nor shop. They work beneath the trees near their houses.... Their tools consist of a small anvil, a goat's skin that serves as a bellows, some hammers, a pair of pincers, and two or three files.... They are always seated, chatting or smoking endlessly.... There are never less than three at work together. One keeps the fire alive by means of bellows made of goat's skin cut in two, or two skins joined together, and closed at the end except for a small nozzle of iron or copper.... The man who blows sits behind the bellows and presses them with his elbows and knees alternately.... In this manner they make quite delicate pieces of workmanship, both in gold and silver, especially the small objects of different shapes called manillas, which the women use to adorn their hair, or as necklaces or bracelets.

Mungo Park, who travelled through Senegambia in 1797–98, left detailed descriptions of both iron-smelting and gold mining, but had only a few words to spare for the goldsmith:

Most of the African blacksmiths are acquainted also with the method of smelting gold, in which process they use an alkaline salt, obtained from a ley of burnt cornstalks evaporated to dryness. They likewise draw the gold into wire, and form it into a variety of ornaments, some of which are executed with a great deal of taste and ingenuity.

These and other early accounts confirm that in Senegambia the same group of craftsmen was responsible for all metalworking, whether in iron, brass, silver or gold. But though capable of working gold, they seem to have been regarded principally as blacksmiths. Today the situation has begun to change under the impact of modern conditions; there are now many

Fig. 114 The technique of hammering gold has been practised in the Sahel since the first millennium A.D. Here a Peul goldsmith near Jenne hammers a rod of gold into a large four-lobed gold earring. Photo: Monique Barbier-Mueller, 1986

Senegalese workers in gold and silver who have not the slightest knowledge of blacksmithing. Yet despite this, there is still no separate name for a goldsmith in most languages of the region.

Over the vast expanse of the Sahara and Sahel the picture is similar. It is, or was

115

Fig. 115   In Mali, as elsewhere in the Sahel, the metalsmith rarely specialises in working gold. He is at the same time a tinker, a blacksmith, a silversmith and a goldsmith, and when occasion demands he also works brass and aluminium. Photo: Musée National du Mali

Fig. 116   Festive jewellery worn by a Jewish woman of the Draa valley, south-western Algeria. Some of these ornaments, notably the cruciform and disc-shaped pendants, are found in similar form in the Sahel. They may perhaps have been introduced to sub-Saharan West Africa by Jewish goldsmiths who are known to have moved south in medieval times. Photo: Jean Besancenot, 1930s.

until recently, rare to find any craftsman who specialises exclusively in making objects of gold. He tends to be a worker in all metals, performing whatever services will bring him a living. He is at the same time a tinker, a maker of iron weapons and tools, and a worker in brass, copper, silver, aluminium and gold (fig. 115). Often he is somewhat feared for his supposed command of magical powers, and he may perform a variety of functions that have no direct connection

with the metal arts – for instance surgeon, herbalist or soothsayer. Much of his income may be derived from these other activities. In the languages of the region the name most commonly applied to him means a blacksmith or general metalworker.

In view of this repeated association with blacksmiths it may be that goldsmithing originated, at least in some parts of the Sahara and Sahel, simply as an extension of the blacksmith's craft. Such a possibility finds support in David's statement of 1744 that the blacksmiths hammered the gold in a cold state to make trinkets. This was an obvious way for a blacksmith to work gold (fig. 114). It may have been an initial step in the development of a goldsmith's craft from local blacksmithing. More sophisticated techniques, such as wire-drawing, filigree work, granulation and lost wax casting, could have been learnt later.

Since there were blacksmiths in West Africa by the first millenium B.C., a goldsmith's art may have emerged locally at a very early period. It is reasonable to assume that some goldsmithing was being carried on as early as the fourth or fifth century A.D., when the trans-Saharan trade began to develop.

The peoples of the Sahara have had contact both with North Africa and with the Sahel zone, perhaps for millennia. From the earliest times these Saharan peoples, both black and white – including Berber, Tuareg and Maures – have shown a passionate liking for jewellery, not simply for its beauty but on account of its supposed magical and protective powers. Since they belonged to the North African cultural world of which the Sahara was but an extension, they would naturally have adopted North African techniques of goldsmithing and silversmithing. Once known in the Sahara, these techniques could readily have been transmitted to the towns along its southern shore.

Knowledge of goldsmithing may also have reached West Africa more directly by way of immigrant North African craftsmen. From time to time professional goldsmiths and other metalworkers from North Africa must have come south along the Saharan trade routes to set up business in the towns of the desert and Sahel. These immigrants included a number of Jews, who were well known for their goldsmithing activities in North Africa. By the fifteenth and sixteenth centuries there were Jewish merchants and goldsmiths at Sijilmasa and the oasis of Tuat; they were also present in Timbuktu and Gao until expelled by Askia Mohammed about 1512. According to some traditions the present goldsmiths of Mauritania are of Jewish origin and have links with southern Morocco.

Such immigrant craftsmen could have introduced North African jewellery forms into the lands south of the Sahara (fig. 116). They may have brought knowledge of filigree working, granulation and lost wax casting, techniques that had been known to Mediterranean goldsmiths for many centuries.

It would not be surprising that North African metalworkers moved south, despite the harsh nature of the Sahara-Sahel region. Here there was a demand for exotic imports, doubtless including Moroccan and Egyptian jewellery – the North African goldsmith Sakan, in the eleventh century, was recorded as having supplied gilded chains for the Sudan trade. The large potential market for such items would have

116

served to attract North African metalsmiths.

The southward migration of metalsmiths would also have been encouraged by the growth of trans-Saharan trade after the mid-first millennium. Every caravan dealing in gold required a man skilled in using weights and scales, who knew how to test the purity of gold-dust and where necessary make it up into jewellery or ingot form. His services were especially valuable in the Sahelian towns at the southern end of the trade routes, where gold-dust and jewellery were regularly traded. Goldsmiths may thus have been employed to travel with the caravans, and encouraged to settle as permanent residents in the Middle Niger towns.

At the courts of some of the great Sahelian kings there was a demand for gold ornaments and jewellery. To meet this demand the rulers may occasionally have engaged foreign goldsmiths. Mansa Musa of Mali, for instance, could conceivably have returned with Egyptian goldworkers after his pilgrimage to Mecca in 1324, since (according to al-Dawadari) he had promised the Mamluk Sultan to establish a coinage in his name.

It is also not unlikely that in the 1590s, when Moroccan armies invaded the towns of the Middle Niger, North African goldsmiths were brought in to supervise the exportation of loot and tribute. Charles Monteil reported a tradition that the oldest weights in Jenne had been brought from Morocco, a fact which would be consistent with the presence of Moroccan gold-smiths.

It is not known for certain how the art of goldsmithing originated in West Africa, but the above discussion has sought to consider the possibilities. These are:

(a) an independent extension of the local blacksmith's craft;
(b) gradual diffusion of knowledge from North Africa via the Saharan peoples;

Fig. 117 The art of the goldsmith flourishes in Senegal. In this postcard of the colonial period, a master goldsmith of Dakar sits behind his anvil while a young assistant tends the bellows. Archives Barbier-Mueller

Fig. 118 In Ghana the techniques of gold-working were highly developed. The Asantehene's goldsmiths used all the techniques known to them to create a rich array of cast, hammered and gold-leafed ornaments for the royal attendants. Photo: E. Elisofon, Kumasi

117

613.- DAKAR — Bijoutiers Sénégalais

(c) direct transfer of knowledge to the Sahel by immigrant North African goldsmiths.

Each of these processes may have contributed to the spread of goldsmithing in West Africa, and it is not necessary to suppose a single origin.

Over the centuries there may have been much movement of goldsmiths in the Sahel. They went wherever they could earn a livelihood, tending to settle in towns with a good market for gold and close to the courts of kings. From time to time they may have been dispersed by political upheavals such as the conquest of ancient Ghana and the Moroccan invasion. These movements would further have spread knowledge of goldsmithing techniques and metalworking in general.

In the Senegambia region, notably in Senegal, goldsmiths proliferated (fig. 117). These craftsmen, like those of Mali, are of diverse origins and belong to many ethnic groups. Most of them designate the goldsmith or jeweller by the same name as the blacksmith, a fact that suggests an ancient connection between the two crafts.

The situation is rather different in the Akan, Baule and lagoons regions of Ghana and Côte d'Ivoire. Here, notably among the Akan, traditional blacksmithing is rare. Although some seventeenth-century accounts speak of the skilled work of coastal "blacksmiths", it seems that the activities of blacksmithing, including ironsmelting, were never common in this forest zone. Instead the Akan relied heavily for their supply of tools, weapons and unmanufactured iron on three major sources: the savanna forges to the north, the large and impressive iron industry of the Bassar region in central

Togo, and European trade. For centuries they received iron goods by overland caravans from the two African sources. The European trade, especially in iron bars, developed in the sixteenth and seventeenth centuries.

Probably for this reason goldsmithing is regarded by the Akan, Baule and lagoons peoples as an activity distinct from blacksmithing. The goldsmith's

119

Fig. 119   Master goldsmiths were active in all parts of the Akan region. They had many workshops in and around Kumasi. This Asante goldsmith is seen working with his assistant about 1900. Photo, probably by E. Perregaux: Basel Mission Archive

Fig. 120   By the lost wax casting process jewellery of fine quality can be made in silver or brass as well as gold. The forms of the brass beads on this Baule necklace are identical to those made in gold. Archives Barbier-Mueller

craft carries great prestige (fig. 118); he would not dream of working iron, and might well be offended by any suggestion that his craft was related to that of the blacksmith. Throughout this region the blacksmith and goldsmith are known by different names, and they may always have been distinct.

It seems likely that the first goldsmiths in the region were active among the northern Akan, in towns such as Begho and Techiman on the border between forest and savanna. Even here goldsmithing may not predate the fourteenth or early fifteenth century. The first Akan goldsmiths may have

learnt their craft from immigrant (or itinerant) foreign goldsmiths of various origins, such as the Mande Diula, the Lorhon and perhaps also Sonrai or Peul metalworkers from the region of Jenne. With the opening up of the Akan goldfields to external trade, goldsmiths began to appear throughout the Akan region (fig. 119). By the seventeenth century, if not before, they were also present among the lagoons peoples and the Baule of Côte d'Ivoire.

Apart from the question of origins, there were other major differences between goldsmiths of the Akan-Baule region and those of Senegambia-Sahel. The Akan and Akan-related smiths drew a significant part of their income from working in brass (fig. 120), in addition to gold. They specialised in casting, and brought the lost wax casting process to a high degree of perfection. Goldsmiths of the Senegambia and Sahel, on the other hand, worked much more frequently with silver, making less use of brass, and their favoured techniques were hammering, cutting, filigree and repoussé work.

These differences were not absolute. West African goldsmiths shared a common pool of technology, and knowledge became widely disseminated over the centuries. The broad regional differences that emerged – and also the regional variations of jewellery style and subject – were the result of cultural preferences, not of limited knowledge or lack of technical proficiency.

The goldsmiths had at their command a variety of techniques, both for creating the basic form and for applying decoration. The following is a description of the basic manufacturing techniques.

Fig. 121   Although lost wax casting was preferred, the Akan produced many items of gold regalia by hammering techniques. This disc-shaped pectoral is of beaten and embossed gold. Cat. 63

Fig. 122   Various stages in the making of a Peul gold earring in a workshop near Jenne. The goldsmith alternately heats a rod of gold over a small charcoal fire and hammers it on his anvil. It requires many hours of work to achieve the perfect form of the finished earring. Photos: Monique Barbier-Mueller, 1986

121

1. Hammering and Cutting

Like the blacksmiths, many goldsmiths fashioned objects by hammering. A pellet, rod or other suitable piece of metal would be hammered to the required thickness and trimmed to shape. If necessary it was heated, bent or curled. Simple gold ornaments may have been made by this means from very early times, for example the gold earring of the first millennium A.D. found at Jenne-Jeno (fig. 9). More complex ornaments such as tubular beads and hollow pendants were constructed from a number of pieces of hammered metal, which were skilfully fitted or joined together.

These techniques are most commonly used in the Sahara, Sahel and Sene-gambia, where a large part of the smith's time is taken up in hammering, cutting and manipulating his metal (fig. 122). The Akan and Baule also practised hammering techniques to produce ornaments such as disc-shaped pectorals (fig. 121), but only a small proportion of their work is made in this way, lost wax casting being preferred.

Fig. 123   Baule goldsmiths in the village of Assabonou produce the thin sheets required for gold-leafing by hammering out a small pellet of gold on the anvil. This work requires skill, patience and dexterity. Photo: Timothy F. Garrard, 1985

Fig. 124   For several hundred years the Akan have used gold leaf to adorn objects of wood or leather. This royal bracelet, carved in a soft white wood, is covered with sheets of gold affixed with glue. In earlier times the sheets were usually secured by tiny staples of gold wire. Cat. 103

2. Gold-leafing

In Ghana and Côte d'Ivoire many items of regalia are carved from wood which is then covered with sheets of beaten gold leaf. This is an economical way to use gold, while at the same time creating large and visually impressive objects. The technique is an old one, for in 1602 Pieter de Marees mentioned that the Akan sometimes gold-plated their sword hilts, and an example of such a sword dating from about the mid-seventeenth century is still preserved in the Danish National Museum. Over the last sixty or seventy years the number of gold-leafed objects has proliferated. Today they are more often seen than the costlier objects of cast gold.

To make the gold sheet, a small pellet of gold is laboriously hammered out on a steel anvil, being repeatedly twisted during the process to maintain an even thickness (fig. 123). This work requires patience and skill. One gram of metal is sufficient to make a sheet several inches square. When the gold is sufficiently thin it is affixed to the wooden model with glue, which has replaced the tiny gold staples used earlier in this century (fig. 124). In Ghana most gold-leafing is today carried out in and around Kumasi. In Côte d'Ivoire it is a speciality of Baule goldsmiths at Assabonou.

While traditional hammered gold leaf is still made, it may eventually be superseded by the industrially manufactured European equivalent, which is many times thinner. In the past some Akan and Baule smiths have been able to obtain this in small quantities, and carvings decorated with European gold leaf can now be seen, some of them by no means recently manufactured.

The art of gold-leafing seems to be confined to the Akan and Baule; elsewhere there is no trace of it today. Its origins are obscure. Possibly the technique was developed in ancient Ghana or Mali as a means of adorning regalia, but of this there is no sure evidence.

123

3. Lost Wax Casting

The lost wax or *cire perdue* method of casting has been frequently described. It is so ancient in West Africa that its precise origins are unknown. Whether it was a technique independently invented in the region or learnt from North Africa or Egypt remains an open question – though given the long cultural contacts with the north through trans-Saharan

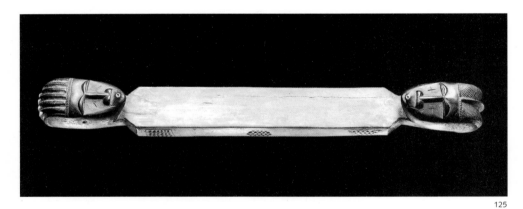

125

Fig. 125   A modelling board is used in the preliminary stages of casting, for rolling wax threads with a wooden spatula. It may take the form of a low stool, or a narrow length of wood that is sometimes fixed between two upright posts. This old Baule modelling board is adorned with two sculptured wooden heads; the modelling spatula was sometimes carved in the same way. Archives Barbier-Mueller

Fig. 126   Three Baule wax models for gold pendant heads, made by Koffi Yao Christophe of Bouake, 1986. Archives Barbier-Mueller

Fig. 127   Two Baule heads cast in silver, one being gilded. These were made by the goldsmith Diby Koffi of Bouake in 1986, after a photograph of a pendant in the Barbier-Mueller collection (fig. 94, top). Archives Barbier-Mueller

trade, an external origin seems highly plausible. In any event lost wax casting has been known in West Africa for more than a thousand years.

By this technique castings could be made in a variety of metals. They exist not only in gold but in silver and brass, occasionally in bronze, copper or aluminium, and even (though very rarely) in iron. Even in places where gold jewellery was not used, such as the Voltaic region and parts of Nigeria, the lost wax casting technique was used to make countless objects of brass.

Most of the major schools of lost wax casting are located in the forest and savanna. Here it was the Akan, together with the Baule and the lagoons peoples of Côte d'Ivoire, who came to excel in gold casting. By this technique they made the magnificent range of finger-rings, bracelets, beads, amulets, sword

ornaments and other objects that have been described in earlier chapters. Goldsmiths among the Kulango also cast some extremely rare pendants in gold, representing bush spirits.

Further north, in the Sahel and Sahara, hammering techniques predominate and lost wax castings are scarce. In these regions it is difficult to point to a single published example of lost wax casting in gold, with the possible exception of some bracelets found in the first millennium tomb of the Berber queen Tin Hinan, at Abalessa. Likewise, no lost-wax castings in gold seem to be known from Senegambia. Here the goldwork is mostly hammered or filigree.

Nevertheless, lost wax casting was not entirely unknown in the desert and semi-desert zones, and formerly it seems to have been practised there more widely than today. Some centuries ago there were smiths in the Mopti-Jenne region of Mali who cast large numbers of bracelets, amulets and figurines in cuprous metal. For this to be possible, costly brass had to be imported from north of the Sahara, and beeswax from the lands to the south. In Mauritania too, according to Maure goldsmiths interviewed in Senegal, lost wax casting was once practised to a limited extent. Even today, in the south-eastern Sahara, the Tuareg still produce their silver "crosses of Agades" by the casting process.

In spite of the apparent absence of cast gold in these regions, it is not impossible that a limited quantity was once produced. In particular there is no obvious reason why the brass-casters of the Mopti-Jenne region should not also have worked in gold, a metal readily available through trade. Such objects would rarely survive and even more rarely come to public notice.

There were a number of variations of the lost wax casting process. The basic technique (which may be described as "solid casting") was as follows. First, a solid wax model was made of the object to be cast. This was invested in one or more coats of slip made from finely pulverised charcoal and clay. When thoroughly dry, the invested model was firmly encased in a mould made from coarser clay mixed with donkey dung or palm-nut fibre. After drying, the mould was heated and inverted over a pot of water, the molten wax draining away through a small duct. This left an empty cavity inside the mould in the exact form of the object to be cast. Molten metal in a crucible could now be poured manually into the mould; alternatively, a crucible containing pieces of metal was attached to the mould, heated and inverted, causing the liquid metal to fill the cavity. The latter was the usual technique of the Akan. This process, which varied in minor details from one workshop to another, resulted in a solid casting in the exact shape of the original wax model.

Another form of the process may be termed "hollow casting". This differed from solid casting in that a solid wax model was not used. Instead, the caster prepared a core made from a mixture of clay and charcoal (or took such a core from his ready-made stock). To make a casting, he began by covering this core with a skin of beeswax, which was then modelled and decorated until it had assumed the form of the casting required. This technique was much used by the Baule and lagoons peoples, for instance to make their small hollow-cast gold heads (figs. 126, 127). The Akan also used it to make objects such as hollow-cast rings and sword ornaments. Cores have the great advantage that they save gold and enable lighter castings to be produced.

126

127

Fig. 128   The Akan used the technique of openwork casting to create finger-rings of great elegance. This example is said by some Asante informants to represent a weaver bird's nest. Others identify it as a kind of toadstool. Cat. 137

Fig. 129   Wax models for beads in the workshop of the chief goldsmith of Kumasi. The designs are formed from wax threads laid over a charcoal core. Photo: Timothy F. Garrard, 1986

Fig. 130   In Ghana and Côte d'Ivoire many objects were made as hollow castings in order to save gold. The form of the object was modelled from a thin sheet of wax placed over a charcoal core that could be removed after casting. These hollow-cast objects from southern Côte d'Ivoire represent a leopard and a pangolin. Cat. 202, 204

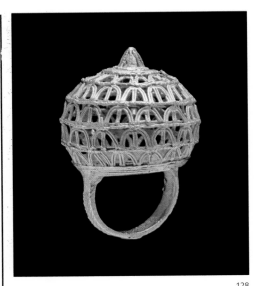

128

Some of the most technically accomplished castings from Ghana and Côte d'Ivoire combine the hollow casting and openwork casting techniques. Parts of the design are constructed from a wax sheet laid over the basic core, while other parts are made from wax threads arranged to produce an openwork effect. Some casters, notably in southeastern Côte d'Ivoire, built up the whole form from wax threads even where an openwork effect was not required.

Yet another variant of the process may be termed "openwork casting". This was primarily a jewellery technique, used especially for making gold objects such as beads, finger-rings, bracelets and bells of openwork form (fig. 128). Here too a core was often used, but instead of modelling a wax skin over it the goldsmith produced an openwork design usually from wax threads (fig. 129). These were arranged in lattice-work, spirals or whatever other design was required.

129

The Making of a Baule Gold Bead

One of the most popular Baule gold bead forms is the disc (*taliɛ*). In some cases the edge of the disc is adorned with tiny granules, a form of ornament known as *wowo nouan*. Usually the granules are placed singly or in pairs, but on some of the finer beads they are arranged in groups of three forming a triangle (cat. no. 230). This triple ornament is called *tondama* after a tree whose seeds occur in triple clusters. Such beads are still made in Bouake by the goldsmith Diby Koffi and his son Koffi Yao. The process of manufacture is as follows:

1. The goldsmith prepares the wax thread (fig. 131) on a well-oiled modelling board such as that shown in fig. 125. He uses a carved wooden spatula (fig. 132). This is a work of extraordinary skill, for the wax thread is sometimes reduced to less than half a millimetre in thickness.

2. He next takes the thin wax thread and with his fingers coils it into a disc on the flat surface of the board (fig. 132).

3. A slender rod of charcoal is then laid across the centre of the disc and pressed into the wax (fig. 133). On top of this a second wax disc of identical size is placed. The two discs are then joined by careful pressure, the charcoal rod being sandwiched between them (fig. 134).

4. On each side of the double disc, where the charcoal rod protrudes, the goldsmith models a short tube from coiled wax thread (fig. 135).

5. It now remains to place the granules around the wax bead. The goldsmith takes another wax thread and with a knife slices it into tiny sections (fig. 136). These sections adhere to the sharp edge of the blade.

6. A glowing piece of charcoal is now passed close to the edge of the blade (fig. 137). The heat causes the tiny segments of wax to melt into globules of equal size. These are called *klana klenzua*, cricket's eggs.

7. When the globules have hardened the goldsmith detaches them one by one and fixes them around the edge of the wax bead in the desired pattern (fig. 138). This is done by simple pressure of the fingers, without the use of further heat.

8. It now remains only to invest the wax model with slip, enclose it in a mould and proceed to the casting stage. Following casting by the *cire perdue* method, the bead is carefully brushed, cleansed and polished. At the same time the charcoal rod which passes through its centre is removed with the aid of a piece of wire, leaving a hollow passage by which the bead can be strung. The result is a finished gold disc-bead complete with granulations (fig. 139).

The example reproduced here is an old bead whose wax threads have a diameter of about 0.35 mm. Modern casters can rarely achieve such fineness. Their wax threads usually have a diameter of 1 mm or more.

Figs. 131–139 Various stages in the making of a Baule gold bead. This is a work of extraordinary skill, requiring much time and patience. Photos: Monique Barbier-Mueller, Jean Paul Barbier and Timothy F. Garrard, Bouake, 1988

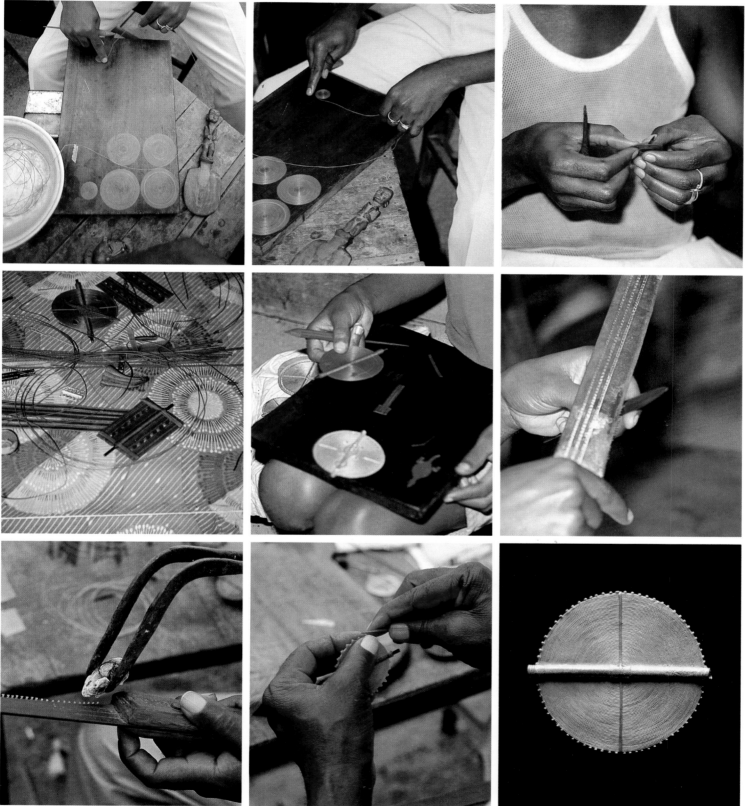

Fig. 140   In this century some castings have been made using the chalky white bone of the cuttlefish as a mould. This Akan gold pendant (based on an American heraldic motif) was produced by such a method. Cat. 100

Fig. 141   Filigree working is among the most highly developed jewellery techniques in Senegal. Pieces of gold or silver are drawn into thin wires with a drawplate, and used to create designs of astonishing beauty and complexity. Cat. 46

4. Direct Casting

In Ghana, Côte d'Ivoire, Burkina Faso and Mali, some smiths made castings directly from natural objects without the use of wax. This technique was developed to its fullest among the Akan, who often used such objects as hard-shelled seeds and fruits, snails, crabs, dried fish, small animals, beetles and insects. Elsewhere the technique was usually limited to groundnuts, locusts and the occasional small lizard.

140

Whatever the object chosen, it was encased in clay and charcoal and, when the mould was completely dry, burned out in the fire. After this the ashes of the object to be cast were, if possible, shaken out of the mould and molten metal poured into the cavity to give an exact replica of the natural object.

Direct castings are almost all of brass. Among goldwork they are found only as occasional ornaments for Akan sandals, bracelets or rings.

5. Cuttlefish Bone Casting

Small gold or silver castings of inferior quality were sometimes made by using the chalky white bone of the cuttlefish as a mould. The process was very simple. A pattern of the object required was pressed firmly into the soft side of the bone, or a design was carved into it. Molten metal was poured into the cavity so produced. The resultant casting was then scrubbed (sometimes in a mixture of alum, salt and water) and polished. This method was used to make medallions, rings, buttons, crucifixes and other small ornaments, and even counterfeit coins.

Cuttlefish bone casting is most common in coastal towns, where the bone can readily be obtained. However, it is also known to many inland goldsmiths, not only in Ghana and Côte d'Ivoire but even in Senegal and Mali. Almost nothing can yet be said about the origins and history of the process.

One of the chain necklaces in the Barbier-Mueller collection has a central pendant produced from a cuttlefish-bone mould. This depicts an American heraldic eagle with shield and thunderbolts (fig. 140) – a good example of the Akan propensity for copying foreign forms.

6. Filigree and Other Wirework

The art of metalworking in filigree finds its greatest development in Senegal, among the Wolof and to a lesser extent among the Tukulor and Maures. With astonishing skill the goldsmith constructs intricate pieces of jewellery from metal threads (fig. 141). This technique can be used to make jewellery of entirely openwork design such as beads, ear-rings, pendants and European-inspired peacocks and butterflies (fig. 31). Alternatively, the filigree can be fixed to a back-plate of sheet metal, giving a solid, massive effect.

Formerly, both gold and silver filigree were made, but today the silver is merely electro-gilded if a golden appearance is required.

The threads are made on a drawplate, a slab of iron in which holes of various diameters have been punched. The wire is drawn through successively finer holes until it is reduced to the diameter required. Drawplates are common in Senegal, and they were also reported from the Gold Coast both in the 1660s and in the late nineteenth century. Jean Barbot and Willem Bosman, in the last quarter of the seventeenth century, both noted that the Akan were making filigree hat-bands of gold and silver wire for sale to Europeans. Drawplates seem never to have been widely used by the Akan, however, and were perhaps confined to a few coastal goldsmiths.

Apart from their use in filigree, metal wires were used in a number of other ways, especially to make chains, chain necklaces and chain bracelets. Some of the designs were African, others inspired by European work.

Decorative Techniques

The main decorative techniques used by the goldsmiths may be briefly summarised. Hammered metal sheet might be decorated in a variety of ways: engraved or incised, stippled, punched or embossed. Small holes of various patterns might be cut into the metal. Alternatively, filigree threads or twisted wires were soldered on to the metal sheet to provide surface decoration. Different effects were achieved by the

use of granulation, a very ancient technique once widely practised in the Mediterranean world. This entailed the soldering of tiny globules to a back-plate, using borax as a flux. The technique was known to most of the Sahelian goldsmiths but not, it would appear, to the Akan or Baule. Tukulor and Wolof jewels are sometimes embellished with tiny applied flat discs of metal, used either for their decorative effect or to keep filigree wires in place.

For lost wax castings the basic form was obtained by cutting or modelling a piece

142

of wax. Further detail could be achieved by adding separately modelled parts, or by applying wax pellets, simple wax threads, or twisted and plaited threads. Alternatively, designs could be engraved on or carved into the wax model. Similar effects could be achieved by engraving or punching the cast metal object.

The goldsmith paid much attention to cleaning and burnishing the finished jewel. Often it was heated or boiled in salt water to which a quantity of alum

and saltpetre (nitrate of potash) had been added. Wolof goldsmiths often put their jewellery in a chemical bath which turns it a violent orange, red or even purplish colour, very different from the pale yellow of pure West African gold. This artificial colouring is highly appreciated by the women of Senegal.

The goldsmiths of Asante used a different technique, covering the finished jewel with finely ground red ochre and immersing it in boiling salt water. After this treatment it was thoroughly scrubbed and then burnished with an animal's tooth. Traces of red ochre can still be seen on some old jewellery from this region.

The debasing of gold has been practised at all periods, but some older jewels can be found in very fine metal (18–22 carats). Twentieth-century works tend to be of base alloy which in some cases falls as low as 3 or 4 carats. Recent castings from Ghana and Côte d'Ivoire are sometimes gilded with fine gold to conceal this poor quality metal.

Conclusion

The ancient art of the West African goldsmith seems doomed to disappear, at least in its traditional form. Changing tastes and social conditions are responsible; except in the remote villages of the interior there is now little demand for the ornate jewels with which ladies bedecked themselves fifty years ago. Traditional forms of women's jewellery have become unfashionable in the large cosmopolitan centres, where the current styles tend to reflect intercontinental culture (fig. 142).

In the more specialised field of regalia, largely confined to the Akan, Baule and lagoons peoples, there remains a

Fig. 142   Today the fashionable ladies of West Africa seek to follow the demands of international fashion, and they have gradually abandoned the traditional jewellery worn by their grandmothers. This Baule woman from Côte d'Ivoire enhances her natural elegance with a display of European jewellery. Photo: Timothy F. Garrard, Bouake

Fig. 143   Despite the rapid pace of change in West Africa some customs have been retained. Splendid displays of gold jewellery and regalia can still be seen at traditional ceremonies, notably in southern Ghana and Côte d'Ivoire. Here the goldsmith's art retains much of its ancient form, and its survival seems assured, at least for some time to come. Carte postale Etienne Nangho, Images de chez Nous

substantial demand. But in these regions the quality of workmanship has declined over the last few decades, and items produced today bear little comparison with those of former times. They are at best indifferent copies, a sad reminder of a tradition past its prime.

Changing conditions have brought about a loss of ancient forms and designs, and a movement away from traditional methods of work. West African goldsmiths now rely increasingly on imported chemicals, acids, tools and appliances. In Dakar one can see broken light bulbs used as flasks for dissolving gold in acid, and car batteries employed for electro-gilding. Gas cylinders are replacing the old charcoal brazier. In Bouake the demand is for European-made crucibles and tools selected from French catalogues. Everywhere the traditional methods of goldsmithing are falling into disuse or being drastically modified by modern conditions.

Foremost among the exponents of the new goldsmithing are the Senegalese, whose influence is today felt far from their homeland. In this century large numbers of Senegalese goldsmiths have migrated to other West African countries. They are now established not only in capital cities – Abidjan, Monrovia, Bamako, Ouagadougou, Lomé – but also in many smaller towns. From one country to another their products are virtually identical, competently made and pleasing to the eye but rarely rising to great heights. While their skill is not in question, a great part of this output can hardly be regarded as traditional. As often as not it is copied from pattern books to meet the demands of an international clientele. This is West African goldsmithing of the future: glittering and technically competent, but far removed from the glorious art of the ancestral goldsmiths.

Plates

In the plates, the order in which the objects are presented sometimes departs from the order of the catalogue entries (pages 220–244). This has been done for aesthetic reasons. A cross-reference to the catalogue entry has therefore been included in the captions for each plate. The items on each plate are numbered from left to right, top to bottom.

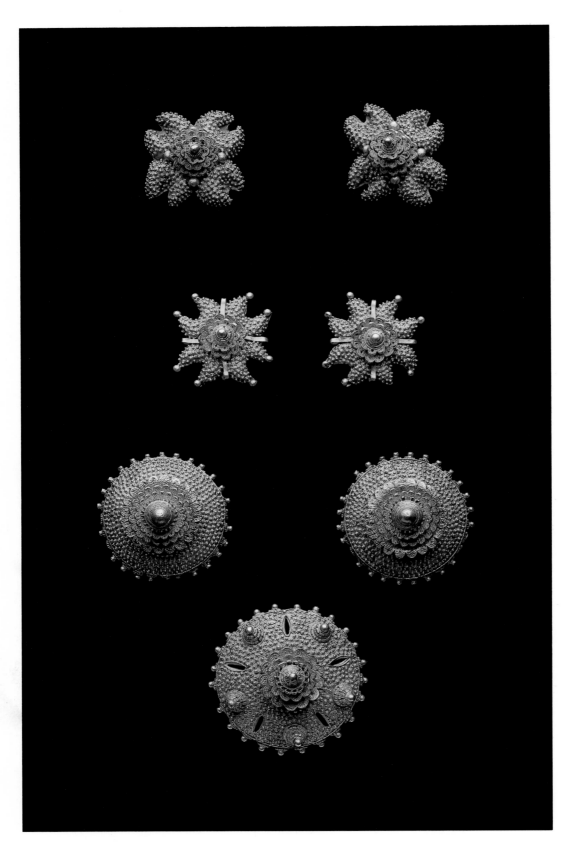

Plate 1

1,2
Senegal
Tukulor/Wolof
Pair of hair ornaments
Inv. 1034-178 A, B.
Cat. 1, description p. 220

3,4
Senegal
Tukulor/Wolof
Pair of hair ornaments
Inv. 1034-177 A, B.
Cat. 2, description p. 220

5,6
Senegal
Tukulor/Wolof
Pair of globular hair ornaments
Inv. 1034-176 B, C.
Cat. 3, description p. 220

7
Senegal
Tukulor/Wolof
Globular hair ornament
Inv. 1034-176 A.
Cat. 4, description p. 220

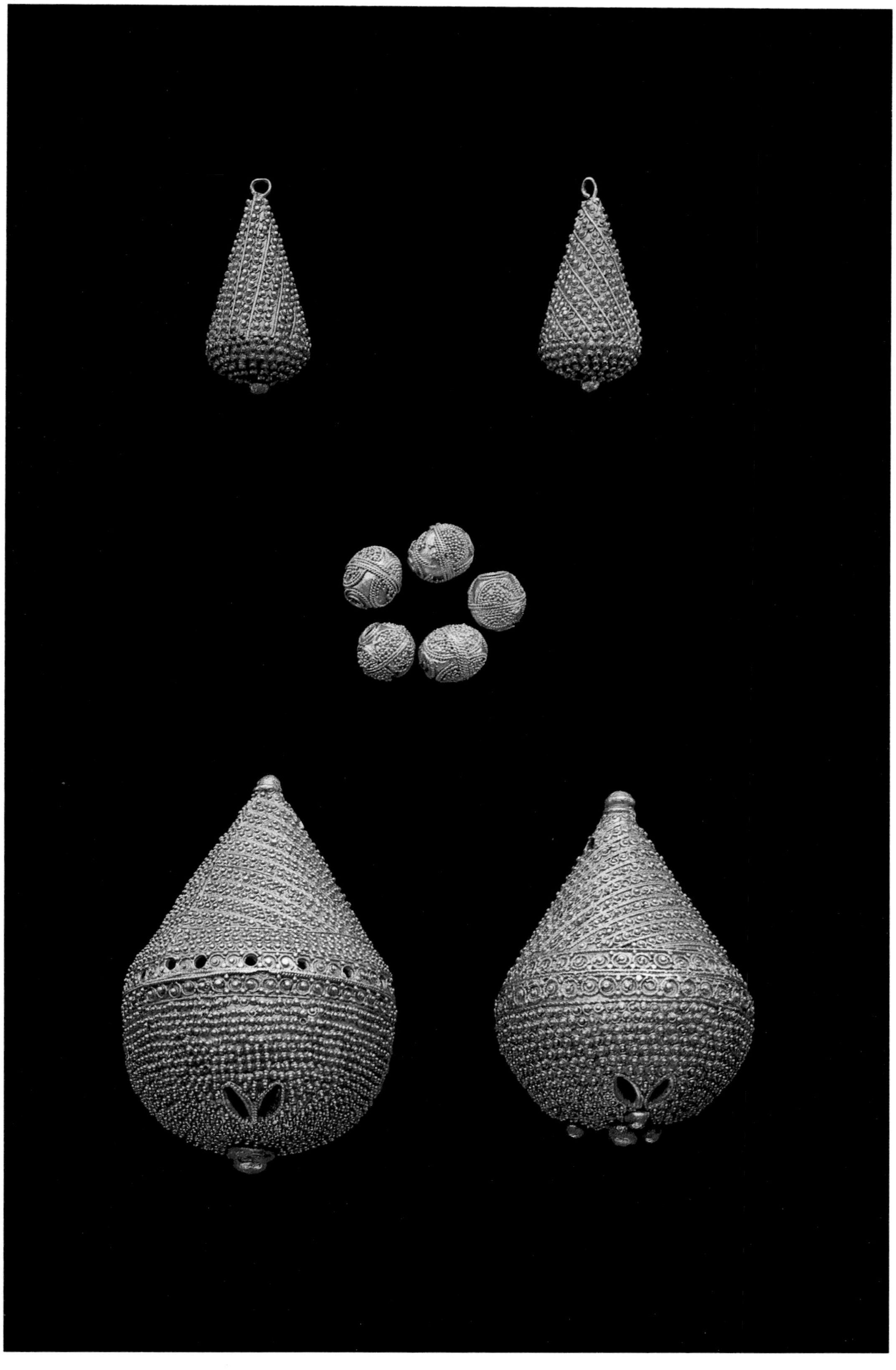

Plate 2

1,2
Senegal
Tukulor/Wolof
Pair of teardrop-shaped hair ornaments
Inv. 1034-180 A, B.
Cat. 7, description p. 220

3
Senegal
Wolof/Tukulor
Five small spherical beads
Inv. 1034-194.
Cat. 8, description p. 220

4
Senegal
Tukulor/Wolof
Teardrop-shaped ornament
Inv. 1034-133 B.
Cat. 5, description p. 220

5
Senegal
Tukulor/Wolof
Teardrop-shaped ornament
Inv. 1034-133 A.
Cat. 6, description p. 220

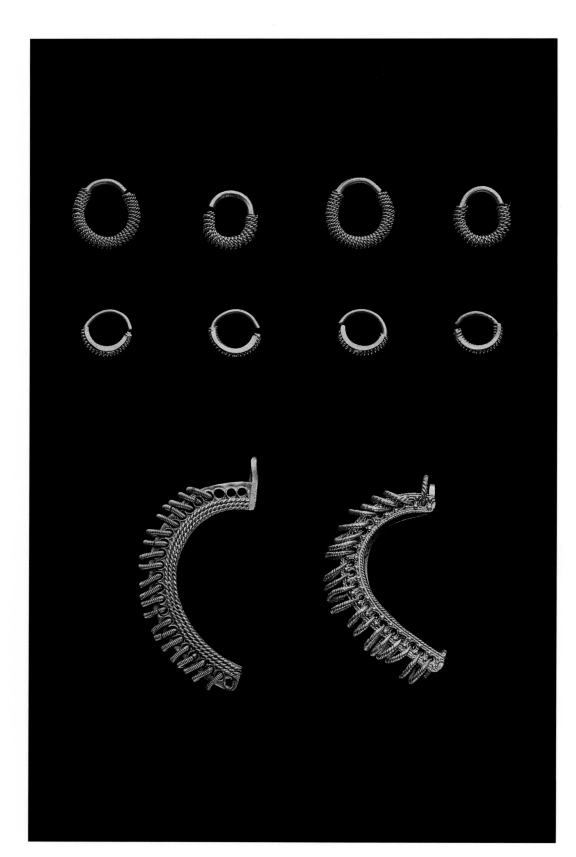

Plate 3

1-8
Senegal
Peul/Tukulor/Wolof
Four pairs of small rings
Inv. 1034-179 C–J.
Cat. 9, description p. 220

9
Senegal
Peul/Tukulor/Wolof/Serer
Curved ear-clip
Inv. 1034-179 B.
Cat. 10, description p. 220

10
Senegal
Peul/Tukulor/Wolof/Serer
Curved ear-clip
Inv. 1034-179 A.
Cat. 11, description p. 220

Plate 4

1,2
Mali, Guinée, Senegal
Peul/Tukulor/Sarakole/Bamana/Sonrai
etc.
Pair of crescent-shaped gold rings
Inv. 1034-161 A, B.
Cat. 12, description p. 220

3,4
Senegal
Wolof
Pair of silver-gilt earrings
Inv. 1034-175 A, B.
Cat. 13, description p. 220

5,6
Senegal
Tukulor/Wolof
Pair of crescent-shaped earrings
Inv. 1034-174 A, B.
Cat. 14, description p. 221

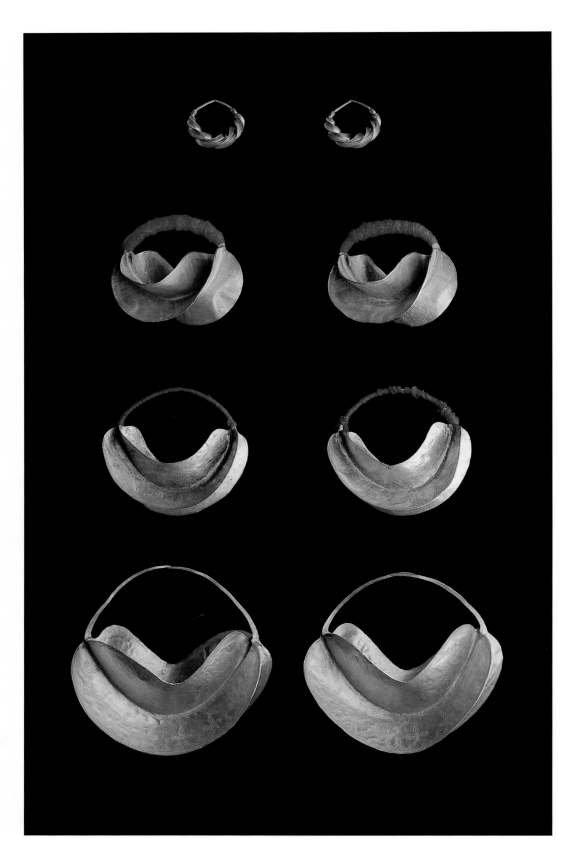

Plate 5

1,2
Mali
Peul/Sonrai
Pair of crescent-shaped earrings
Inv. 1034-160 A, B
Cat. 15, description p. 221

3,4
Mali
Peul
Pair of hammered earrings
Inv. 1004-28 A, B.
Cat. 16, description p. 221

5,6
Mali
Peul
Pair of hammered earrings
Inv. 1004-135 A, B.
Cat. 17, description p. 221

7,8
Mali
Peul
Pair of hammered earrings
Inv. 1004-69 A, B.
Cat. 18, description p. 221

Plate 6

1,2
Mali
Peul
Pair of hammered earrings
Inv. 1004-120 A, B.
Cat. 19, description p. 221

3,4
Mali
Peul
Pair of hammered earrings
Inv. 1004-134 A, B.
Cat. 20, description p. 221

5,6
Mali
Peul
Pair of hammered earrings
Inv. 1004-137 A, B.
Cat. 21, description p. 221

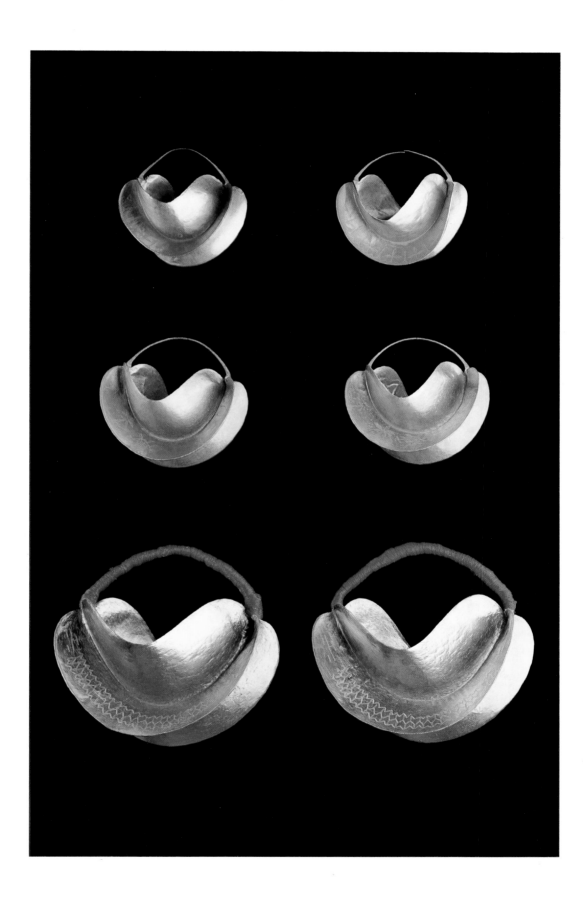

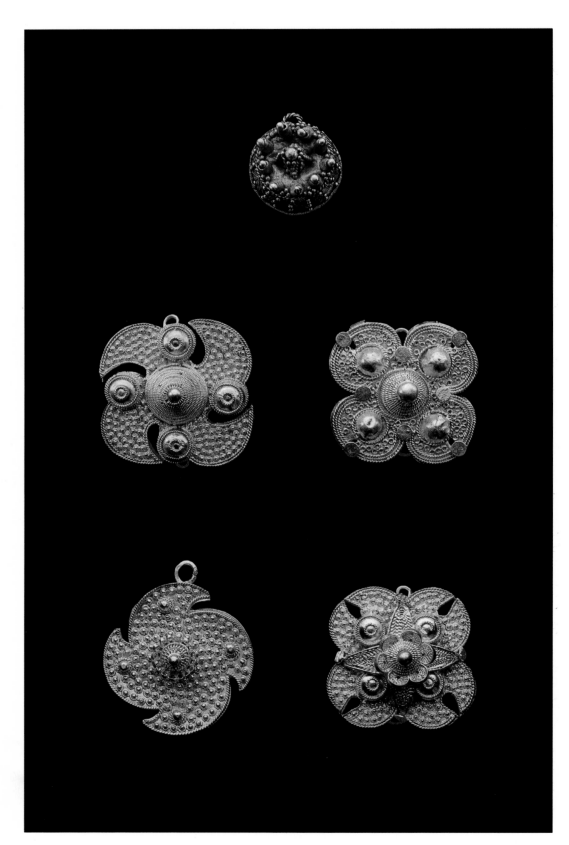

Plate 7

1
Mauritania
Maure
Crown-shaped ornament
Inv. 1034-188.
Cat. 22, description p. 221

2
Senegal or Mali
Tukulor/Sarakole
Throat ornament
Inv. 1034-185.
Cat. 26, description p. 221

3
Mali or Senegal
Tukulor/Peul
Throat ornament
Inv. 1034-153.
Cat. 23, description p. 221

4
Senegal
Tukulor
Throat ornament
Inv. 1034-186.
Cat. 25, description p. 221

5

Senegal or Mali
Tukulor/Sarakole
Throat ornament
Inv. 1034-187.
Cat. 24, description p. 221

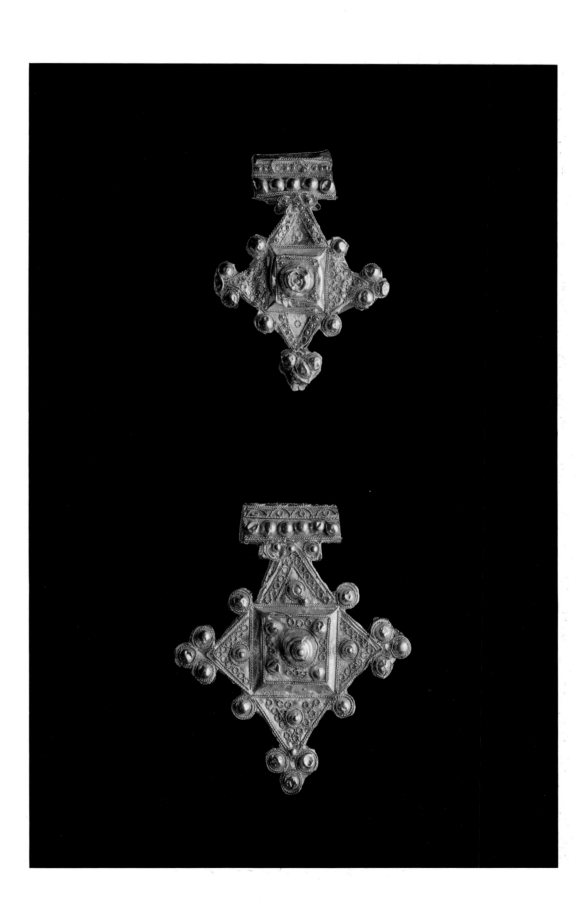

Plate 8

1
Mali or Mauritania
Maure/Tukulor/Peul (?)
Cruciform pendant
Inv. 1034-226.
Cat. 28, description p. 222

2
Mali or Mauritania
Maure/Tukulor/Peul (?)
Cruciform pendant
Inv. 1034-227.
Cat. 27, description p. 222

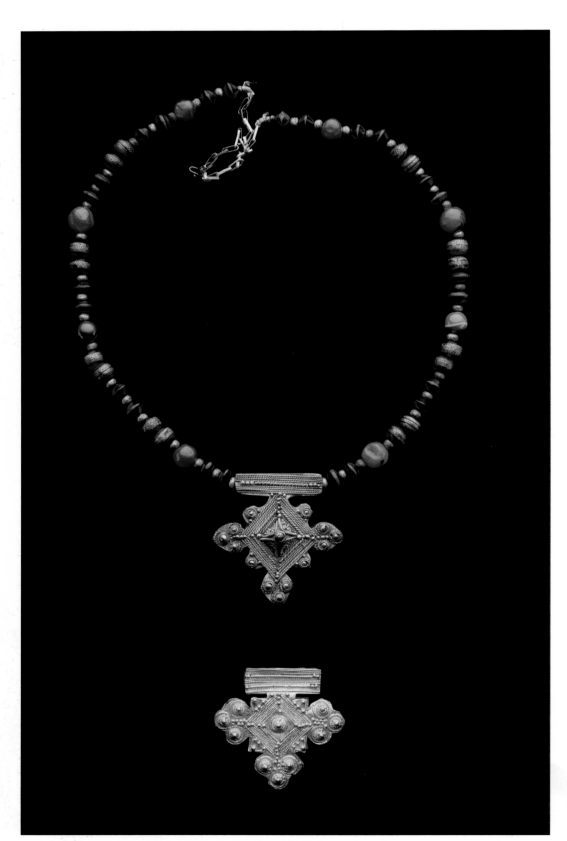

Plate 9

1
Mauritania
Maure
Cruciform pendant on a necklace
Inv. 1034-183.
Cat. 29, description p. 222

2
Mauritania
Maure
Cruciform pendant
Inv. 1034-181.
Cat. 30, description p. 222

Plate 10

1
Senegal
Tukulor/Wolof
Bicone-shaped bead
Inv. 1034-157.
Cat. 33, description p. 222

2
Senegal
Tukulor/Wolof
Bicone-shaped bead
Inv. 1009-91.
Cat. 34, description p. 222

3
Senegal
Tukulor/Wolof
Pendant of elongated cylinder form
Inv. 1034-189.
Cat. 35, description p. 222

4
Mali
Bamana/Sarakole
Bicone-shaped pendant
Inv. 1034-190.
Cat. 32, description p. 222

5
Mali or Senegal
Peul/Tukulor
Bicone-shaped pendant with chain
Inv. 1034-127.
Cat. 31, description p. 222

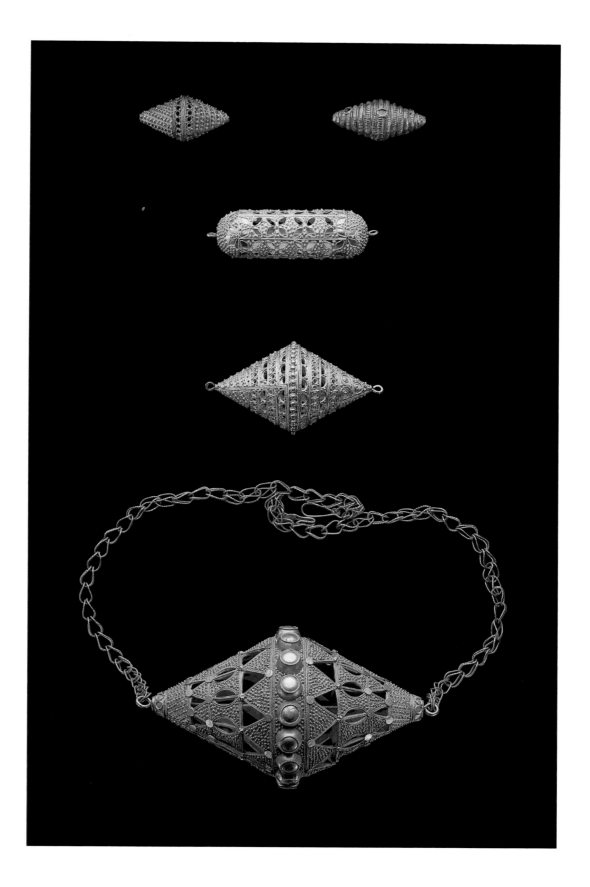

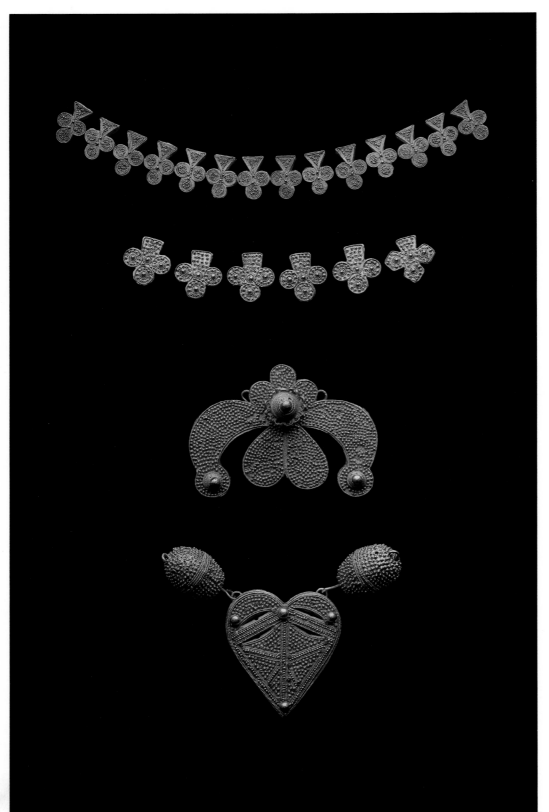

Plate 11

1
Senegal
Tukulor
Fourteen ornaments in the form of trefoils
Inv. 1034-128.
Cat. 36, description p. 222

2
Senegal
Tukulor
Six ornaments in the form of trefoils
Inv. 1034-152.
Cat. 37, description p. 222

3
Senegal
Tukulor
Pendant
Inv. 1034-158.
Cat. 38, description p. 222

4
Senegal
Tukulor
Pendant in the form of a heart
Inv. 1034-130
Cat. 39, description p. 222

Plate 12

1
Senegal
Tukulor
Pendant in the form of a star, with a chain
of globular beads
Inv. 1034-129.
Cat. 40, description p. 223

2
Senegal
Wolof
Necklace of oval wire beads
Inv. 1034-134.
Cat. 41, description p. 223

Plate 13

1
Senegal
Wolof
Pendant of filigree flowers with a wire chain
Inv. 1034-125.
Cat. 42, description p. 223

2
Senegal
Wolof
Necklace ensemble
Inv. 1034-126.
Cat. 43, description p. 223

Plate 14

1,2
Senegal
Wolof
Pair of bracelets
Inv. 1034-132 A, B.
Cat. 44, description p. 223

3,4
Senegal
Wolof
Pair of bracelets
Inv. 1034-131 A, B.
Cat. 45, description p. 223

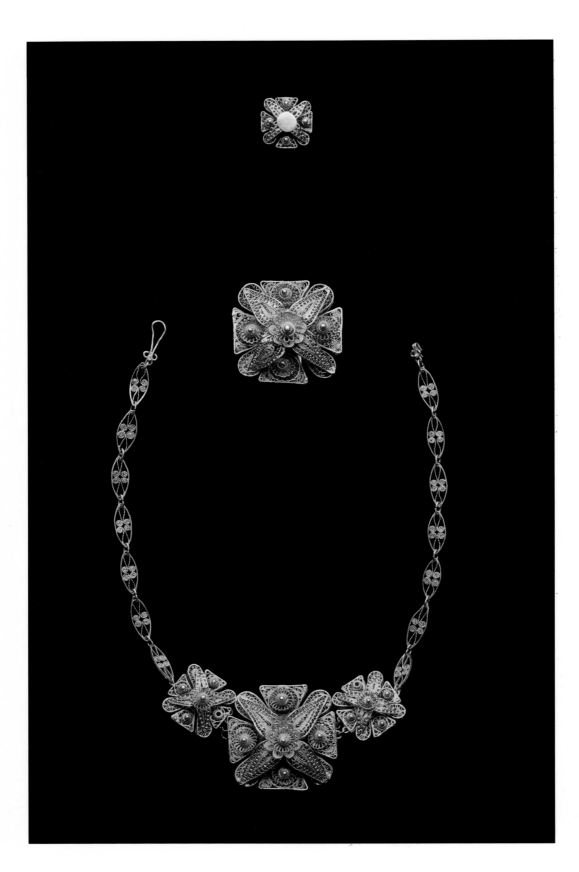

Plate 15

Senegal
Wolof
Set of filigree jewellery comprising a
finger-ring, a bracelet and a necklace
Inv. 1000-44, A, B, C.
Cat. 46, description p. 223

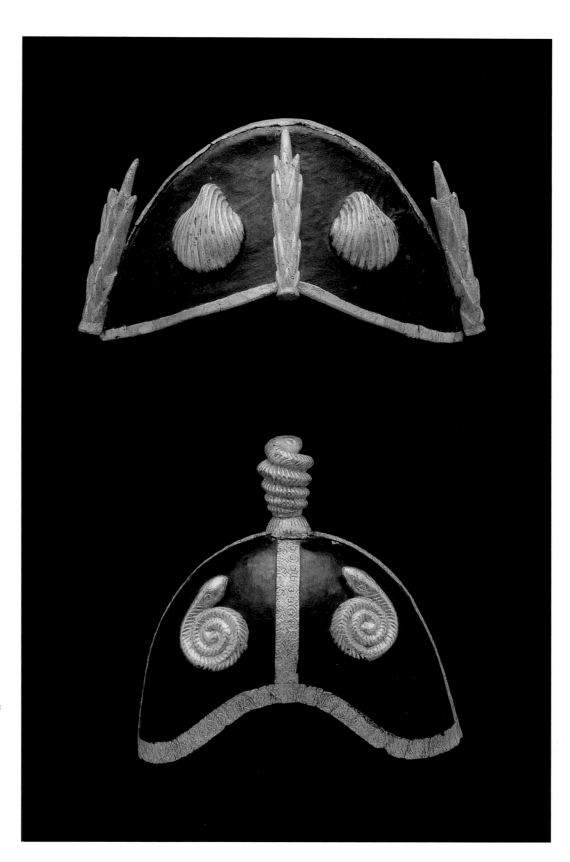

Plate 16

1
Ghana
Akan
Helmet of antelope skin, decorated with
wooden ornaments covered with gold leaf
Inv. 1009-83.
Cat. 48, description p. 223

2
Ghana
Akan: Asante
Helmet of antelope skin with wooden
decorations covered with gold leaf
Inv. 1009-84.
Cat. 49, description p. 223

Plate 17

1
Ghana
Akan: Asante
Crown of wood covered with gold leaf,
lined with velvet
Inv. 1009-133.
Cat. 50, description p. 223

2
Ghana
Akan
Head-dress of goatskin with wooden
plaque covered with gold leaf
Inv. 1009-115.
Cat. 55, description p. 224

Plate 18

1
Ghana
Akan
Head-dress of goatskin with an amulet
covered with a sheet of gold
Inv. 1009-113.
Cat. 54, description p. 224

2
Ghana
Akan
Head-dress of goatskin with an amulet
covered with a sheet of gold
Inv. 1009-112.
Cat. 53, description p. 224

3
Ghana
Akan
Head-dress of goatskin with an amulet
covered with a sheet of gold
Inv. 1009-114.
Cat. 52, description p. 224

4
Ghana
Akan
Head-dress of goatskin with an amulet
covered with a sheet of gold
Inv. 1009-127.
Cat. 51, description p. 223

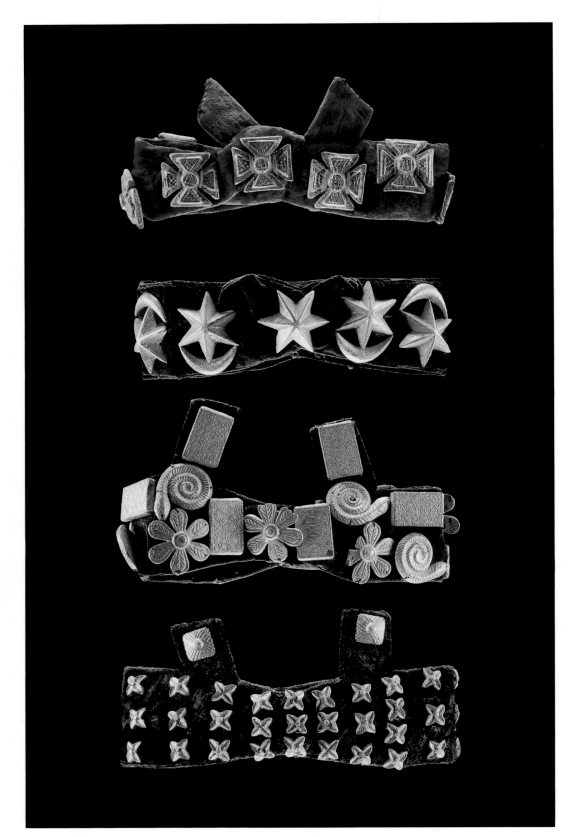

Plate 19

1
Ghana
Akan
Headband of velvet with wooden
decorations covered with gold leaf
Inv. 1009-40.
Cat. 59, description p. 224

2
Ghana
Akan
Headband of velvet with wooden
decorations covered with gold leaf
Inv. 1009-57.
Cat. 58, description p. 224

3
Ghana
Akan
Headband of velvet with wooden
decorations covered with gold leaf
Inv. 1009-43.
Cat. 57, description p. 224

4
Ghana
Akan
Headband of velvet with wooden
decorations covered with gold leaf
Inv. 1009-19.
Cat. 56, description p. 224

Plate 20

1
Ghana
Akan
Hairpin of ivory with a gold finial
Inv. 1034-163.
Cat. 47, description p. 223

2
Ghana
Akan
Leaf-shaped ornaments for a hat
Inv. 1009-50 A, B, C, D.
Cat. 60, description p. 224

Plate 21

1
Ghana
Akan
Disc-shaped pectoral
Inv. 1034-203.
Cat. 63, description p. 225

2
Ghana
Akan: Asante or Adanse
Disc-shaped pectoral
Inv. 1034-209.
Cat. 64, description p. 225

3
Ghana
Akan
Disc-shaped pectoral
Inv. 1034-62.
Cat. 65, description p. 225

4
Ghana
Akan
Disc-shaped pectoral
Inv. 1034-219.
Cat. 66, description p. 225

5
Ghana
Akan
Disc-shaped pectoral
Inv. 1034-142.
Cat. 67, description p. 225

6
Ghana
Akan
Disc-shaped pectoral
Inv. 1034-72.
Cat. 68, description p. 225

Plate 22

Ghana
Akan
Disc-shaped pectoral suspended from fibre
cords
Inv. 1034-240.
Cat. 69, description p. 225

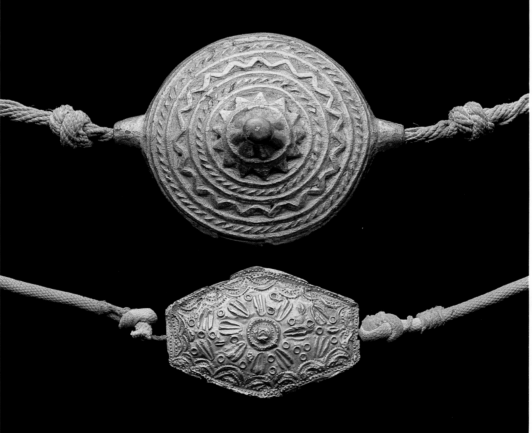

Plate 23

1
Ghana
Akan: probably Asante
Disc-shaped pectoral on a cord
Inv. 1034-229.
Cat. 70, description p. 225

2
Ghana
Akan
Disc-shaped pectoral of carved wood
covered with gold leaf
Inv. 1034-152.
Cat. 71, description p. 225

3
Ghana
Akan
Six-sided amulet attached to a woven cord
Inv. 1034-204.
Cat. 82, description p. 226

Plate 24

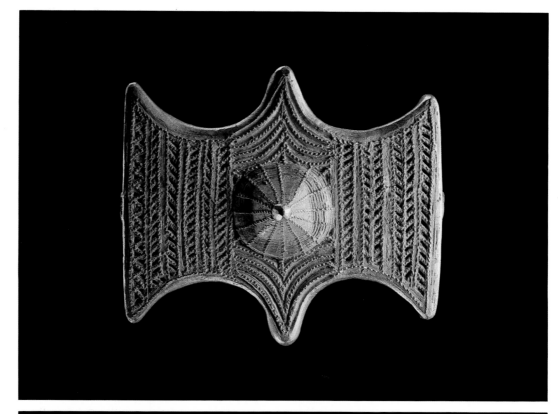

1
Ghana
Akan: Asante
Pectoral of unusual form
Inv. 1034-205.
Cat. 72, description p. 225

2, 3, 4
Ghana
Akan
Disc-shaped beads
Inv. 1034-170, 1034-34, 1034-33.
Cat. 78, 73, 75, descriptions pp. 225, 226

5, 6, 7
Ghana
Akan
Disc-shaped beads
Inv. 1034-30, 1034-169, 1034-32.
Cat. 76, 79, 77, descriptions pp. 225, 226

8
Ghana
Akan
Bead in the form of an amulet
Inv. 1034-212.
Cat. 81, description p. 226

9
Ghana
Akan
Disc-shaped bead
Inv. 1034-29.
Cat. 74, description p. 225

Plate 25

Ghana
Akan
Necklace of 108 beads
Inv. 1034-60.
Cat. 83, description p. 226

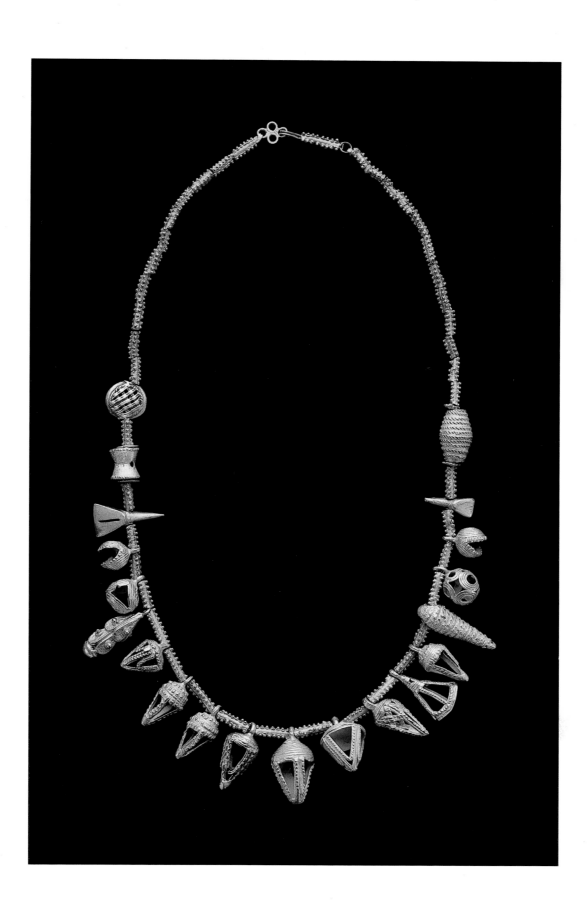

Plate 26

Ghana
Akan
Necklace of 63 beads
Inv. 1034-61.
Cat. 84, description p. 226

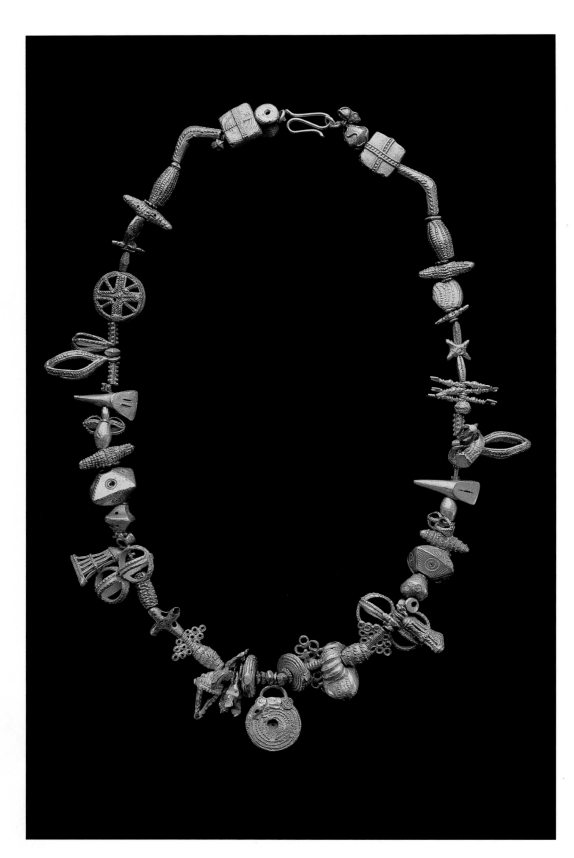

Plate 27

Ghana
Akan
Necklace of 103 beads
Inv. 1034-53.
Cat. 85, description p. 226

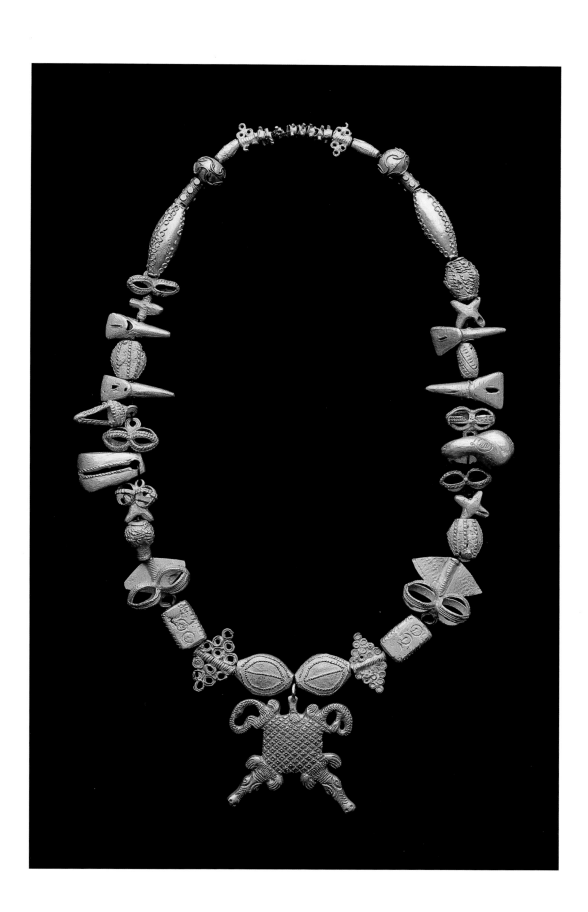

Plate 28

Ghana
Akan
Necklace of 49 beads
Inv. 1034-52.
Cat. 86, description p. 226

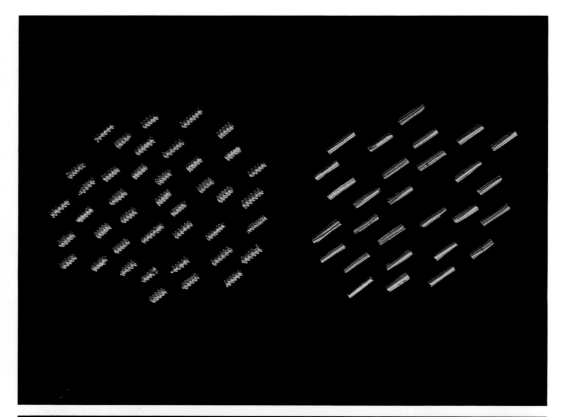

Plate 29

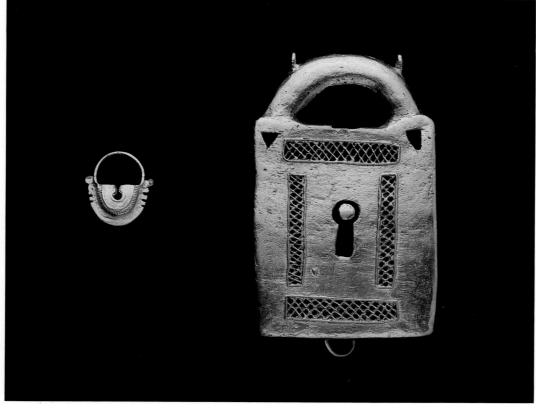

1
Ghana
Akan
String of 41 elongated beads
Inv. 1034-51.
Cat. 87, description p. 226

2
Ghana
Akan
String of 28 small beads
Inv. 1034-50.
Cat. 88, description p. 226

3
Ghana
Akan
Pendant in the form of a padlock
Inv. 1034-214.
Cat. 93, description p. 227

4
Ghana
Akan
Padlock
Inv. 1034-206.
Cat. 172, description p. 234

Plate 30

1
Ghana
Akan
Pendants of a stool, two swords, and a
fetish object
Inv. 1009-131.
Cat. 96, description p. 227

2,3
Ghana
Akan
Two pellet-bells
Inv. 1034-166 A, B.
Cat. 89, description p. 226

4,5
Ghana
Akan
Two bells
Inv. 1034-162 A, B.
Cat. 90, description p. 226

6
Ghana
Akan
Sandal ornament in the form of a palm
beetle
Inv. 1034-167.
Cat. 161, description p. 233

7,8
Ghana
Akan
Two sandal ornaments
Inv. 1034-211 A, B.
Cat. 162, description p. 233

9
Ghana
Akan
Hollow square bead
Inv. 1034-213.
Cat. 80, description p. 226

10
Ghana
Akan
Pendant of a stylised cutlass
Inv. 1034-215.
Cat. 97, description p. 227

11
Ghana
Akan
Pendant of a gunpowder flask
Inv. 1034-216
Cat. 92, description p. 226

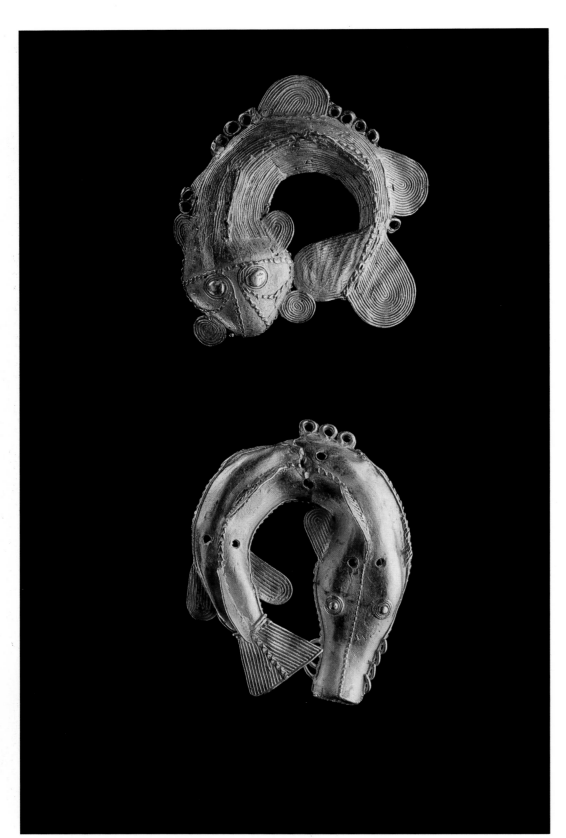

Plate 31

1
Ghana
Akan
Pendant representing a fish
Inv. 1034-63.
Cat. 95, description p. 227

2
Ghana
Akan: probably Asante
Pendant representing a fish
Inv. 1034-231.
Cat. 94, description p. 227

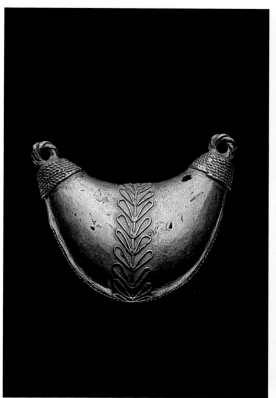

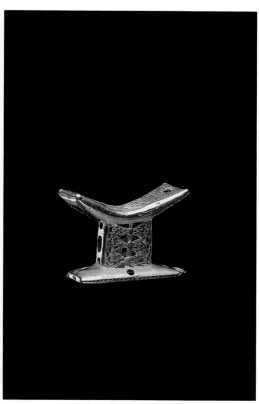

Plate 32

1
Ghana
Akan: probably Asante
Pellet bell
Inv. 1034-207.
Cat. 173, description p. 234

2
Ghana
Akan
Pendant of a royal stool
Inv. 1034-228.
Cat. 91, description p. 227

3
Ghana
Akan
Neck-chain with central pendants of a
cutlass, bill-hook and cocoa pods
Inv. 1034-54.
Cat. 99, description p. 227

Plate 33

1
Ghana
Akan
Neck-chain with a pendant of an eagle
Inv. 1034-47.
Cat. 100, description p. 227

2
Ghana
Akan
Pair of jawbones
Inv. 1034-208 A, B.
Cat. 175, description p. 235

3
Ghana
Akan
Pendant ornament of a man plucking
cocoa pods with a bill-hook
Inv. 1034-217.
Cat. 98, description p. 227

Plate 34

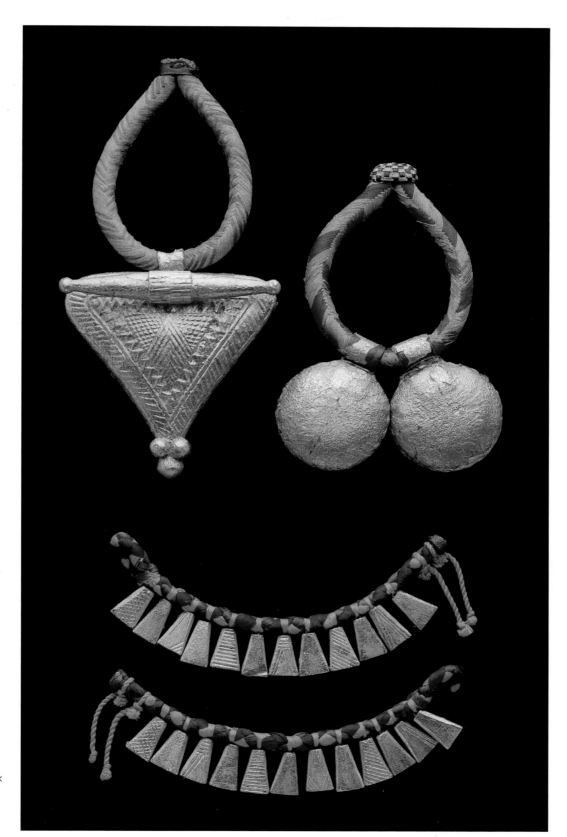

1
Ghana
Akan
Two elbow amulets of carved wood
covered with gold leaf, suspended from a
silk cord
Inv. 1009-58.
Cat. 101, description p. 227

2
Ghana
Akan
Elbow ornament of two amulets covered
with gold leaf
Inv. 1031-30.
Cat. 102, description p. 228

3
Ghana
Akan
Pair of ankle bands each consisting of a silk
cord with twelve wooden ornaments
covered with gold leaf
Inv. 1009-59 A, B.
Cat. 160, description p. 233

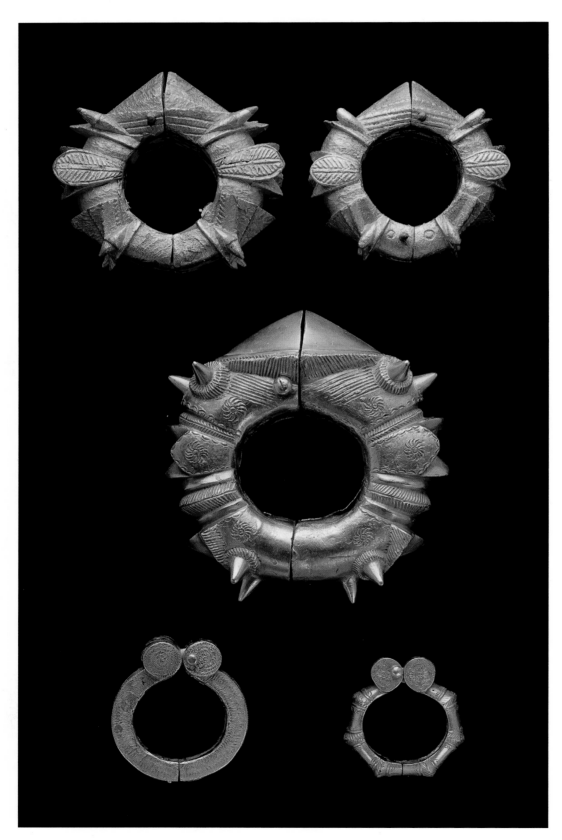

Plate 35

1
Ghana
Akan
Chief's bracelet of carved wood covered
with gold leaf
Inv. 1031-76.
Cat. 103, description p. 228

2
Ghana
Akan
Chief's bracelet of carved wood covered
with gold leaf
Inv. 1031-305.
Cat. 104, description p. 228

3
Ghana
Akan
Chief's bracelet
Inv. 1031-321.
Cat. 107, description p. 228

4
Ghana
Akan
Queen-mother's bracelet
Inv. 1031-66.
Cat. 110, description p. 228

5
Ghana
Akan
Queen-mother's bracelet
Inv. 1031-23.
Cat. 109, description p. 228

Plate 36

1
Ghana
Akan
Chief's bracelet
Inv. 1031-65.
Cat. 108, description p. 228

2
Ghana
Akan
Chief's bracelet
Inv. 1031-18.
Cat. 106, description p. 228

3
Ghana
Akan: probably Asante
Chief's bracelet
Inv. 1031-17.
Cat. 105, description p. 228

4
Ghana
Southern Akan
Bracelet of plaited wires ornamented with
two cannons and stylised flowers or fruit
Inv. 1031-21.
Cat. 112, description p. 228

5
Ghana
Southern Akan
Bracelet of plaited wires ornamented with
two groups of birds pecking nuts
Inv. 1031-15.
Cat. 111, description p. 228

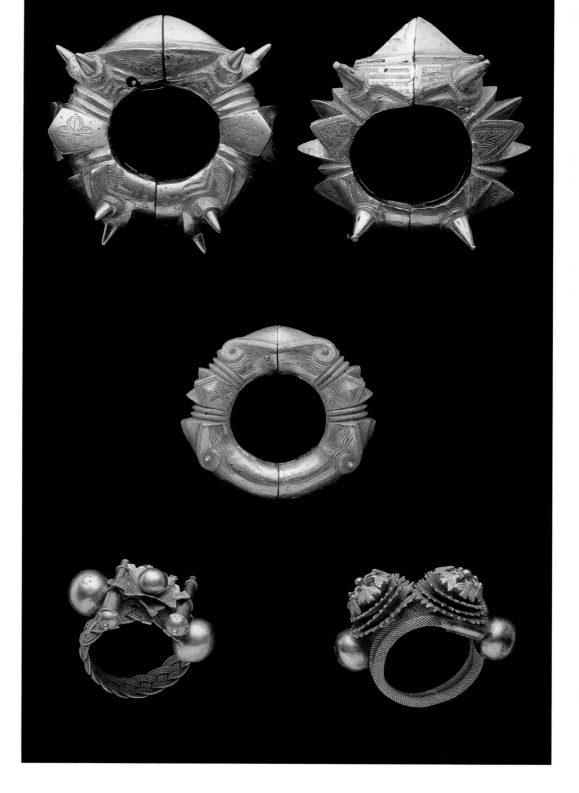

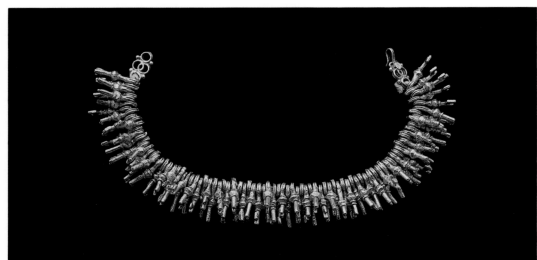

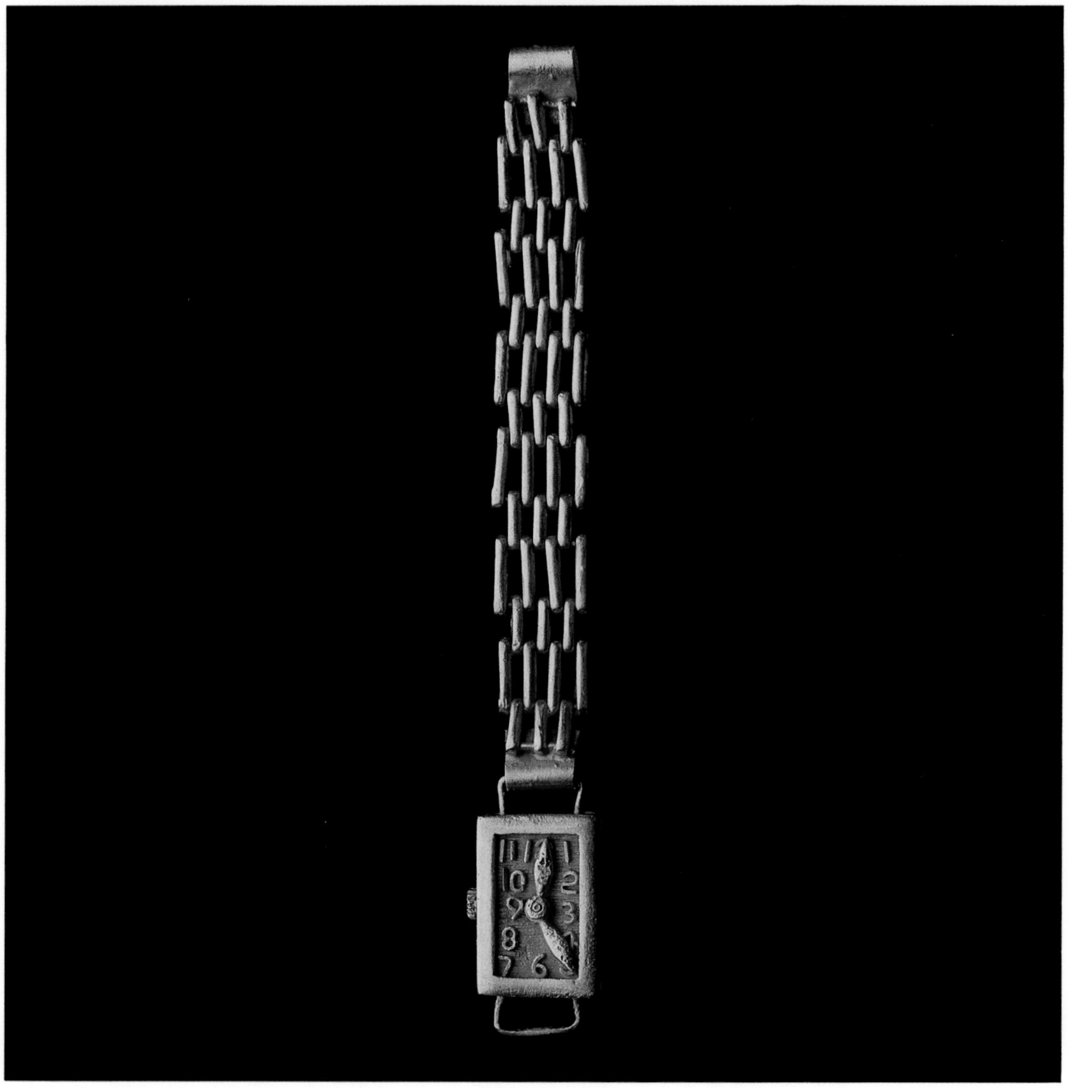

Plate 37

1
Ghana
Akan
Bracelet of ninety small keys
Inv. 1031-67.
Cat. 113, description p. 229

2
Ghana
Akan
Bracelet in the form of a European
wristwatch on a chain
Inv. 1031-322.
Cat. 114, description p. 229

Plate 38

1
Ghana
Akan
Finger-ring in the form of a twisted knot
Inv. 1033-14.
Cat. 131, description p. 230

2
Ghana
Akan
Finger-ring in the form of a twisted knot
Inv. 1033-28.
Cat. 128, description p. 230

3
Ghana
Akan
Finger-ring in the form of a twisted knot
Inv. 1033-33.
Cat. 129, description p. 230

4
Ghana
Akan
Ring with a design of three twisted coils
Inv. 1033-44.
Cat. 126, description p. 230

5
Ghana
Akan
Finger-ring in the form of a twisted knot
Inv. 1033-22.
Cat. 130, description p. 230

6
Ghana
Akan
Ring with six twisted lobes
Inv. 1033-16.
Cat. 125, description p. 230

7
Ghana
Southern Akan
Finger-ring with a circular central motif
Inv. 1033-32.
Cat. 116, description p. 229

8
Ghana
Akan
Finger-ring with an openwork sphere
Inv. 1033-7.
Cat. 137, description p. 231

9
Ghana
Southern Akan
Finger-ring
Inv. 1033-31.
Cat. 115, description p. 229

10
Ghana
Southern Akan
Finger-ring with an anvil
Inv. 1033-20.
Cat. 120, description p. 229

11
Ghana
Southern Akan
Finger-ring with a pair of bellows
Inv. 1033-30.
Cat. 121, description p. 229

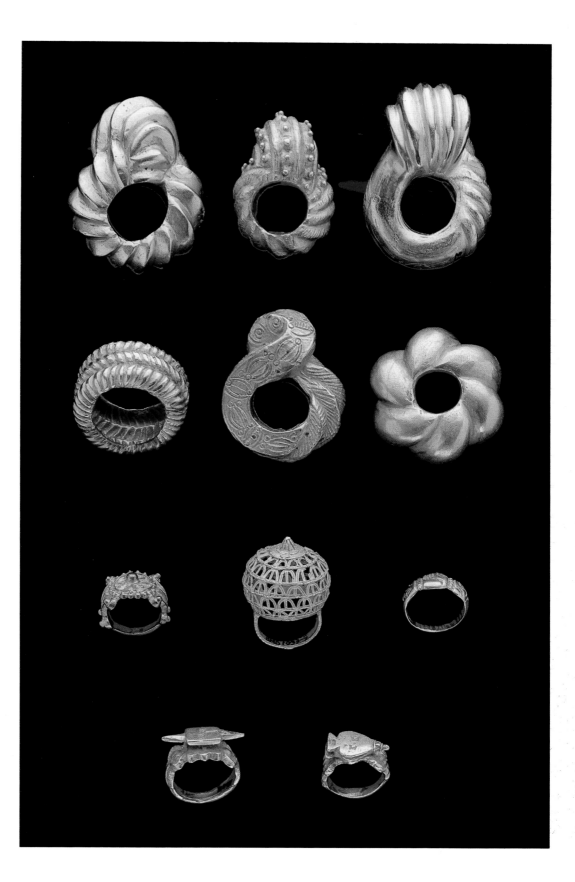

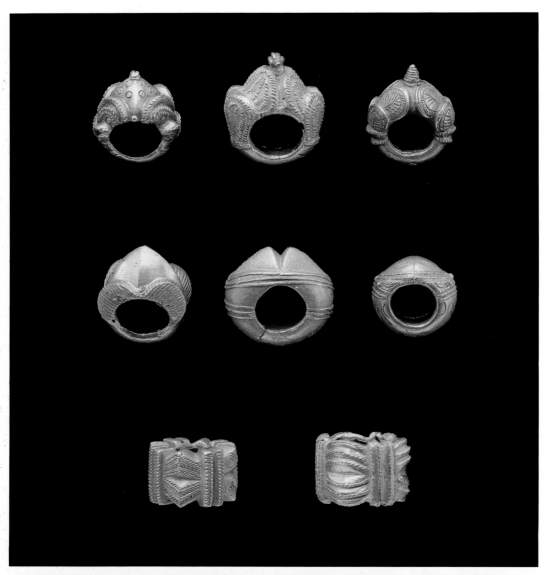

Plate 39

1, 3
Ghana
Akan
Finger-rings with a bud-like protuberance
Inv. 1033-37, 1033-35.
Cat. 132, 133, descriptions p. 230

2
Ghana
Akan
Finger-ring with foliate designs
Inv. 1033-24.
Cat. 134, description p. 230

4, 5, 6
Ghana
Akan
Finger-rings with a lozenge-shaped bezel
Inv. 1033-12, 1033-38, 1033-36.
Cat. 118, 119, 117, descriptions p. 229

7
Ghana
Akan
Finger-ring representing tied canes
Inv. 1033-74.
Cat. 135, description p. 230

8
Ghana
Akan
Ring probably representing tied canes or
ropes
Inv. 1033-42.
Cat. 127, description p. 230

9, 10
Ghana
Akan
Rings with an oval bezel
Inv. 1033-39, 1033-40.
Cat. 122, 123, descriptions p. 229

11
Ghana
Akan
Ring with a heart bearing the initials
"K.D."
Inv. 1033-41
Cat. 124, description p. 230

Plate 40

1
Ghana
Akan
Finger-ring perhaps representing a flower
Inv. 1033-99.
Cat. 136, description p. 230

2
Ghana
Akan
Finger-ring covered with numerous spikes
Inv. 1033-15.
Cat. 138, description p. 231

3
Ghana
Akan
Finger-ring covered with spikes
Inv. 1033-25.
Cat. 139, description p. 231

4
Ghana
Akan
Finger-ring of an oil-palm tree
Inv. 1033-21.
Cat. 140, description p. 231

5
Ghana
Akan
Finger-ring of an oil-palm tree
Inv. 1033-13.
Cat. 141, description p. 231

6
Ghana
Akan
Finger-ring with a human head
Inv. 1033-26.
Cat. 148, description p. 232

7
Ghana
Akan
Finger-ring with four cannons and a
gunpowder keg
Inv. 1033-76.
Cat. 146, description p. 232

8
Ghana
Akan
Finger-ring with four cannons and a
gunpowder keg
Inv. 1033-11.
Cat. 147, description p. 232

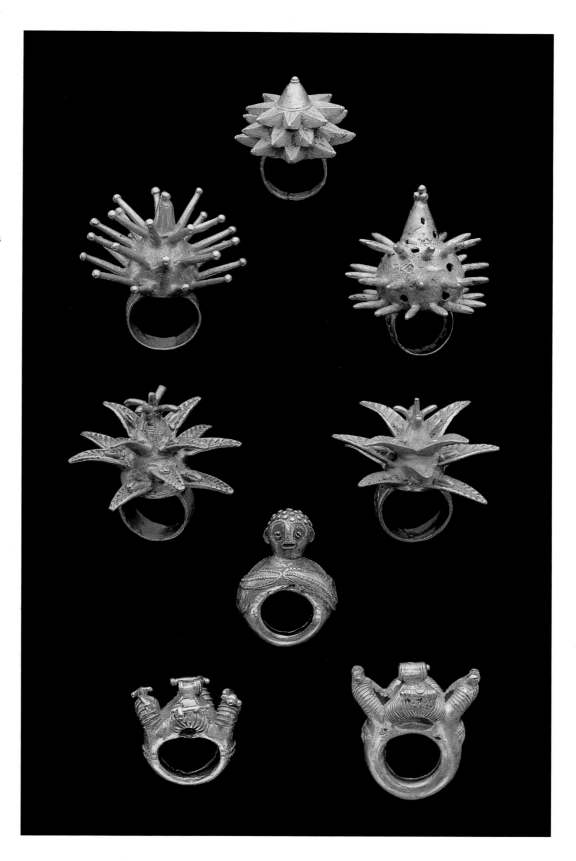

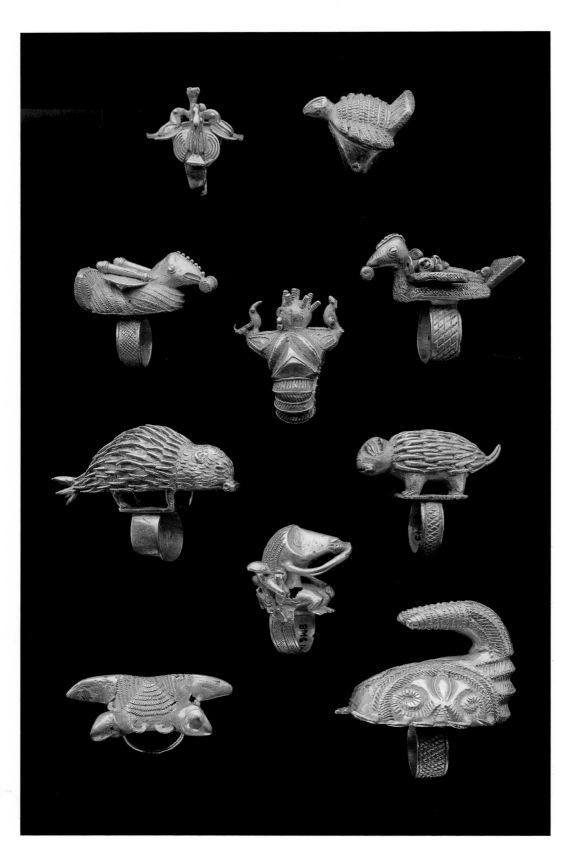

Plate 41

1
Ghana
Akan
Finger-ring of four birds pecking palm-nuts
Inv. 1033-19.
Cat. 143, description p. 231

2
Ghana
Akan
Finger-ring of a bird
Inv. 1033-84.
Cat. 142, description p. 231

3
Ghana
Akan
Finger-ring of a bird carrying a gunpowder
keg and two cannons
Inv. 1033-48.
Cat. 144, description p. 231

4
Ghana
Akan
Finger-ring of a bird carrying gunpowder
kegs and cannons
Inv. 1033-27.
Cat. 145, description p. 231

5
Ghana
Akan
Finger-ring of a human head with two
birds
Inv. 1033-77.
Cat. 149, description p. 232

6
Ghana
Akan: Asante
Finger-ring of a porcupine
Inv. 1033-78.
Cat. 150, description p. 232

7
Ghana
Akan: Asante
Finger-ring of a porcupine
Inv. 1033-43.
Cat. 151, description p. 232

8
Ghana
Akan
Finger-ring of a hunter shooting a monkey
Inv. 1033-17.
Cat. 152, description p. 232

9
Ghana
Akan
Finger-ring of two crocodiles with a single body
Inv. 1033-83,
Cat. 153, description p. 232

10
Ghana
Akan
Finger-ring of a scorpion
Inv. 1033-49.
Cat. 154, description p. 232

Plate 42

1
Ghana
Akan
Finger-ring of a frog
Inv. 1033-29.
Cat. 155, description p. 233

2
Ghana
Akan
Finger-ring of a frog
Inv. 1033-18.
Cat. 156, description p. 233

3
Ghana
Akan
Finger-ring of a mudfish
Inv. 1033-85.
Cat. 158, description p. 233

4
Ghana
Akan
Finger-ring of a mudfish
Inv. 1033-71.
Cat. 157, description p. 233

5
Ghana
Akan
Finger-ring of a mudfish
Inv. 1033-23.
Cat. 159, description p. 233

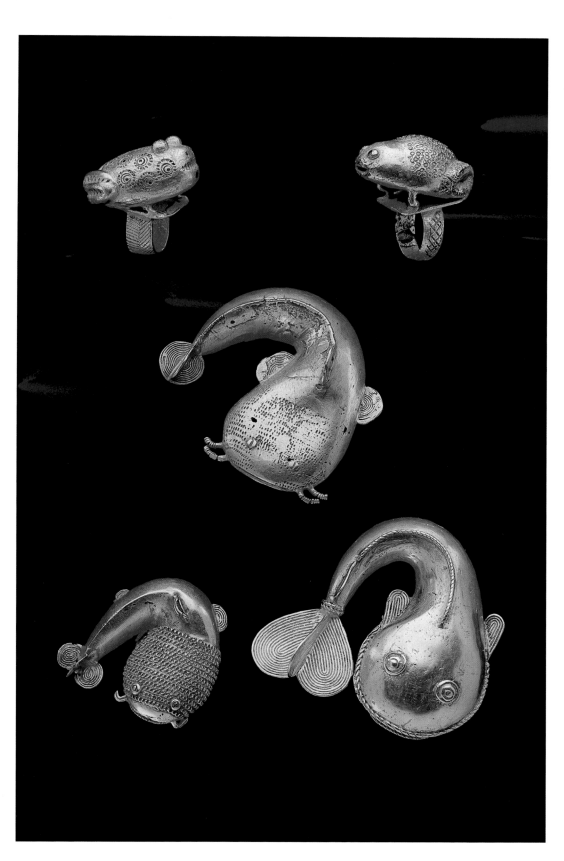

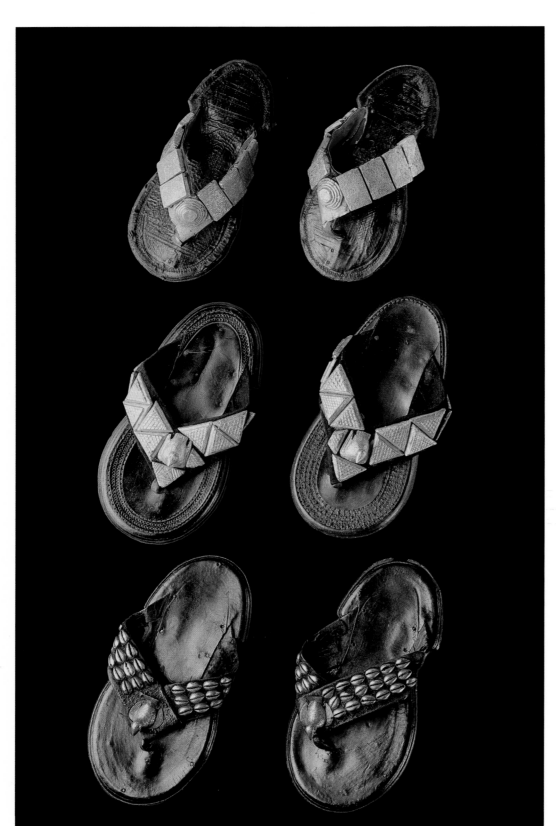

Plate 43

1
Ghana
Akan
Pair of chief's leather sandals, with talismans of carved wood covered with gold leaf
Inv. 1009-66 A, B.
Cat. 163, description p. 233

2
Ghana
Akan
Pair of chief's leather sandals, with ornaments of carved wood covered with gold leaf
Inv. 1009-53 A, B.
Cat. 164, description p. 233

3
Ghana
Akan
Pair of chief's leather sandals, decorated with cowry shells and a bird
Inv. 1009-129 A, B.
Cat. 165, description p. 233

Plate 44

1
Ghana
Akan
Horse-tail whisk, the handle with amulets of carved wood covered with gold leaf
Inv. 1009-34.
Cat. 166, description p. 233

2
Ghana
Akan
Horse-tail whisk, the leather handle covered with gold foil, and with two amulets of leather and gold
Inv. 1009-85.
Cat. 167, description p. 233

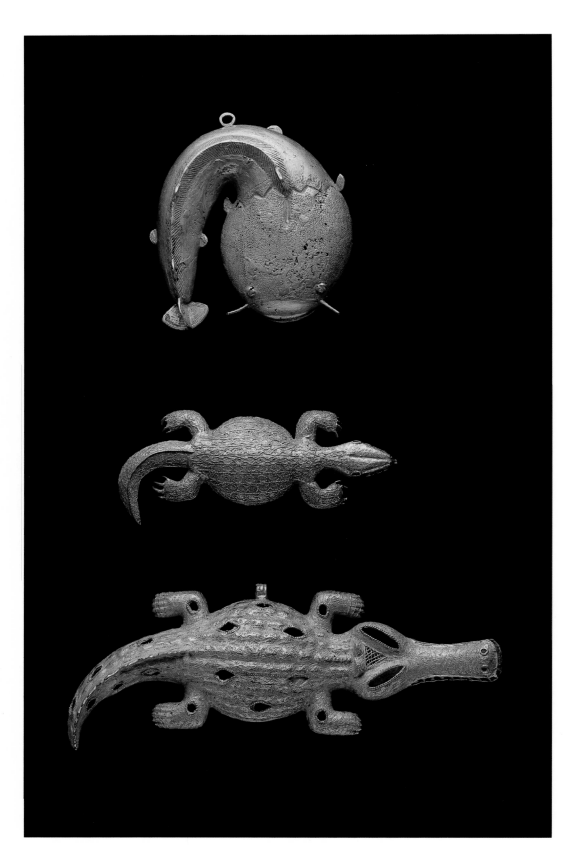

Plate 45

1
Ghana
Akan: probably Asante
Sword ornament of a mudfish
Inv. 1034-171.
Cat. 168, description p. 234

2
Ghana
Akan: northern Asante
Sword ornament of a skink or monitor
lizard
Inv. 1009-63.
Cat. 169, description p. 234

3
Ghana
Akan: Asante
Sword ornament of a crocodile
Inv. 1009-69.
Cat. 170, description p. 234

Plate 46

1
Ghana
Akan: northern Asante
Sword ornament of a lion
Inv. 1009-62.
Cat. 171, description p. 234

2
Ghana
Akan
Disc-shaped ornament
Inv. 1034-44.
Cat. 61, description p. 224

3
Ghana
Akan
Ornament in the form of a cockle-shell
Inv. 1034-168.
Cat. 174, description p. 234

4
Ghana
Akan
Disc-shaped ornament
Inv. 1034-42.
Cat. 62, description p. 225

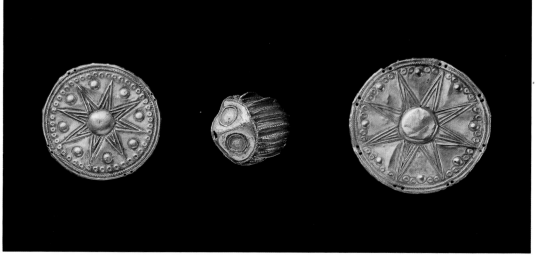

Plate 47

1
Ghana
Akan
Sword with an iron blade and a carved wooden pommel covered with gold leaf
Inv. 1009- 42.
Cat. 176, description p. 235

2
Ghana
Akan
Sword with an iron blade, the carved wooden pommel covered with gold leaf
Inv. 1009-35.
Cat. 177, description p. 235

Plate 48

1
Ghana
Akan
Sword with an iron blade an a carved
wooden pommel covered with gold leaf
Inv. 1009-36.
Cat. 178, description p. 235

2
Ghana
Akan
Sword with an iron blade and a carved
wooden pommel covered with gold leaf
Inv. 1009-17.
Cat. 179, description p. 235

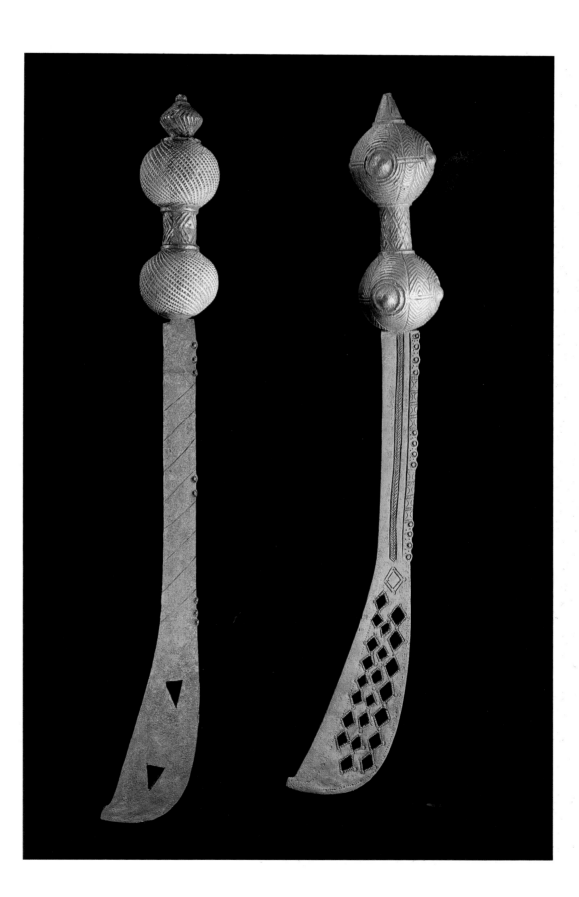

Plate 49

1
Ghana
Akan: Asante
Linguist staff finial. Carved wood covered
with gold leaf.
Inv. 1009-31.
Cat. 181, description p. 235

2
Ghana
Akan
Umbrella finial. Carved wood covered with
gold leaf.
Inv. 1009-70.
Cat. 180, description p. 235

3
Ghana
Akan
Linguist staff finial. Carved wood covered
with gold leaf.
Inv. 1009-60.
Cat. 182, description p. 235

Plate 50

1
Ghana
Akan
Linguist staff with a finial showing one man
eating from a bowl while another man
looks on. Carved wood covered with gold
leaf.
Inv. 1009-52.
Cat. 183, description p. 235

2
Ghana
Akan
Linguist staff with a finial showing a man
scraping bark from a tree. Carved wood
covered with gold leaf.
Inv. 1009-55.
Cat. 184, description p. 235

3
Ghana
Akan
Linguist staff top of a bush-cow with three
birds perching among its horns. Carved
wood covered with gold leaf.
Inv. 1009-65.
Cat. 185, description p. 235

Plate 51

1
Ghana
Akan
Linguist staff with a finial showing an elephant and a bush-cow. Carved wood covered with gold leaf.
Inv. 1009-56.
Cat. 186, description p. 236

2
Ghana
Akan
Linguist staff representing birds on its finial and staff. Carved wood covered with gold leaf.
Inv. 1009-128.
Cat. 187, description p. 236

Plate 52

1
Côte d'Ivoire
South-eastern region
Downward-pointing crescent moon
Inv. 1034-78.
Cat. 188, description p. 236

2
Côte d'Ivoire
South-eastern region
Downward-pointing crescent moon with
cut-out triangles
Inv. 1034-25.
Cat. 190, description p. 236

3
Côte d'Ivoire
South-eastern region
Downward-pointing crescent moon with
openwork designs
Inv. 1034-36.
Cat. 189, description p. 236

4
Côte d'Ivoire
Lagoons area
Hair ornament in the form of a crescent
Inv. 1034-267.
Cat. 191, description p. 236

5
Côte d'Ivoire
South-eastern region
Downward-pointing crescent moon
Inv. 1034- 24.
Cat. 192, description p. 236

6
Côte d'Ivoire
South-eastern region
Downward-pointing crescent moon with a
human face
Inv. 1034-22.
Cat. 193, description p. 236

7
Côte d'Ivoire
South-eastern region
Downward-pointing crescent moon with a
human face
Inv. 1034-230.
Cat. 194, description p. 237

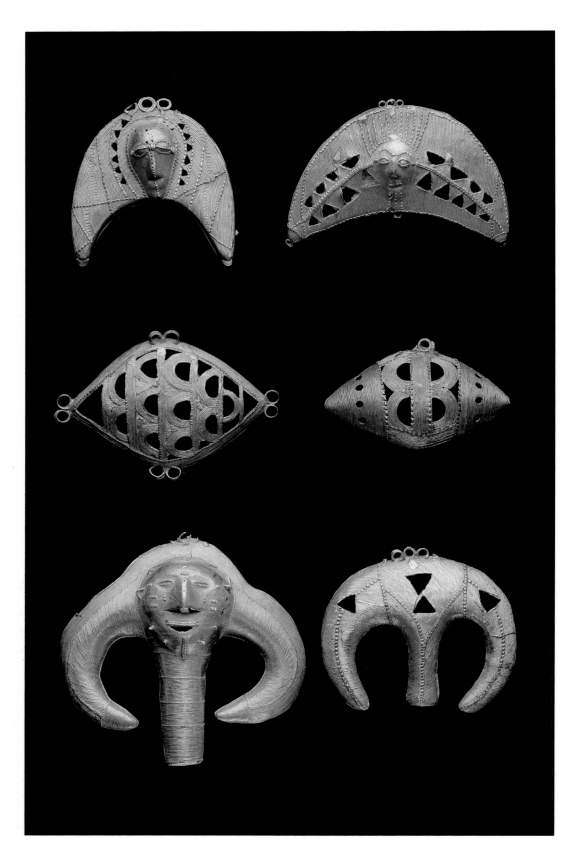

Plate 53

1
Côte d'Ivoire
South-eastern region
Downward-pointing crescent moon with a
human face
Inv. 1034-3.
Cat. 196, description p. 237

2
Côte d'Ivoire
Lagoons area
Downward-pointing crescent moon with a
human face
Inv. 1034-1.
Cat. 195, description p. 237

3
Côte d'Ivoire
Lagoons area
Lozenge-shaped ornament
Inv. 1034-27.
Cat. 197, description p. 237

4
Côte d'Ivoire
Lagoons area
Lozenge-shaped ornament
Inv. 1034-26.
Cat. 198, description p. 237

5
Côte d'Ivoire
Lagoons area
Human face on a stylised ram's head with
downward-curving horns
Inv. 1034-40.
Cat. 199, description p. 237

6
Côte d'Ivoire
Lagoons area
Stylised ram's head with horns pointing
downwards
Inv. 1034-20.
Cat. 200, description p. 237

Plate 54

1
Côte d'Ivoire
Lagoons area (?)
Elephant
Inv. 1007-73.
Cat. 201, description p. 238

2
Côte d'Ivoire
Lagoons area (?)
Stylised leopard
Inv. 1034-5.
Cat. 202, description p. 238

3
Côte d'Ivoire
South-eastern region
Pangolin
Inv. 1007-71.
Cat. 204, description p. 238

4
Côte d'Ivoire
Lagoons area
Cow
Inv. 1007-72.
Cat. 203, description p. 238

Plate 55

1
Côte d'Ivoire
Probably lagoons area
Chicken
Inv. 1034-57.
Cat. 205, description p. 238

2
Côte d'Ivoire
Lagoons area
Chicken holding a seed in its beak
Inv. 1034-139.
Cat. 206, description p. 239

3
Côte d'Ivoire
Lagoons area
Tortoise
Inv. 1034-4.
Cat. 208, description p. 239

4
Côte d'Ivoire
Lagoons area
Catfish
Inv. 1034-21.
Cat. 207, description p. 239

Plate 56

1
Côte d'Ivoire
Lagoons area
Convex disc
Inv. 1034-56.
Cat. 210, description p. 239

2
Côte d'Ivoire
Lagoons area
Tortoise, freshwater terrapin or turtle
Inv. 1034-37.
Cat. 209, description p. 239

3
Côte d'Ivoire
Lagoons area
Human face in the centre of an open hand
Inv. 1034-2.
Cat. 211, description p. 239

4
Côte d'Ivoire
Unknown provenance
Pendant of a human head
Inv. 1034-10.
Cat. 212, description p. 239

5
Côte d'Ivoire
Unknown provenance
Pendant of a human head
Inv. 1034-11.
Cat. 213, description p. 240

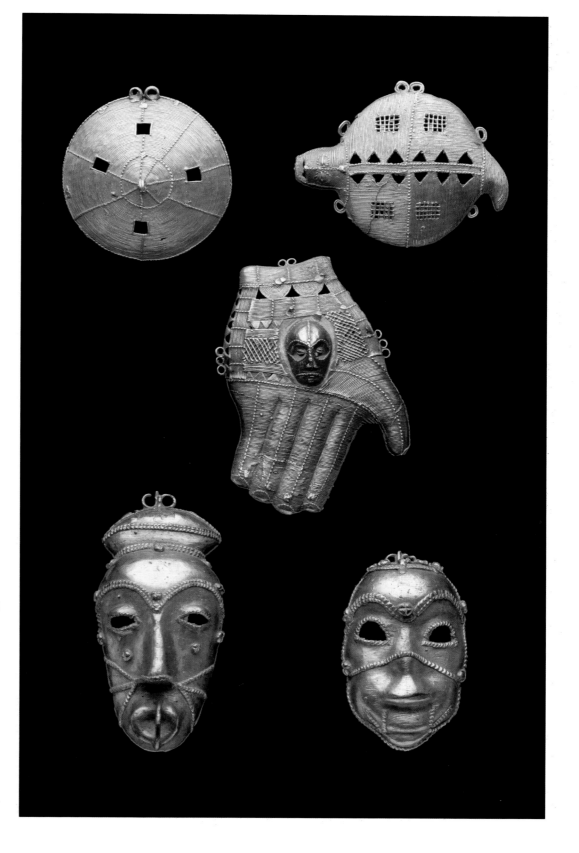

Plate 57

1
Côte d'Ivoire
Baule
Pendant of a human head
Inv. 1034-41.
Cat. 215, description p. 240

2
Côte d'Ivoire
Baule
Pendant of a human head
Inv. 1034-140.
Cat. 216, description p. 240

3
Côte d'Ivoire
Baule
Pendant of a human head
Inv. 1034-184.
Cat. 217, description p. 240

4
Côte d'Ivoire/Ghana border region
Perhaps Anyi or Abron
Human head
Inv. 1034-38.
Cat. 214, description p. 240

Plate 58

1
Côte d'Ivoire
South-eastern region
Pendant of a stylised human head
Inv. 1034-16.
Cat. 224, description p. 242

2
Côte d'Ivoire
Baule
Pendant of a human head
Inv. 1034-18.
Cat. 219, description p. 241

3
Côte d'Ivoire
Baule
Pendant of a human head
Inv. 1034-6.
Cat. 218, description p. 240

4
Côte d'Ivoire
South-eastern region
Pendant of a human head
Inv. 1034-8.
Cat. 221, description p. 241

5
Côte d'Ivoire
South-eastern region
Pendant of a human head
Inv. 1034-9.
Cat. 223, description p. 241

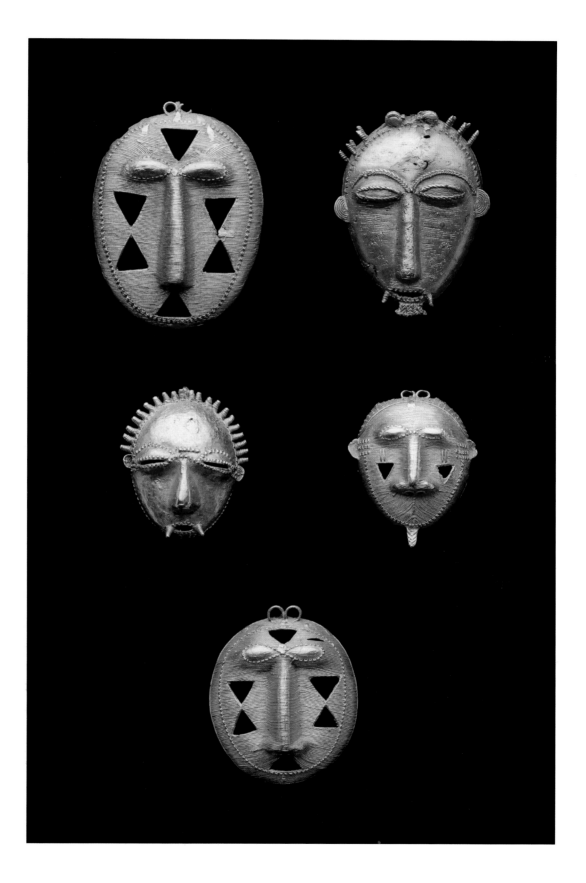

Plate 59

1
Côte d'Ivoire
Western lagoons area (?)
Pendant of a human head
Inv. 1034-58.
Cat. 225, description p. 242

2
Côte d'Ivoire
South-eastern region
Pendant of a human head
Inv. 1034-7.
Cat. 222, description p. 241

3
Côte d'Ivoire
South-eastern region
Pendant of a human head
Inv. 1034-17.
Cat. 220, description p. 241

4
Côte d'Ivoire
South-eastern region (?)
Pendant of a human head on an elongated
plaque
Inv. 1034-12.
Cat. 226, description p. 242

Plate 60

1
Côte d'Ivoire
Baule
Necklace of 27 beads
Inv. 1034-223.
Cat. 230, description p. 242

2
Côte d'Ivoire
Baule
Pendant of a human face on an openwork
medallion
Inv. 1034-220.
Cat. 227, description p. 242

3
Côte d'Ivoire
Baule
Large tubular bead
Inv. 1034-221.
Cat. 229, description p. 242

4
Côte d'Ivoire
Baule
Bead of openwork design, incorporating a
human face
Inv. 1034-222.
Cat. 228, description p. 242

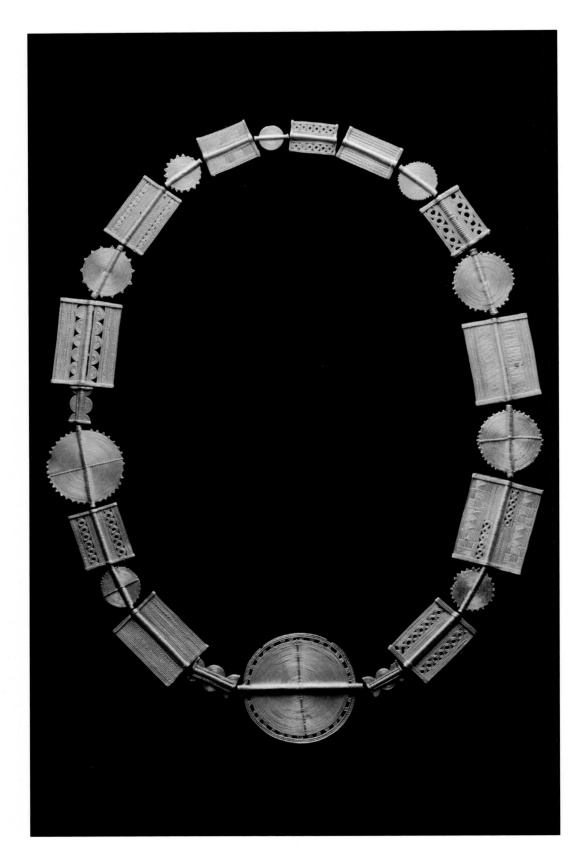

Plate 61

Côte d'Ivoire
Baule
Necklace of 23 beads, mostly discs and
rectangles
Inv. 1034-232.
Cat. 231, description p. 242

Plate 62

Côte d'Ivoire
Baule
Necklace of 23 beads and a small pellet bell
Inv. 1034-235.
Cat. 232, description p. 242

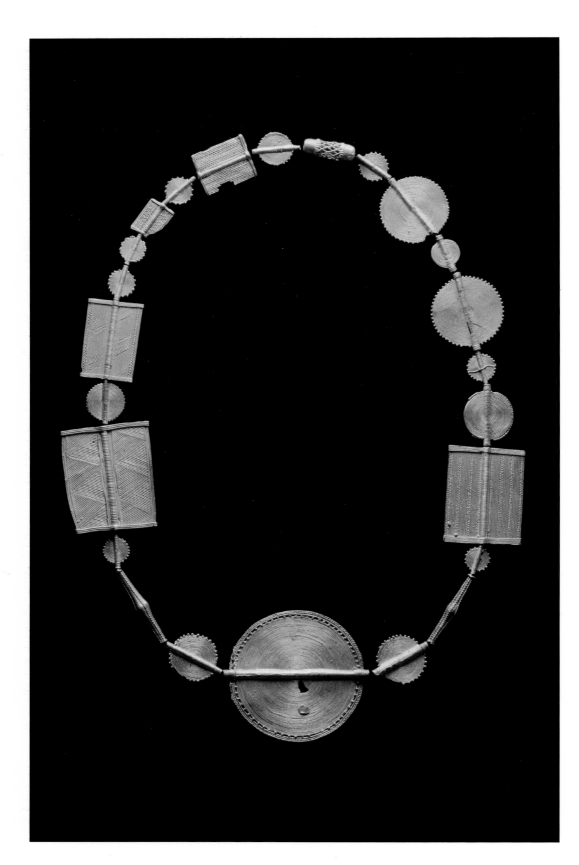

Plate 63

Côte d'Ivoire
Baule
Necklace of 24 beads comprising discs,
rectangles and tubular forms
Inv.1034- 233.
Cat. 233, description p. 243

Plate 64

Côte d'Ivoire
Baule
Necklace of 23 gold and 3 silver beads
Inv. 1034-191.
Cat. 234, description p. 243

Plate 65

Côte d'Ivoire
Baule
Necklace of 21 beads
Inv. 1034-193.
Cat. 236, description p. 243

Plate 66

Côte d'Ivoire
Baule
Necklace of 21 beads
Inv. 1034-192.
Cat. 235, description p. 243

Plate 67

Côte d'Ivoire
Baule
Necklace of 19 beads
Inv. 1034-218.
Cat. 237, description p. 243

Plate 68

1
Côte d'Ivoire
Baule
Disc-shaped spiral bead
Inv. 1034-172.
Cat. 238, description p. 243

2
Côte d'Ivoire
Baule
Disc-shaped spiral bead with an openwork
design
Inv. 1034-39.
Cat. 239, description p. 243

3
Côte d'Ivoire
Baule
Disc-shaped spiral bead
Inv. 1034-225.
Cat. 240, description p. 243

4
Côte d'Ivoire
Baule
Disc-bead with crocodile motif
Inv. 1034-298.
Cat. 241, description p. 243

5
Côte d'Ivoire
Baule
Pellet bell from a necklace
Inv. 1034-299.
Cat. 242, description p. 243

6
Côte d'Ivoire
Baule (?)
Pendant in the form of a bellows
Inv. 1034-19.
Cat. 243, description p. 243

7
Côte d'Ivoire
Lagoons area (?)
Triangular hair ornament
Inv. 1034-269.
Cat. 244, description p. 244

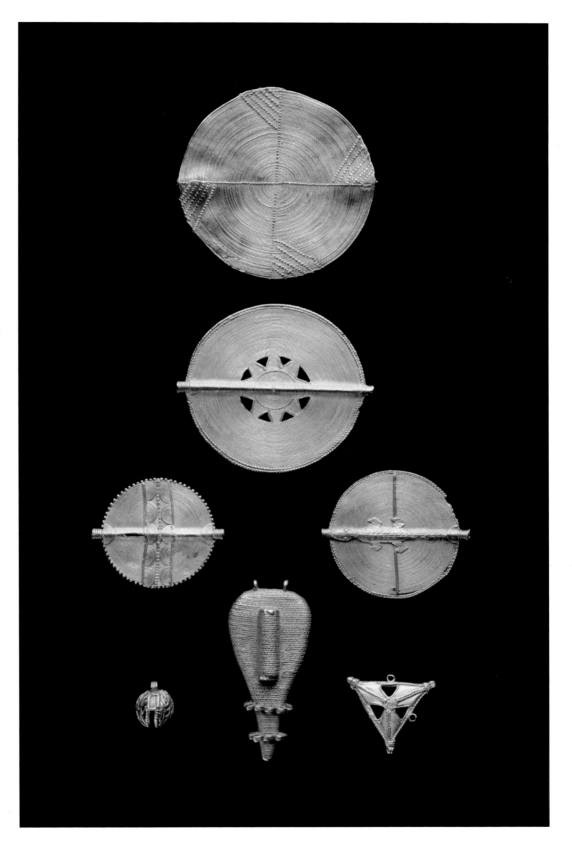

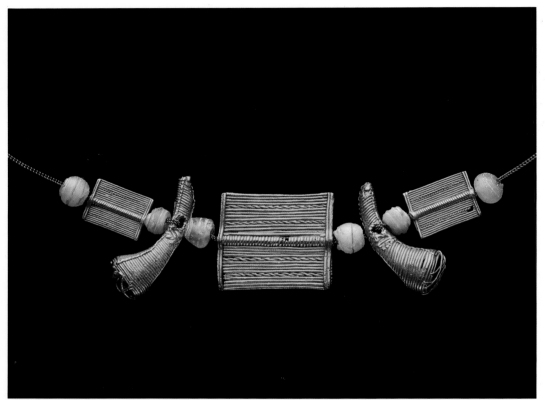

Plate 69

1
Côte d'Ivoire
Baule
Beads incorporated into a European necklace
Inv. 1034-13.
Cat. 245, description p. 243

2
Côte d'Ivoire
South-eastern region
Finger-ring with a dome-shaped bezel, decorated with three crocodiles
Inv. 1033-3.
Cat. 247, description p. 244

3
Côte d'Ivoire
Baule
Finger-ring with a motif of two birds
Inv. 1033-94.
Cat. 246, description p. 243

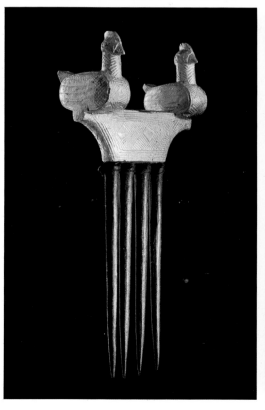

Plate 70

1
Côte d'Ivoire
Baule
Amulet of carved wood covered with gold leaf
Inv. 1034-182.
Cat. 248, description p. 244

2
Côte d'Ivoire
Baule
Comb of carved wood covered with gold leaf
Inv. 1007-178.
Cat. 251, description p. 244

3
Côte d'Ivoire
Baule
Comb of carved wood covered with gold leaf
Inv. 1007-183.
Cat. 250, description p. 244

4
Côte d'Ivoire
Baule
Hairpin of carved wood covered with gold leaf
Inv. 1007-102.
Cat. 249, description p. 244

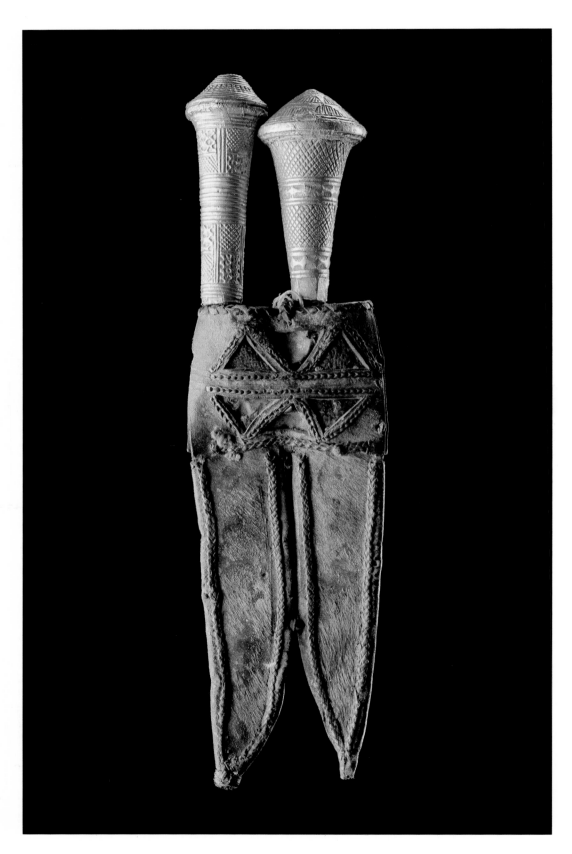

Plate 71

Côte d'Ivoire
Baule
Two knives with gold-leafed handles in a
double sheath
Inv. 1007-169.
Cat. 252, description p. 244

Plate 72

1
Côte d'Ivoire
Baule
Fly-whisk handle surmounted by a parrot.
Carved wood covered with gold leaf.
Inv. 1007-15.
Cat. 253, description p. 244

2
Côte d'Ivoire
Baule
Horse-tail fly-whisk, the carved wooden
handle covered with gold leaf
Inv. 1007-100.
Cat. 254, description p. 244

Catalogue

1
Senegal
Tukulor/Wolof

Pair of hair ornaments, each in the form of four opposed crescents covered with granulation, and with a filigree flower in the centre. Silver-gilt, circa mid-20th century.

These ornaments are called *kɔngere* or *ti tɔɔnde* (Tukulor), *khop* or *khop ak pɛp* (Wolof).

Size: each 3.8 cm
Weight: each 10 gm
1034-178 A, B   **Plate 1**

2
Senegal
Tukulor/Wolof

Pair of hair ornaments, each in the form of four opposed crescents covered with granulation, and with a filigree flower in the centre. Silver-gilt, circa mid-20th century.

Size: each about 4 cm
Weight: each 15 gm
1034-177 A, B   **Plate 1**

3
Senegal
Tukulor/Wolof

Pair of globular hair ornaments of silver-gilt, each with granulation, applied globules, and a central filigree flower. Circa mid-20th century.

Ornaments of this form are worn in a cluster together with the teardrop-shaped pendants called *khoulalat*, attached to the hair or wig above the temple. They are called *kaje* or *kaaje*, "stone" (Tukulor, Peul, Bamana), *kadie* or *kadia* (Wolof), *taroho* or *kange katinte* (Sarakole), and *tundi, aluban* or *anuban* (Sonrai).

Size: each 4.3 cm
Weight: each 30 gm
1034-176 B, C   **Plate 1**

4
Senegal
Tukulor/Wolof

Globular hair ornament of silver-gilt, with openwork designs, granulation, applied globules, and small cones of twisted wire, a filigree flower in the centre. Circa mid-20th century.

Size: 5.3 cm
Weight: 31 gm
1034-176 A   **Plate 1**

5
Senegal
Tukulor/Wolof

Teardrop-shaped ornament of silver-gilt, with openwork designs and surface granulation. Circa mid-20th century.

Ornaments of this form were worn in a cluster at the temple, attached to the hair or to a wig. They are called *khoulalat, khoulalate* or *khoulalatou* (Tukulor, Wolof, Peul, Bamana, Sonrai).

Size: 6.4 cm
Weight: 34 gm
1034-133 B   **Plate 2**

6
Senegal
Tukulor/Wolof

Teardrop-shaped ornament (*khoulalat*) of silver-gilt, with openwork designs and surface granulation. Circa mid-20th century.

Size: 5.5 cm
Weight: 28 gm
1034-133 A   **Plate 2**

7
Senegal
Tukulor/Wolof

Pair of small teardrop-shaped hair ornaments of silver-gilt, with surface granulation. Circa mid-20th century.

Size: each about 3.5 cm
Weight: each 6 gm
1034-180 A, B   **Plate 2**

8
Senegal
Wolof/Tukulor

Five small spherical beads of silver-gilt, with designs formed by granulation.

These beads are made by most goldsmiths in Senegal. They are constructed from two separate half-spheres of metal which are soldered together. The application of small granules to form distinct patterns is a work requiring great skill, but it is usually performed by assistants rather than by the master goldsmith himself.

Size: each bead 1.1 cm
Weight: 4 gm
1034-194   **Plate 2**

9
Senegal
Peul/Tukulor/Wolof

Four pairs of small rings of twisted wire, used as earrings or hair ornaments. Gilded silver. Third quarter of 20th century.

These rings are named as *kwotɛnɛ* (Peul), *dɔbbɛ hortonde* (Tukulor), and *dibe, dobe* or *krania* (Wolof).

Diameters from 1.3 to 2 cm
Weight per pair: 2, 2, 3 and 5 gm
1034-179 C–J   **Plate 3**

10
Senegal
Peul/Tukulor/Wolof/Serer

Curved ear-clip of silver-gilt, with 21 small attached rings. Circa mid-20th century.

These clips enable a woman to wear multiple rings in her ears without having a separate hole pierced for each ring. They are named as *gorgor* or *gɔlgɔl* (Sonrai, Peul), *yɛlkɛlɛ* or *hanyere nup* (Peul), *nyɛnyɛmɛ* (Sarakole, Bamana), *nyanyama* (Tukulor, Wolof), and *tioup tioup, diaro nop* or *diare nop* (Wolof).

Size: 6.5 cm
Weight: 12.5 gm
1034-179 B   **Plate 3**

11
Senegal
Peul/Tukulor/Wolof/Serer

Curved ear-clip of silver-gilt, with 21 small attached rings. Circa mid-20th century.

Size: 5.2 cm
Weight: 9.5 gm
1034-179 A   **Plate 3**

12
Mali, Guinée, Senegal
Peul/Tukulor/Sarakole/Bamana/Sonrai etc.

Pair of crescent-shaped twisted gold rings. Probably 20th century.

Twisted rings, worn in the ears, in the nose or on the forehead, are one of the most ancient forms of gold jewellery known in West Africa. They have probably been made since the first millennium A.D. From the eleventh century onwards there is mention of these "twisted gold rings of Wangara" as an important trade commodity. Gold-dust obtained from the mines was melted down and fashioned into such rings, each one probably of a specific weight. These were then traded to North African and European merchants for export.

Such crescent-shaped rings may still be seen throughout the Sahel, from the Atlantic coast in the west to the town of Gao in the east. They are made and worn by many ethnic groups including the Peul, Tukulor, Sarakole, Bamana and Sonrai. Some Dogon women also wear them. Women milk-sellers and market traders among the Peul and Tukulor enhance their often striking natural beauty by a dazzling display of such rings.

Among the many names for these rings are *kwotɛnɛ kange* (Peul), *dɔbbɛ hortonde* (Tukulor), *taro mere* (Sarakole), *misifuru, "cow intestines"* (Bamana), *tolomi* or *hanyo korbɔ* (Sonrai), and *dibe, dibe misifuru* or *dobe* (Wolof).

A Sonrai informant said that when worn on the forehead they could also be called *mutukal* (a name derived from the Arabic mithqal). This was, he explained, because Arab gold dinars or mithqals had formerly been worn in the same way.

Size: 2.9 and 3 cm
Weight: 25.5 and 26.5 gm
1034-161 A, B   **Plate 4**

13
Senegal
Wolof

Pair of silver-gilt earrings in plaited wire, adorned with small discs covered in granulation.

These earrings date from the first half of the 20th century. They are called *dibe batou nganar*, "earrings with the eyes of the fowl".

The use of small applied discs is a feature borrowed by Wolof and Tukulor goldsmiths from European filigree jewellery.

Size: each 3.6 cm
Weight: each 20 gm
1034-175 A, B   **Plate 4**

14
Senegal
Tukulor/Wolof

Pair of hollow crescent-shaped earrings of silver-gilt, with a ribbed design. Circa mid-20th century.

These are called *hortonde* or *dɔbbɛ hortonde* (Tukulor), *keupeul dibe* or *kupɛlɛ* (Wolof).

Size: each 4 cm
Weight: each 17 gm
1034-174 A, B   **Plate 4**

15
Mali
Peul/Sonrai

Pair of crescent-shaped gilded brass earrings. 20th century.

These earrings were hammered from a rod of brass, a technique requiring much patience and skill. They are probably the work of a Peul or Sonrai goldsmith.

Such rings are called *kwotɛnɛ kange* (Peul), *tolomi* or *fɛɛta* (Sonrai), *kang dobi* or *foori* (Sarakole), *dɔbbɛ, fɔɔri* or *hortonde wɛɛba* (Tukulor), and *dibe* or *dibe tap* (Wolof).

Size: each 3.3 cm
Weight: each about 5 gm
1034-160 A, B   **Plate 5**

16
Mali
Peul

Pair of hammered and twisted gold earrings consisting of four lobes, each lightly engraved with abstract designs. The suspension bands are covered with scarlet thread, which protects the ears from injury while at the same time enhancing the dramatic effect of these ornaments.

These are of Peul workmanship from the region of Jenne, probably from the first half of the 20th century.

Such large earrings are called *kwotɛnɛ kange*, pl. *kwotɛnɛje kange* (Peul), *hortonde wɛɛba* or *foori* (Tukulor), *fɛɛta* or *tolomi* (Sonrai), *tado karanyɛ* (Sarakole).

Size: each 7.5 cm
Weight: each 53 gm
1004-28 A, B   **Plate 5**

17
Mali
Peul

Pair of hammered gold earrings, lightly engraved on two lobes. The suspension bands are covered with scarlet thread. Base bold, circa mid-20th century.

Earrings of this style, in which the lobes are not twisted, are said to come from the Macina region, although today they are also made in Mopti.

Size: each 8.5 cm
Weight: each 19 gm
1004-135 A, B   **Plate 5**

18
Mali
Peul

Pair of hammered gold earrings, engraved on two lobes. Probably third quarter of the 20th century.

Size: each about 11 cm
Weight: each about 54 gm
1004-69 A, B   **Plate 5**

19
Mali
Peul

Pair of hammered gold earrings, engraved on two lobes. 20th century.

Size: 13 and 13.3 cm
Weight: 90 and 92 gm
1004-120 A, B   **Plate 6**

20
Mali
Peul

Pair of hammered gold earrings, engraved on two lobes with trees, cows, human figures and abstract designs. Commissioned in 1986 from Amadou Diallo, a goldsmith of Mopti.

Size: each 15.5 cm
Weight: each 120 gm
1004-134 A, B   **Plate 6**

21
Mali
Peul

Pair of hammered gold earrings, engraved on two lobes. Commissioned by Monique Barbier-Mueller in 1986 from Amadou Diallo, a goldsmith of Mopti.

This pair of earrings is remarkable for its size and weight, totalling 610 grams of gold. Only the richest of Peul women could afford to commission such a work, which represented the ultimate display of wealth. Both the form and the size are traditional. In the 1790s Mungo Park observed that part of the gold of Bambuk was converted into ornaments for the women, "but in general these ornaments are more to be admired for their weight than their workmanship. They are massy and inconvenient, particularly the ear-rings, which are commonly so heavy as to pull down and lacerate the lobe of the ear; to avoid which, they are supported by a thong of red leather, which passes over the crown of the head from one ear to the other."

Size: 23.7 and 24.7 cm
Weight: 300 and 310 gm
1004-137 A, B   **Plate 6**

22
Mauritania
Maure

Crown-shaped ornament of silver-gilt, surmounted by ten small cones. Sheet metal with twisted thread designs and granulation; small loop for suspension.

Such ornaments are worn on the forehead or in the hair.

Size: 1.4 cm
Weight: 4 gm
1034-188   **Plate 7**

23
Mali or Senegal
Tukulor/Peul

Silver-gilt ornament in the form a quatrefoil, worn on a short chain at the throat. This example is recent, dating probably from the third quarter of the 20th century; older examples are of finer workmanship.

Throat ornaments of quatrefoil or swastika form are worn by Peul and Tukulor women in Mali, Guinée and Senegal. The form may be ancient. This example is constructed from sheet metal adorned with wire decoration and small applied discs, with larger globules in the centre and in each lobe.

Such ornaments are called *koloni* (Peul, Tukulor, Bamana, Sonrai, Sarakole, Wolof), or *pɛlɛl* or *pɛlal* (Tukulor).

Size: 3.7 cm
Weight: 12 gm
1034-153   **Plate 7**

24
Senegal or Mali
Tukulor/Sarakole

Silver-gilt throat ornament in the form of a quatrefoil surmounted by a flower. Twisted thread decoration and granulation, with four spheres between the leaves.

Size: 3.6 cm
Weight: 14 gm
1034-187   **Plate 7**

25
Senegal
Tukulor

Silver-gilt ornament in the form of a swastika.

These ornaments are worn by women at the throat on a short chain. The design is called "claws of the lion" in several languages: *sɛgɛnɛ mbarode* (Tukulor) and *keuru weyu gainde* (Wolof).

Size: 3.9 cm
Weight: 12 gm
1034-186   **Plate 7**

26
Senegal or Mali
Tukulor/Sarakole

Silver-gilt throat ornament in the form of a swastika, with a central cone flanked by four spheres. Sheet metal with twisted thread decoration and granulation.

This design, according to one goldsmith at Dakar, is of Sarakole origin.

Size: 3.5 cm
Weight: 14 gm
1034-185   **Plate 7**

27

Mali or Mauritania

Maure/Tukulor/Peul (?)

Cruciform pendant of 18 carat gold.

This jewel has been constructed from sheets of hammered gold with the addition of twisted thread and pellet designs.

Comparable ornaments of gold are very rarely seen in the Sahel today. Most are now of silver (which in some cases may be gilded). Their form is typical of Maure jewellery, but some may also have been produced by the Tukulor, Peul and other peoples of the Sahel.

Ornaments of this form are familiar from the Atlantic coast of Senegal and Mauritania to the Middle Niger region. They evidently travelled even further afield: this example and the following one came to light in the Asante region of Ghana, where they were owned by an Akan dignitary. It is not known how they reached the Akan region. Their slightly battered appearance, and the fact that they are of fine gold, suggests that they are of appreciable age. They may date from the 18th or 19th century.

Size: 8 cm

Weight: 25 gm

1034-227 **Plate 8**

28

Mali or Mauritania

Maure/Tukulor/Peul (?)

Cruciform pendant of 18 carat gold.

This jewel is a smaller version of the last, and has been constructed in the same way. The two were found together in the Asante region of Ghana. It may date from the 18th or 19th century.

Size: 7 cm

Weight: 16.5 gm

1034-226 **Plate 8**

29

Mauritania

Maure

Cruciform pendant of gilded silver, on a necklace of ninety beads of silver, glass, carnelian and ebony.

This cross is of sheet metal decorated with twisted thread and pellet designs. Sixteen of the accompanying beads are of ebony inlaid with silver.

Such pendants are called *boghdad* (Maure), *diola* (Sarakole) or *korbasirire* (Peul).

Size: pendant 4.7 cm

1034-183 **Plate 9**

30

Mauritania

Maure

Cruciform pendant (*boghdad*) of gilded silver.

This jewel is constructed from sheet metal with the addition of twisted thread and pellet designs. 20th century.

Size: 4.5 cm

Weight: 12 gm

1034-181 **Plate 9**

31

Mali or Senegal

Peul/Tukulor

Large bicone-shaped gold pendant with chain, probably late 19th or early 20th century.

This ornament is constructed from soldered cones of sheet metal, pierced with openwork designs and adorned with granulation, twisted wires, small applied discs and punched half-spheres. The chain is of twisted gold wire.

Such pendants are found principally in Mali and Senegal, where they are highly prized. Some of the finest, such as this example, are Peul or Tukulor work, though the Sonrai and Sarakole also made them. Smaller versions in decadent style (often of silver rather than gold) are produced by Bamana and Wolof smiths. The form may be traced back at least a thousand years in the Middle East. It was probably introduced to West Africa through trans-Saharan trade.

In Mali these bicone-shaped pendants are worn by rich women as the centrepiece of a necklace. They are called *korɔwal, kuruwel* or *kolowa* (Peul, Tukulor, Sonrai), *kanjɛlɛ* (Sarakole), and *dola* or *dora* (Sarakole, Bamana, Wolof). Acquired by J. Müller before 1939

Size: 11 cm

Weight: 94 gm

1034-127 **Plate 10**

32

Mali

Bamana/Sarakole

Bicone-shaped pendant of gilded silver with openwork designs, twisted wire ornament and granulation.

Size: 7.6 cm

Weight: 26 gm

1034-190 **Plate 10**

33

Senegal

Tukulor/Wolof

Bicone-shaped bead of silver-gilt, circa mid-20th century.

This is a small Senegalese version of the bicone form, made from cones of sheet silver with added granulations.

Size: 3.8 cm

Weight: 6 gm

1034-157 **Plate 10**

34

Senegal

Tukulor/Wolof

Small bicone-shaped bead of silver-gilt. Circa mid-20th century.

Size: 4 cm

Weight: 12 gm

1009-91 **Plate 10**

35

Senegal

Tukulor/Wolof

Silver-gilt pendant of elongated cylinder form, openwork with granulation.

Pendants of this form are named as *bouserade* or *bouserare* (Tukulor, Wolof), or *kororo*, "weaver's shuttle" (Sonrai). They are said to be based on an old Moroccan design.

Size: 7.3 cm

Weight: 20 gm

1034-189 **Plate 10**

36

Senegal

Tukulor

Series of fourteen silver-gilt ornaments in the form of small trefoils. Circa first half of the 20th century.

These ornaments are worn on the forehead, or sometimes on a necklace. Senegalese informants usually identify them as Tukulor work. The trefoil motif is said to be traditional. These examples show the elegant design and fine granulation of older Senegalese work.

They are named as *yendiass* or *trefal* (Tukulor), *trefal* or *thɛɛrɛ trèfle* (Wolof).

Size: each about 2 cm

Weight: each about 1 gm

1034-128 **Plate 11**

37

Senegal

Tukulor

Six silver-gilt trefoils. Third quarter of the 20th century.

Size: each 2.2 cm

Weight: each 2.7 gm

1034-152 **Plate 11**

38

Senegal

Tukulor

Silver-gilt pendant of uncertain form, perhaps representing a stylised butterfly. Sheet metal with granulation, twisted wire, filigree and large globules. Circa mid-20th century.

This unusual pendant may be a Tukulor version of the Wolof butterfly ornaments that were in vogue earlier in this century; the original inspiration is European. A goldsmith of Dakar, interviewed in 1986, regarded it as an untraditional fantasy.

It is named as *mɛrɛgal* (Tukulor), *digeul* or *degeul* (Wolof).

Size: 8.2 cm

Weight: 46 gm

1034-158 **Plate 11**

39

Senegal

Tukulor

Silver-gilt pendant in the form of a heart, suspended between two hollow ovoid beads. Probably first half of the 20th century.

This elegant jewel is constructed from hammered sheet metal adorned with granulation, twisted wires and several larger globules, together with small applied discs. In style it is Tukulor, but the motif is European-inspired. The small applied discs also reveal European influence.

It is named as *fɛdal* (Tukulor), *tchor, thɛɛrɛ tchor* or *nieti thɛɛrɛ* (Wolof), *kange nunkola* or *yinkola* (Sarakole).

Size of pendant: 5.7cm
Weight: 48 gm
1034-130 **Plate 11**

40
Senegal
Tukulor

Silver-gilt pendant in the form of a seven-lobed star, suspended from a chain of 32 globular beads. Probably first half of the 20th century.

This ornament is constructed from hammered sheet silver, profusely adorned with granulation, twisted wires and small applied discs. A larger globule is placed in the centre of each lobe. Some Senegalese point out that its massive style is characteristic of Tukulor work (although the seller, a merchant in the Marché Tilène, Dakar, claimed that it was a Wolof jewel from St. Louis). The small applied discs indicate influence from European methods of jewellery manufacture.

The pendant is named as *hɔdere* (Tukulor), *bideou*, "star" (Wolof), or *pɛmɛ* (Sarakole).

Size of pendant: 9 cm
Weight: 96 gm
1034-129 **Plate 12**

41
Senegal
Wolof

Necklace consisting of ten oval silver-gilt wire beads. 20th century.

This necklace is named as *tchakh ratakhal* or *tchokh ratakhal ak raw nyar*.

Size: 47 cm
Weight: 45 gm
1034-134 **Plate 12**

42
Senegal
Wolof

Massive silver-gilt pendant of filigree flowers, suspended from a wire chain.

This is a typical example of the French-influenced jewellery produced by Wolof goldsmiths earlier in this century. It is named as *digeul ak khop* or *thɛɛrɛ khop*, the chain being called *yakhou diane* ("the eyes of the snake") or *tchakh*.

Size: 10.8 cm
Weight: 170 gm
1034-125 **Plate 13**

43
Senegal
Wolof

Necklace ensemble of silver-gilt with an ornate central pendant representing a basket of flowers, two side-pendants of flowers, four openwork spherical beads and a wire chain.

This is a fine example of early 20th century Wolof filigree work with French-inspired designs. The town of St. Louis at the mouth of the Senegal river was a noted centre for the production of such jewellery in colonial times. The central pendant is called *kostime* or *cheno panie*.

Size of pendant: 10 cm
Weight: 160 gm
1034-126 **Plate 13**

44
Senegal
Wolof

Pair of silver-gilt bracelets made from flexible plaited wire, adorned with sheet metal bands and spherical terminals. First half of the 20th century.

These are named as *lamour raou* or *lamou lat*. They are also called *lamou batou nganar* ("the eyes of the fowl").

Size: each 7.5 cm
Weight: each 45 gm
1034-132 A, B **Plate 14**

45
Senegal
Wolof

Pair of hollow silver-gilt bracelets constructed from sheet metal, each with six large and twelve small half-spheres ornamented with spiral wirework. They are said to be Wolof work in the style of St. Louis and date from around the mid-20th century.

They are named as *kɛwɛ, lamou kɛwɛ*; also as *batou ngainde* ("they eyes of the lion").

Size: each 9.2 cm
Weight: each about 85 gm
1034-131 A, B **Plate 14**

46
Senegal
Wolof

Set of filigree jewellery in silver-gilt, comprising a finger-ring, a bracelet, and a necklace incorporating three pendants, all with flower-shaped motifs.

The workmanship of these items of jewellery is typical of the St. Louis goldsmiths working in the colonial period.

Date: early to mid-20th century.
Size: ring 3.3 cm, bracelet 7.5 cm, necklace 51 cm
Weight: ring 25 gm, bracelet 70 gm, necklace 160 gm
1000-44 A, B, C **Plate 15**

47
Ghana
Akan

Hairpin (*ntiriba* or *tiduaba*) of ivory, with a gold finial in the form of a flower.

Hairpins were of European inspiration. They first came into use on the Fanti coast in the late nineteenth century. Most are of brass, but this rare and beautiful example is in gold and ivory. It may have come from the jewellery of an Akan queen-mother and dates perhaps from the late 19th or early 20th century.

The gold is of 16–17 carats.
Size: 9.2 cm
Weight: 5.5 gm
1034-163 **Plate 20**

48
Ghana
Akan

Helmet (*krɔbɔnkyɛ*) of antelope skin, decorated with ribbons of sheet gold and carved wooden ornaments covered with gold leaf.

These helmets were probably inspired by some kind of European hat, perhaps military, of the 18th or early 19th century. They are worn by a chief's sword-bearers and gun-carriers. On this example the designs are of palm fruits (*mmɛtoma so abɛ*) and cockle shells (*adam*). Among the Akan and the Baule red cockle shells have for centuries been a popular form of decoration for belts and other items of stool paraphernalia. In the wealthier chiefdoms they are not infrequently copied in gold.

Size: 24 cm
1009-83 **Plate 16**

49
Ghana
Akan: Asante

Sword-bearer's helmet (*krɔbɔnkyɛ*) of antelope skin, divided into four panels by ribbons of sheet gold, each panel containing a coiled snake of carved wood covered with gold leaf. The helmet is topped by another coiled wooden snake covered with gold leaf.

This helmet may date to the 1920s or 30s. The ribbons of sheet gold are embossed with a tiny floral pattern. The snakes would represent a proverb such as the following:

Anibereɛ na ɔwɔ de ka.
A snake bites when it is angered.
(Let sleeping dogs lie.)

This may be interpreted as a warning to potential enemies or the populace at large not to be troublesome.

Size: 20 cm
1009-84 **Plate 16**

50
Ghana
Akan: Asante

Crown of wood covered with gold leaf, the interior lined with black velvet.

The form of this crown is based on a European model, possibly the British imperial crown. One significant modification has been made: the cross at the top of the original has been replaced by a cluster of three pods of the okra plant (gombo).

Size: 20.3 cm
1009-133 **Plate 17**

51
Ghana
Akan

Head-dress of goatskin, to which is attached a large circular amulet (*sɛbɛ*) covered with a sheet of beaten and embossed gold.

Muslim amulets were eagerly sought by the Akan. They sometimes enclose Arabic verses from the Koran or some magic formula. This unusual item of headgear, worn by certain attendants of a chief, may perhaps date from the 19th or early 20th century.

Size of amulet: 10 cm
Weight: 70 gm. About 18 carats.

1009-127 **Plate 18**

52
Ghana
Akan

Head-dress of goatskin, to which is attached a large rectangular leather amulet covered with a sheet of beaten and embossed gold.

The gold covering of this amulet is of very fine workmanship. It may date from the 19th or early 20th century.

Size of amulet: 11.6 cm
Weight: 67 gm. About 17 carats

1009-114 **Plate 18**

53
Ghana
Akan

Head-dress of goatskin, with attached rectangular amulet covered with beaten and embossed gold.

This is another fine example of repoussé goldwork, similar in age to the last.

Size of amulet: 12.6 cm
Weight: 78 gm. About 17 carats

1009-112 **Plate 18**

54
Ghana
Akan

Head-dress of goatskin, with attached rectangular amulet covered with beaten and embossed gold.

Size of amulet: 13.5 cm
Weight: about 135 gm. About 17 carats

1009-113 **Plate 18**

55
Ghana
Akan

Head-dress of goatskin, to which is attached a rectangular wooden plaque covered with gold leaf. In this example the plaque imitates the form of a leather amulet. Perhaps 20th century.

Size of amulet: 14.7 cm

1009-115 **Plate 17**

56
Ghana
Akan

Chief's headband (*abotire*) of black velvet, decorated with numerous four-pointed stars of carved wood covered with gold leaf.

In some proverbs the stars represent people and are contrasted with the moon, representing the chief. The stars remain unchanged while the moon waxes and wanes; in the same way the

people are always there though chiefs may come and go. Hence the following proverb:

Nyankonsoromma na ɔman wɔ no na nye osrane.

The stars: the state belongs to them forever but not to the moon.
(The state belongs to the people and not to the chief.)

Size: 30 cm

1009-19 **Plate 19**

57
Ghana
Akan

Chief's headband (*abotire*) of black velvet, decorated with flowers, snakes and rectangular amulets of carved wood covered with gold leaf.

The ornaments represented on this hat are said to be *mfofoo* (a flower found in the bush), *ɔnanka* or *ɔnanka bobonini* (the puff-adder) and *nsɛbɛ* (talismans). They are explained as meaning that the chief is protected against danger: the snake hides in the *mfofoo* shrub and lies in wait, but the chief is protected by his talismans.

Size: 26 cm

1009-43 **Plate 19**

58
Ghana
Akan

Chief's headband (*abotire*) of black velvet, decorated with a row of six-pointed stars and crescent moons of carved wood covered with gold leaf.

The following proverb was cited for this hat in Kumasi:

Kyɛkyɛ-pɛ-awarɛ (awadeɛ), enti na ɔbɛn bosome da biara.

The evening star, desirous of being married, always stays close to the moon.

(The evening star is always seen close to the moon. This design signifies faithfulness. It was explained as meaning that if a woman loves a man she will try to stay near him. In the political context it would indicate that the people love their chief and will support him.)

Size: 27.5 cm

1009-57 **Plate 19**

59
Ghana
Akan

Chief's headband (*abotire*) of red velvet, decorated with a row of Maltese crosses in carved wood covered with gold leaf.

The Akan sometimes call this cross design *busuyideɛ* or *mmusuyideɛ*, "that which drives away evil spirits". It was formerly regarded as a powerful symbol to avert misfortune and evil (*abusudeɛ*), and for this reason was used to protect the chief's person. It appeared as a design on palace walls, and also on royal hats and *adinkra* cloths. Like the swastika (of which it may be a variant), it seems to have been originally regarded by the Akan as a magic protective symbol.

Today knowledge of traditional Akan symbolism is declining with the spread of school education, and it has become common for younger informants to interpret the design in other ways. In Asante (1986) the designs on this head-band were interpreted both as a butterfly (*afafantɔ*) and as a hawk's tail (*asansatoɔ*). In the words of one man:

Asansa ekyini a okyini no nti na yɛ de toɔ no. Ɛno ma ɔhene tumi nya tumi bi.

The hawk roams about daily so its tail was put on the crown to signify the strength of the king.

Size: cross 4.2 cm, total 65.5 cm

1009-40 **Plate 19**

60
Ghana
Akan

Four leaf-shaped ornaments for a chief's hat, in beaten gold.

In Asante these ornaments are identified as leaves of the fern (*aya*). They are interpreted in several ways. According to some they mean that the chief is popular, attracting people round him just as ferns grow on and around the palm tree. Others see them as a symbol of fearlessness ("I am not afraid of you"), or of ability to endure hardship. In either case, like much of the symbolism in Akan royal art, they are intended to reflect the prestige and power of the chief.

Two of these ornaments are of 16.5 and 18 carats. They date from around the first half of the 20th century.

Size: 11, 14.7, 12.7 and 10.9 cm
Weight: 4, 7, 6 and 3,5 gm

1009-50 A, B, C, D **Plate 20**

61
Ghana
Akan

Disc-shaped ornament of beaten gold, with a central "sunburst" design surrounded by smaller spheres.

The large series of disc-shaped Akan objects seems to have been inspired by Sahelian jewellery, including Arabic dinars. The Akan used such ornaments in various ways. Some were nailed to stools, chairs and caskets. Others were hung from state swords, falling into the class of ornaments known as *abosodeɛ*. They were also sewn on to the front of the monkey-skin caps worn by royal heralds. The present disc was probably used on a cap, for along its edge are four tiny pairs of holes, too small for nails but sufficiently large for threads.

In Asante this disc is called *tadeɛ*, meaning a pool of water. Its designs were interpreted as *nsoroma*, a star, and *tanoa*, leaves of a water plant covering the surface of the pool. It may be intended to symbolise the chief surrounded by his people.

This disc may date from the late 19th or early 20th century.

Size: 5.6 cm
Weight: 8 gm

1034-44 **Plate 46**

62
Ghana
Akan

Disc-shaped ornament of beaten gold, with a central "sunburst" design surrounded by smaller spheres. Perhaps late 19th or early 20th century.

This disc has eight pairs of small holes along its edge. It may be from a herald's hat.

Size: 6.7 cm
Weight: 7 gm

1034-42 **Plate 46**

63
Ghana
Akan

Disc-shaped pectoral of beaten gold with 15 points around the edge.

This kind of pectoral is called *awisiado*, *ewisiado* or *akrafokɔnmu*.

This pectoral is embossed with four palm beetles and foliate motifs. The central boss and each of the 15 points are covered with twisted gold wire.

It may date from the 19th or early 20th century.

Size: 15.5 cm
Weight: 90 gm. About 17 carats, alloyed with silver

1034-203 **Plate 21**

64
Ghana
Akan: Asante or Adanse

Disc-shaped pectoral of cast gold with elaborate spiral designs.

Probably first half of the 20th century. Pectorals of this design were produced by goldsmiths both in Kumasi (Asante) and Obuasi (Adanse), and similar though inferior castings are still made.

Size: 8.9 cm
Weight: 84 gm

1034-209 **Plate 21**

65
Ghana
Akan

Disc-shaped pectoral of cast gold, with an openwork design resembling a seven-petalled flower.

This finely cast pectoral may date from the late 19th or early 20th century.

Size: 8.1 cm
Weight: 41 gm. 12 carats

1034-62 **Plate 21**

66
Ghana
Akan

Circular pectoral of cast gold, resembling a flower with 16 petals. 20th century.

Size: 11.8 cm
Weight: 157 gm. 6 carats

1034-219 **Plate 21**

67
Ghana
Akan

Disc-shaped pectoral of beaten gold, with embossed designs of flowers, fern leaves (?) and cowry shells. Probably first half of the 20th century.

Size: 12 cm
Weight: 26.6 gm. About 16 carats, alloyed with silver

1034-142 **Plate 21**

68
Ghana
Akan

Disc-shaped pectoral of beaten gold, with embossed designs of flowers, leaves, ferns (?), cowry shells etc. Probably first half of the 20th century.

Size: 15.6 cm
Weight: 33 gm. 15 carats

1034-72 **Plate 21**

69
Akan

Disc-shaped pectoral of beaten gold, suspended from seven fibre cords.

This pectoral is decorated with triangular motifs arranged in four concentric circles. The work is particularly fine and may date from the 19th century.

Size: 10.6 cm
Weight: 127 gm. 14 carats, alloyed with silver

1034-240 **Plate 22**

70
Ghana
Akan: probably Asante

Disc-shaped pectoral of beaten gold with embossed designs, on a white cord.

The unusual purity of the metal (20–21 carats) suggests that this pectoral may have been made directly from newly mined gold-dust, without the usual alloy of brass or silver. It is fine work and may date from the 19th century.

Size: 5cm
Weight: 18 gm

1034-229 **Plate 23**

71
Ghana
Akan

Disc-shaped pectoral of carved wood covered with gold leaf, suspended from a cord of white threads. 20th century.

Size: 13.2 cm

1034-152 **Plate 23**

72
Ghana
Akan: Asante

Cast gold pectoral of unusual form. Probably 20th century.

Size: 11 cm
Weight: 122 gm. About 10 carats

1034-205 **Plate 24**

73
Ghana
Akan

Flat disc-shaped gold bead of openwork design.

Despite its battered and worn appearance this bead is a very fine casting, and probably of considerable age. It may well date from the 17th or 18th century, making it the oldest item of West African gold in the Barbier-Mueller collection. Beads of this form are called *dwinneɛ* in Asante.

Size: 3.1 cm
Weight: 2.5 gm

1034-34 **Plate 24**

74
Ghana
Akan

Flat disc-shaped gold bead of openwork design, made up of three concentric rows of spirals round a central spiral.

This bead falls into the general category of *dwinneɛ*, but its design is also known in Asante as *akyekyedeɛ akyi* (or *akyiri*), "the back of the tortoise". The spirals are thought to resemble the plates on the carapace of a tortoise.

This is a fine casting that dates perhaps from the late 18th or 19th century. The rim of the bead has been constructed from wax threads.

Size: 3.6 cm
Weight: 6.5 gm

1034-29 **Plate 24**

75
Ghana
Akan

Flat disc-shaped gold bead of openwork design, incorporating five spirals around a central spiral.

This bead is called *akyekyedeɛ akyi*. It may date from the nineteenth century.

Size: 3.2 cm
Weight: 4.5 gm

1034-33 **Plate 24**

76
Ghana
Akan

Flat disc-shaped gold bead of openwork design, with spirals and loops.

This ornate little casting is identified as *akyekyedeɛ akyi*. It probably dates from the 19th century.

Size: 3.3 cm
Weight: 9 gm

1034-30 **Plate 24**

77
Ghana
Akan

Flat disc-shaped gold bead with linear wax thread designs.

This bead is called *dwinneɛ*. It may date from the 19th or early 20th century.

Size: 3.5 cm
Weight: 6 gm

1034-32 **Plate 24**

78
Ghana
Akan

Flat disc-shaped gold bead. Openwork with wax thread designs.
19th-early 20th century.
Size: 4.1 cm
Weight: 5.9 gm
1034-170   **Plate 24**

79
Ghana
Akan

Flat disc-shaped gold bead. Openwork with wax thread designs.
19th-early 20th century.
Size: 2.9 cm
Weight: 4 gm
1034-169   **Plate 24**

80
Ghana
Akan

Hollow square gold bead with incised or impressed designs.
The Akan call this kind of bead *mankata*, a name derived from Sir Charles McCarthy, a British governor who was defeated and killed in battle against the Asante in 1824.
Size: 3.5 cm
Weight: 8 gm
1034-213   **Plate 30**

81
Ghana
Akan

Silver-gilt bead in the form of a six-sided amulet (*suman*). Sheet metal.
The form of this bead is based on that of a leather amulet containing magic ingredients or a verse from the Koran.
Size: 2.5 cm
Weight: 3.5 gm
1034-212   **Plate 24**

82
Ghana
Akan

Six-sided amulet of beaten gold with repoussé designs, attached to a white woven cord.
This is a protective charm (*suman*), worn by a chief next to the skin.
Size: 8.8 cm
Weight: 31 gm. 18 carats
1034-204   **Plate 23**

83
Ghana
Akan

Necklace of 108 gold beads.
Gold necklaces such as this, made up of numerous small beads of different forms, were highly prized. Chiefs wore multiple strands on their wrists and forearms, and round their ankles. Queen-mothers also wore them as

necklaces. Many of the individual beads have proverbial significance. In general, such an assemblage of beads is referred to as *mpempenadeɛ*, and individual beads as *kɔnmuadeɛ*. The whole necklace is usually called *suman*, which suggests that it is regarded as being made up of amulets and "fetishes", i.e. objects of magical, religious or spiritual significance.
Among the beads on this and the following three necklaces are the following:

adwinneɛ ketewa	a small circular bead
aba	small seed
abia	kind of seed
fotɔ aba	small black seed
bese saka	kola nuts
akɔnkɔdeɛ	silk-cotton husk
burodua	corn cob
ahohoa	small snail
apupuo	type of water-snail
sedeɛ	cowry shell
akokono	palm grub
akɔtɔsen or *mɛtwee*	crab's teeth
adusen, edusen	canine teeth
dodomsen, dodomseɛ	molar tooth
akoko ani	chicken's eye
akyekyedeɛ akyi	back of the tortoise
akyimpirebuo, atsimpirebuo	weaver bird's nest
nsoroma	star
nkwantanan	crossroads
pɔkorɔ	knot, gold nugget
pɔkɔwa	small gold nugget
papaseɛ	"things sewn together"
mankata	"Sir Charles McCarthy"
krado	padlock
safoa	key
dɔnnɔ	drum
ankorɛmma	barrel
totoa	gunpowder flask
dɔnnɔmma	small open bell
atinka, atenka	pellet bell
ahwenewa, ahweneɛ dua	type of square talisman
gyabum	type of fetish amulet
kɔkɔrɔ	a tubular bead.

The beads on the present necklace are small and of fine workmanship. Most date probably from the 19th century.
Length: 49.5 cm
Weight: 84 gm
1034-60   **Plate 25**

84
Ghana
Akan

Necklace of 63 small gold beads.
The Akan name this necklace *suman*. Many of the openwork pendant beads represent the silk-cotton husk (*akɔnkɔdeɛ*). The necklace may date from the 19th century.
Length: 49.5 cm
Weight: about 52 gm
1034-61   **Plate 26**

85
Ghana
Akan

Necklace of 103 small gold beads of various forms, with a small gold padlock in the centre.
This is an example of a *suman* necklace. Many of its beads may date from the 19th century.
Size: 49.5 cm
Weight: about 95 gm
1034-53   **Plate 27**

86
Ghana
Akan

Necklace of 49 gold beads with a central pendant of a double crocodile.
Most of the beads on this *suman* necklace probably date from the 20th century. The central motif of the double crocodile represents the same proverb as No. 153 (finger-ring).
Size: 60 cm
Weight: 86 gm
1034-52   **Plate 28**

87
Ghana
Akan

String of 41 small beads with granular edges.
These are also called *mɛtwee* or *akɔtɔsen.* They probably date from the 20th century.
Size of beads: 0.4 to 1.1 cm
Weight of string: 24 gm
1034-51   **Plate 29**

88
Ghana
Akan

String of 28 elongated beads with granular edges, probably of gilded brass.
Beads of this kind are often called *mɛtwee* or *akɔtɔsen* ("crab's teeth").
Probably 20th century.
Size: each bead approx. 1.3 cm
Weight of string: about 20 gm
1034-50   **Plate 29**

89
Ghana
Akan

Two gold pellet-bells (*tɔreɛ* or *atinka*) of openwork design for a necklace or bracelet.
19th–20th century.
Size: each 2.2 cm
Weight: each 4.8 gm. About 8 carats
1034-166 A, B   **Plate 30**

90
Ghana
Akan

Two gold bells (*nnonnoma*) of openwork design for a necklace or bracelet.
19th–20th century.
Size: each 2.3 cm
Weight: each about 3 gm
1034-162 A, B   **Plate 30**

91
Ghana
Akan

Gold pendant of a royal stool (dwa), perhaps for a necklace or bracelet.

Bowdich (1817) mentioned that the Asantehene Osei Bonsu wore strings of gold ornaments on his ankles; these were "of the most delicate workmanship" and they included stools. The present casting could have been used in this way. It is exceptionally fine, and may date from the 18th or 19th century.

Size: 3.5 cm
Weight: 9.5 gm. 12 carats

1034-228   **Plate 32**

92
Ghana
Akan

Gold pendant of a gunpowder flask (totoa) for a necklace.

Probably 19th century.

Size: 3 cm
Weight: 7 gm

1034-216   **Plate 30**

93
Ghana
Akan

Gold pendant of a padlock (krado), for a bracelet or necklace.

Among the Fanti, according to Christensen (1959), there was a kind of charm called siri "made to confuse an opponent in court, in which the proper ingredients may be placed on a padlock and the name of an opponent pronounced as it is locked. A similar procedure may also be used to cause the death of someone, since it is believed that the act of closing the padlock 'locks up his soul'."

This pendant dates from the 20th century.

Size: 3.2 cm
Weight: 6.5 gm

1034-214   **Plate 29**

94
Ghana
Akan: probably Asante.

Gold pendant of a fish, possibly intended to represent a catfish with barbels.

There can be little doubt that this pendant was cast in the 18th or 19th century. It has a fineness and delicacy that are never equalled on castings produced in this century. The gold is relatively pure (about 20 carats).

Size: 6 cm
Weight: about 27 gm

1034-231   **Plate 31**

95
Ghana
Akan

Gold pendant perhaps representing a mudfish or catfish (pitire).

According to Mrs Peggy Appiah of Kumasi, this represents the proverb:

Adwene: meredwene me man ho.

The fish: I am always thinking of the welfare of my State.

(Used of a person who has a sense of responsibility to the society in which he lives.)

This is a relatively old casting of fine quality, and the gold is notably pure. It may date from the late 18th or 19th century.

Size: 6.4 cm
Weight: 26.5 gm. 20–21 carats

1034-63   **Plate 31**

96
Ghana
Akan

Silver-gilt pendants of a stool, a pair of swords, and a fetish object resembling a broom.

Chiefs and rich men wore such pendants attached to a long gold chain.

This group dates to about the mid-20th century.

Size: 7.1 cm
Weight: 131 gm. 2–3 carats (alloy predominantly silver)

1009-131   **Plate 30**

97
Ghana
Akan

Silver-gilt (?) pendant of a stylised cutlass and digging stick.

Such a pendant was worn on a long gold chain.

20th century.

Size: 5.7 cm
Weight: 11 gm

1034-215   **Plate 30**

98
Ghana
Akan

Pendant ornament of a man plucking cocoa pods with a bill-hook. Alloyed gold or gilded silver.

Cocoa (kookoo) brought wealth to Ghana during the second and third quarters of this century. This pendant is said to indicate that the owner's wealth is derived from cocoa.

The pendant has been constructed from sheet metal, with the addition of the small cast figure of a man with bill-hook. It would have been worn suspended from a long gold chain.

Circa mid-20th century.

Size: 10 cm
Weight: 80 gm

1034-217   **Plate 33**

99
Ghana
Akan

Silver-gilt neck-chain consisting of eight lengths of chain worked in various ways, interspersed with six elongated wirework beads, and with central pendants of a cutlass, bill-hook and cocoa pods.

Ornate gold chains (atweaban) have long been popular among wealthy Akan. They are often

worn by chiefs. This example, from around the second quarter of the 20th century, may have belonged to a rich cocoa farmer. It incorporates cocoa pods (kookoo) made from sheet metal, and a cutlass and bill-hook (sekan and kɔtɔkorɔ) made by hammering.

Length of chain: 93 cm
Weight: about 150 gm

1034-54   **Plate 32**

100
Ghana
Akan

Gold neck-chain with a central pendant of an eagle (ɔkɔdeɛ) in silver-gilt.

The eagle is regarded by the Akan as a brave and powerful bird that can be killed only by the gun or the snake. In Asante it is referred to by the saying: Gye tuo, gye ɔwɔ, "I fear the gun, I fear the snake." Ross (1982, p. 64) cites the proverb from which this saying derives:

Ɔkɔdeɛ ɔnsuro wuramu aboa biara gye ɔwɔ ne otuo nko ara.

Except for the snake and the gun, the eagle fears nothing.

The central pendant on this chain illustrates the Akan habit of copying foreign forms; the goldsmith has taken as his model the American heraldic eagle with shield and thunderbolts. The pendant was produced from a cuttlefish-bone mould rather than by lost wax casting. It dates probably from the second or third quarter of the 20th century.

Size: chain 137 cm, pendant 5.5 cm
Weight: 90 gm

1034-47   **Plate 33**

101
Ghana
Akan

Two elbow amulets (nsatire) of carved wood covered with gold leaf, suspended from a cord of yellow and green silk. One is triangular, the other narrow and elongated. They form part of the various amulets (asuman) used to protect the person of the chief.

Among other kinds of protective elbow amulet are ɛfa ne ɛfa (a pair of disc-shaped amulets) and akomfɛmtikorɔ (a bunch of three leather amulets resembling guinea-fowl heads). These might be worn by any of the more important chiefs. In addition, on certain occasions the Asantehene wears a very large triangular gold ornament suspended from his neck, which is known as adaaboɔ.

One man in Kumasi named the present triangular amulet as asansatoɔ, a hawk's tail or hawk's bottom. Sixty years ago Rattray also mentioned that a triangle with smaller cones at each corner was known in Asante as woaso sansa to, "you have held a hawk's bottom", meaning that you have taken great risks to achieve your present position. While these interpretations are not known to all, it is widely agreed that the triangular design emphasises the greatness of the chief.

Size: 25.5 cm

1009-58   **Plate 34**

102
Ghana
Akan

Chief's elbow ornament (*bafurum sɛbɛ*) of two circular amulets covered with gold leaf, suspended from a cord of red, yellow and green silk.

Such amulets were believed to afford magical protection for the chief. Today they have acquired a secondary significance, being called *ɛfa ne ɛfa*, "side by side". This indicates, according to one Asante man, that "we are all together; when settling a case we must satisfy both sides."

The multicoloured cord is known as *abakɔn kaa*, "elbow ring".

Size: 18 cm
1031-30   **Plate 34**

103
Ghana
Akan

Chief's bracelet of carved wood covered with gold leaf.

These ornate royal bracelets are known as *benfra*, *benfena* or *berenfena*.

Size: 12.6 cm
1031-76   **Plate 35**

104
Ghana
Akan

Chief's bracelet of carved wood covered with gold leaf.

Size: 11 cm
1031-305   **Plate 35**

105
Ghana
Akan: probably Asante
Chief's bracelet of cast gold.

This superb example of an Akan royal bracelet is hollow-cast and was made in two identical halves, each modelled over a clay core. The basic form was constructed with wax threads that were subsequently smoothed, a curious technique not infrequently found among older Akan jewellery. In recent times this technique has not been used; instead the basic form is constructed from a sheet of wax modelled over the core.

The surface of this bracelet is decorated with modelled designs, the most prominent of which are four pairs of ram's horns (*dwannimɛn* or *dwennimɛn*). These indicate the power and strength of the chief, referring to the proverb that when the horns of two rams clash in a fight, one must give way to the other.

Added detail is provided by patterns of incised lines and small circles. Two rectangular apertures on the inner part of the bracelet have been neatly covered with applied plates of gold. The two halves of the bracelet are secured by a small pin.

This bracelet dates from the 19th century. It was formerly in the collection of Sir Cecil Armitage, a colonial official who served on the Gold Coast between 1895 and 1920. Armitage took part in the Asante campaign of 1896, when British troops entered Kumasi, seized the Asantehene Prempeh and sent him into exile. It is possible that the bracelet was an item of booty obtained on this occasion; if so, it may have formed part of the Asantehene's regalia. Acquired by J. Müller before 1942.
Published by Charles Ratton in 1951 (no. 83)

Size: 10.8 cm
Weight: 220 gm
1031-17   **Plate 36**

106
Ghana
Akan

Chief's bracelet of cast gold.

This bracelet is remarkable for its size, but the workmanship is inferior to that of no. 105. The four pairs of projecting spikes appear to have been soldered on after the initial casting was made. Casting imperfections have been filed away. Foliate and other designs are crudely incised in a manner typical of much twentieth-century Akan goldsmith's work. Like all bracelets of this type, the casting was made in two identical halves which are secured by a pin.

The bracelet was probably made in the 1920s or 1930s.
Acquired by J. Müller before 1942. Published in Soupault, 1957, p. 71

Size: 12 cm
Weight: 445 gm
1031-18   **Plate 36**

107
Ghana
Akan

Chief's bracelet of cast gold.

This unusually massive example of the type may date from the second or third quarter of the 20th century.

Size: 16.5 cm
Weight: 675 gm. 3–4 carats, heavily alloyed with silver
1031-321   **Plate 35**

108
Ghana
Akan

Chief's bracelet of cast gold.

This example has incised quatrefoil and star designs. The workmanship is typical of the second and third quarters of the 20th century.

Size: 12.3 cm
Weight: 340 gm. 3–4 carats, alloyed with silver
1031-65   **Plate 36**

109
Ghana
Akan

Queen-mother's bracelet of cast gold.

Gold bracelets of this form, known as *babadua*, are generally reserved for the use of a queen-mother (*ɔhemmaa*). They are hollow-cast in two parts which are secured by a pin. This example is of fine workmanship, and may date from the second half of the 19th or the early 20th century.

Size: 6.3 cm
Weight: 111 gm
1031-23   **Plate 35**

110
Ghana
Akan

Queen-mother's bracelet of cast gold.

Although lacking the knobbed angular joints of the last example, this bracelet was also named as *babadua* by Asante informants (1986). It is hollow-cast in two parts and secured by a pin. The incised decorations are crude, and it may date from around the second quarter of the 20th century.

Size: 7.8 cm
Weight: 105 gm. About 7 carats, heavily alloyed with silver
1031-66   **Plate 35**

111
Ghana
Southern Akan

Gold bracelet of plaited wires, ornamented with two groups of birds pecking nuts.

This style of bracelet, influenced by foreign techniques, was probably first produced by Fanti goldsmiths working in the coastal towns of southern Ghana during the nineteenth century. In the colonial period jewellery of this kind became popular among the Akan, and was copied by goldsmiths in many inland towns.

The bracelet incorporates four distinct goldsmithing techniques. Two ropes of flexible plaited wire are used for the basic form, imitating European work. These are secured at each end by a hollow globe finial of sheet metal. Two filigree ornaments are attached to the bracelet, each representing three tiers of foliage. In the centre of the topmost tier is a casting of six birds pecking a fruit.

The filigree and cast motifs represent the following Akan proverb:

Sɛ abɛ bere a, nnomaa nyinaa di bi.

When the palm nuts ripen all birds partake of them.

(When opportunity arises everyone takes advantage of it. If you have money all the family will come to you. When you are important everyone follows you.)

This bracelet dates from the late 19th or early 20th century. It is the kind of jewellery commissioned by rich Akan for their private use. Ex coll. André Lhote. Published in *Les Arts Africains*, Cercle Volney, Paris, 1955 (No. 141)

Size: 10 cm
Weight: 280 gm
1031-15   **Plate 36**

112
Ghana
Southern Akan

Gold bracelet of plaited wires, ornamented with two cannons and stylised flowers or fruit.

This bracelet is constructed from twisted and plaited wires, sheet metal globules and cannons, and soldered squares of sheet metal embossed with foliate designs. It is a more recent example of European-influenced Akan jewellery, dating from about the second quarter of the 20th century. A virtually identical example is published in Kamer, 1979, fig. 46.

The cannons on this bracelet might represent a variety of Akan proverbs such as the following:

(1) *Oprɛmo ntwere nnan.*
   A cannon does not miss game.
   (A powerful person gets what he or she wants.)

(2) *Wodi oburoni adeɛ a, woko aprɛmo ano.*
   If you inherit from a white man, you fight with cannons.
   (If you take over a person's responsibilities you also take on his powers.)

Size: 8.4 cm
Weight: 102 gm
1031-21   **Plate 36**

113
Ghana
Akan

Bracelet of ninety small keys (*safoa*, pl. *nsafoa*).

The Akan attached great importance to keys, which they saw as a symbol of power. From the fifteenth century onwards they obtained them from Europeans in trade, and by 1601 it was reported that the Akan wore them in bunches on the body. Later it became the custom for bunches of keys to be kept among the stool property of the various Akan states. These signified the power and wealth of the state, and they were publicly exhibited at festivals. In Asante there was a court official, the Nsafoahene, who had custody of the Asantehene's keys. He wore them on his arm or round his neck to show his rank.

Among the various proverbs for keys is the following:

Asɛm bi na ehini asɛm bi safoa.

One question acts as the key to another.

In Kumasi, where this form of bracelet is well known, it is called *basahia*. This example may date from the late 19th or early 20th century. The chief goldsmith of Kumasi still makes such bracelets on commission, though the workmanship is inferior and the keys merely gilded brass.

Size: diameter of bracelet 9.5 cm
Weight: about 89 gm
1031-67   **Plate 37**

114
Ghana
Akan

Cast gold bracelet in the form of a European wristwatch on a chain.

Since colonial times some Akan chiefs have worn cast gold replicas of European watches to emphasise their status. These castings indicate the power of the chief to control events, since he is in control of time. Two other examples have been published (Cole and Ross, 1977, fig. 393), and a few Akan watches are known in brass.

Size: 15.2 cm
Weight: 30 gm. 3–4 carats, heavily alloyed with silver
1031-322   **Plate 37**

115
Ghana
Southern Akan

Gold finger-ring (*ɛkawa*).

This ring is not a traditional Akan design, but imitates a European gold ring. It has incuse designs, and may have been made in a mould of cuttlefish bone rather than by lost wax casting. Fanti goldsmiths made such rings in the Akan coastal towns during the 19th century.

Size: 2.2 cm
Weight: 5.5 gm
1033-31   **Plate 38**

116
Ghana
Southern Akan

Gold finger-ring with a circular central motif surrounded by pellets.

This appears to be another example of coastal goldsmith's work based on a European design, and may date from the late 19th or early 20th century. An Asante informant offered the interpretation that it was *atanfoɔ atwa me ho ahyia*, "the enemies around me".

Size: 2.3 cm
Weight: 10 gm
1033-32   **Plate 38**

117
Ghana
Akan

Gold finger-ring with lozenge-shaped bezel.

This may be an imitation of a European ring set with a stone. It may date from the 19th or early 20th century.

Size: 3 cm
Weight: 13 gm
1033-36   **Plate 39**

118
Ghana
Akan

Gold finger-ring with a prominent lozenge-shaped bezel arising from four stylised leaves.

This ring is also European-inspired. It may date from the late 19th or early 20th century.

Size: 4 cm
Weight: 16 gm
1033-12   **Plate 39**

119
Ghana
Akan

Gold finger-ring with a lozenge-shaped bezel divided into two.

This ring is also European-inspired. It may date from the late 19th or early 20th century.

Size: 3.9 cm
Weight: 20 gm
1033-38   **Plate 39**

120
Ghana
Southern Akan

Gold finger-ring with an anvil.

This small ring of relatively fine gold is another example of goldsmith's work from southern Ghana. It probably dates from the nineteenth century, and may have been made in one of the coastal Fanti towns.

The band of the ring imitates a European form, and on each side is portrayed a human figure with upraised arms, crudely rendered in relief. The central motif is a goldsmith's or blacksmith's anvil (*siaseɛ* or *tunsuobo*). This anvil is said to represent the trade by which the ring's owner obtained his wealth.

The anvil bears the initials "K. K." punched with a small European die. These were almost certainly the initials of the person who commissioned the ring, placed on it to confer added prestige and as a mark of ownership. The custom of using initials is evidently European-inspired, and probably originated in the 19th century on the Fanti coast, where literacy was not unknown. Such initials (and sometimes full names and dates) are found both on gold rings and silver spoons; the custom of using them continued throughout the colonial period.

Size: 3 cm
Weight: 14.8 gm. 15 carats
1033-20   **Plate 38**

121
Ghana
Southern Akan

Gold finger-ring with a pair of bellows (*afa*).

This ring is so similar in style to the last that it may be the work of the same goldsmith. The bellows are stamped with the initials "K. K.", and the die appears identical to that used on no. 120.

The band of this ring is decorated with imitation rococo scroll-work. The central motif, a pair of bellows of European form, is said by many informants to indicate the means by which the owner obtained his living. These bellows may have been used by a goldsmith or blacksmith. They illustrate a proverb such as the following:

Afa na ɛboa odwumfoɔ ma no tono, anka adwumfo nni ahooden.

It is the bellows that help a blacksmith to forge, without them he would be helpless.

This ring probably dates from the 19th century.

Size: 2.5 cm
Weight: 15 gm
1033-30   **Plate 38**

122
Ghana
Akan

Gold finger-ring of ribbed design with an oval bezel.

This ring is of fine workmanship, carefully constructed from wax threads. The design imitates a European form, perhaps a signet ring. In Asante (1986) the ribbed design was referred to as *aya*, a fern leaf, and the central bezel as *pono*, a table.

Date: perhaps late 19th century.

Size: 3.2 cm

Weight: 16 gm. About 9–10 carats

1033-39 **Plate 39**

123
Ghana
Akan

Base gold ring with an oval bezel inscribed with the initials "K. K."

This ring imitates another European form. It probably dates from the first half of the 20th century.

Size: 3.1 cm

Weight: 66 gm

1033-40 **Plate 39**

124
Ghana
Akan

Base gold ring of a heart (*akoma*) inscribed with the initials "K. D."

The heart motif is of European origin. This ring probably dates from the first half of the 20th century.

Size: 3 cm

Weight: 68 gm

1033-41 **Plate 39**

125
Ghana
Akan

Gold ring with a twisted design of six transverse lobes.

The inner diameter of this ring is only 1.4 cm, too small to fit the fingers of most adult Akan. It is more likely to be a pipe ring, used to adorn the long bamboo cane of a chief's tobacco pipe.

It may date from the 19th century.

Size: 4.6 cm

Weight: 40 gm

1033-16 **Plate 38**

126
Ghana
Akan

Gold ring with a design of three twisted coils. Alloyed with cuprous metal.

With an inner diameter of 2.5 cm this may be a thumb-ring rather than a finger-ring. Some Asante identified it (1986) as a thumb-ring used only by chiefs. The design was named as *kokoromutika*, and the twisted coils were also referred to as *aya*, ferns.

It may date from the first half of the 20th century.

Size: 3.7 cm

Weight: 27.5 gm

1033-44 **Plate 38**

127
Ghana
Akan

Gold ring with a design probably representing canes or ropes tied in three places.

This was also identified as a chief's thumb-ring and named as *kokoromutika*. The inner diameter is 2.4 cm.

It may date from the first half of the 20th century.

Size: 3.2 cm

Weight: 25 gm

1033-42 **Plate 39**

128
Ghana
Akan

Gold finger-ring in the form of a twisted knot (*pɔkɔrɔ*), decorated with rows of applied pellets.

According to some, this design represents a gold nugget.

The model for this fine ring was initially constructed from wax threads. It may date from about the late 19th century.

Size: 5 cm

Weight: 45 gm. About 18–19 carats

1033-28 **Plate 38**

129
Ghana
Akan

Gold finger-ring in the form of a twisted knot (*pɔkɔrɔ*).

The model for this ring appears to have been constructed in part from wax threads, which were subsequently smoothed over. It is ornamented with incised designs.

It may date from the 19th or early 20th century.

Size: 5.9 cm

Weight: 42 gm

1033-33 **Plate 38**

130
Ghana
Akan

Gold finger-ring in the form of a twisted knot (*pɔkɔrɔ*), the surface covered with incised foliate designs.

Perhaps late 19th or early 20th century.

Size: 5 cm

Weight: 33 gm

1033-22 **Plate 38**

131
Ghana
Akan

Gold finger-ring in the form of a twisted knot (*pɔkɔrɔ*).

Perhaps early 20th century.

Size: 5.7 cm

Weight: 37 gm

1033-14 **Plate 38**

132
Ghana
Akan

Gold finger-ring with a bud-like protuberance surrounded by stylised leaves.

According to Kwasi Agyare, the chief goldsmith of Kumasi, this motif represents the proverb:

Bese pa ne konini ahahan yɛtase no obanyansafoɔ.

Leaves of two kinds of kola we gather with wisdom.

(The leaves of the two kinds of kola are very similar and it needs skill and experience to separate them. You have to take care in dealing with problems, and separate them carefully.)

This ring may date from the first half of the 20th century.

Size: 3.6 cm

Weight: 17 gm. About 8–9 carats

1033-37 **Plate 39**

133
Ghana
Akan

Gold finger-ring with a bud-like protuberance surrounded by stylised leaves.

Proverb as for no. 132.

This ring may date from the late 19th or early 20th century.

Size: 3.9 cm

Weight: 17 gm

1033-35 **Plate 39**

134
Ghana
Akan

Gold finger-ring with foliate designs and a small seed or cocoa pod.

The owner's initials "J.K." are roughly incised on one side of the band.

It may date from the early 20th century.

Size: 4.2 cm

Weight: 29 gm

1033-24 **Plate 39**

135
Ghana
Akan

Gold finger-ring of stylised form, said to represent tied *babadua* canes.

One Asante informant explained that the canes, like the chief, are very strong and can last for many years. The fact that two canes are tied together was not remarked on, though it may have some proverbial significance.

Another man named this ring as *kokoromutika*, and said it was used only by chiefs.

The ring may date from the 19th or early 20th century.

Size: 3.4 cm

Weight: 20 gm

1033-74 **Plate 39**

136
Ghana
Akan

Gold finger-ring perhaps representing a flower.

Size: 4.4 cm

Weight: 28.7 gm. 9–10 carats

1033-99 **Plate 40**

137

Ghana

Akan

Gold finger-ring with an openwork sphere topped by a small cone.

This ring may be interpreted in more than one way. According to Cole and Ross (1977, pp. 36–38 and fig. 56), it represents a bird's nest, referring to the idea that whenever a chief ventures away he will always return home, as a bird would to its nest. This interpretation was not offered during recent fieldwork in Asante (1986); instead, several people including the chief goldsmith of Kumasi named the design as *frumempu*, *frumaampun* or *fruma ampuru*. This is said to be a strong-smelling white toadstool. Two informants added that it resembled a navel. Its appearance as a finger-ring motif was explained by such statements as: "It is rare and that is why we used it," and "It was beautiful and very strange. People were surprised and copied it."

Presumably there is, or was, some proverb relating to this toadstool that would explain its real significance as a ring motif. Unfortunately no such proverb was known to any of the persons questioned.

Rings of this form are often worn by Akan chiefs. The design is an old one. A small and delicately cast example was acquired in Kumasi in 1840 by a visiting missionary; it is now in the Museum für Völkerkunde in Basel.

This ring is of fine workmanship and smaller than most recent examples. It may date from the 19th century.

Size: 4.2 cm

Weight: 16 gm

1033-7   **Plate 38**

138

Ghana

Akan

Gold finger-ring of onion-shaped form covered with numerous spikes.

According to some people in Kumasi, the object shown on this ring is a kind of cocoon called *kotoku-saa-bobe*. They cite several versions of a proverb:

(1) *Kotoku-saa-bobe, onkasa nso ohome.*
   The grub: it does not talk but it breathes.
   (A stranger's character is not easily known.)

(2) *Woay kotoku-saa-bobe; onni ano na ohome.*
   You have become like the grub that has no mouth but breathes.
   (Said of a quiet but wicked person.)

Other Asante identify the design as a kind of fruit of the same name; they add that "it doesn't speak but it breathes." It is said to represent a chief who is calm but capable of exerting his authority when opposed.

There is evidently some confusion between cocoons and a similarly named fruit or seed. According to Mrs Peggy Appiah of Kumasi there is a climbing shrub named *kotoku-saa-burobe* (Morinda spp.) whose fruits have protuberances with hollows at their centre. This may well be the fruit referred to by some Asante informants.

Among the Baule of Côte d'Ivoire a similar name, *kotoku-saa-lome*, is applied to the fruit of a tree. It is said to have a bitter taste, and may perhaps be a kind of lime (*lomi, lome, dome*). A Baule goldsmith at Bouake gave this name to a small brass-casting representing a bunch of three fruits (worn strung on a necklace). He cited for it a Baule proverb alluding to the fruit's bitter taste:

Kotokun-saa-lome: se ɔ wo mwalɔ be kloɛ sangɛ ɔ mantan be, be kloɛ kun.

The *kotokun-saa-lome* fruit says: When I am far from you you love me, but when I am near you hate me.

This relatively large ring probably dates from the first half of the 20th century.

Size: 5.5 cm

Weight: 43 gm

1033-15   **Plate 40**

139

Ghana

Akan

Gold finger-ring of onion-shaped form covered with numerous spikes.

This is another representation of *kotoku-saa-bobe*. On this example the bulbous shape is pierced with small holes. It probably dates from the second or third quarter of the 20th century.

Size: 5 cm

Weight: 43 gm

1033-25   **Plate 40**

140

Ghana

Akan

Gold finger-ring of an oil palm tree.

The oil palm is a source of wealth and prosperity for many Akan. It is a common symbol among royal finger-rings, where it represents the strength, stability and permanence of the chief. Variants of the following proverb are often cited:

Nnua nyinaa bɛwoso ma aka abɛ.

All trees bend in the wind except the oil palm.

(The chief can weather all storms. He remains firm and stable in time of crisis).

Rings of this design are still made, for instance by the chief goldsmith of Kumasi. Some younger Asante, unfamiliar with the design, identify it as *aborobɛ*, the pineapple, but it is clearly intended to be an oil palm (*abɛ*), the small fruits being visible at the base of each leaf.

This ring may date from the second or third quarter of the 20th century.

Size: 5.5 cm

Weight: 55 gm

1033-21   **Plate 40**

141

Ghana

Akan

Gold finger-ring of an oil palm tree.

This ring is almost identical to the last. It may

date from the second or third quarter of the 20th century.

Size: 5.3 cm

Weight: 50 gm

1033-13   **Plate 40**

142

Ghana

Akan

Gold finger-ring of a bird with outstretched wings. 20th century.

Size: 3.9 cm

Weight: 13.5 gm. About 12 carats

1033-84   **Plate 41**

143

Ghana

Akan

Gold finger-ring of four birds pecking palm-nuts.

This motif represents the proverb:

Sɛ abɛ bere a, nnomaa nyinaa di bi.

When the palm nuts ripen all birds partake of them.

(When opportunity comes everyone takes advantage of it. If you have money all the family will come to you. When you are important everyone follows you.)

This ring is a fine small casting and may date from the second half of the 19th century.

Size: 4.6 cm

Weight: 22.5 gm. 9 carats, alloyed with brass and silver

1033-19   **Plate 41**

144

Ghana

Akan

Gold finger-ring of a bird carrying a gunpowder keg in its beak and a cannon on each wing. The bird's body is in the form of a knot, symbolising wisdom (*nyansapɔ*, "wisdom knot").

This ring represents the well-known Akan proverb:

Adwetakyi anomaa werɛmfoɔ te prɛmo so.

The courageous bird Adwetakyi sits on cannons.

(A brave man faces all odds; he is always ready to face the enemy.)

This is a finely cast ring which may date from the second half of the nineteenth century.

Size: 5.1 cm

Weight: 41 gm

1033-48   **Plate 41**

145

Ghana

Akan

Gold finger-ring of a bird carrying gunpowder kegs and cannon in its beak and on its neck, wings and tail.

This work is of less fine quality, the bird's feathers being incised with a spatula and the band of the ring crudely cross-hatched. The metal appears to be alloyed with silver.

Proverb as for no. 144.

This ring probably dates from about the second quarter of the 20th century.

Size: 5.8 cm
Weight: 40 gm

1033-27 **Plate 41**

146
Ghana
Akan

Gold finger-ring of four arched forms each carrying a cannon, and a central pyramid bearing a gunpowder keg.

This motif probably indicates readiness to face the enemy, with a proverb similar to that of No. 144.

The basic form has been constructed from wax threads which were subsequently smoothed. The ring may date from the 19th century.

Size: 3.9 cm
Weight: 24 gm

1033-76 **Plate 40**

147
Ghana
Akan

Gold finger-ring of four arched forms each carrying a cannon, and a central cone bearing a gunpowder keg. There is a small stylised ram's head motif on each side of the ring, on the upper part of the band.

Taken together, the motifs on this ring evidently refer to courage and strength.

The ring may date from the late 19th or early 20th century. In 1986 the chief goldsmith of Kumsai made a ring of almost identical design.

Size: 5.2 cm
Weight: 36 gm

1033-11 **Plate 40**

148
Ghana
Akan

Gold finger-ring with a human head.

One goldsmith in Kumasi named this ring as *ahwɛhwɛba*. Other people in Kumasi thought that it represented the proverb:

Ti korɔ nnkɔ agyina.

One head does not make a council.

(There should be consultation when an important decision is to be made).

In common with some other examples of older Akan goldwork, this ring was initially constructed from wax threads that were subsequently smoothed over. It is likely to date from the 19th century.

Size: 4.7 cm
Weight: 26 gm. 17 carats

1033-26 **Plate 40**

149
Ghana
Akan

Gold finger-ring of a human head with one bird in front of it and another behind.

The motif on this ring may be a variant of the *ti*

korɔ nnkɔ agyina theme (no. 148). Alternatively it may represent a trophy head, i.e. the head of a defeated enemy.

The ring probably dates from the 19th century.

Size: 5 cm
Weight: 28.3 gm. About 8.5 carats

1033-77 **Plate 41**

150
Ghana
Akan: Asante

Gold finger-ring of a porcupine eating a corn-cob.

This Asante royal finger-ring conveys the idea that just as the procupine eats a corn-cob, so will the Asante devour their enemies.

The porcupine (*kotɔkɔ*) is the symbol of the Asante nation. As early as the 1740s the Asantehene's soldiers were referring to themselves as *Asante kotɔkɔ*, and in modern times this has become the name of a popular football team.

The animal usually depicted in Asante art is the crested porcupine (*Hystrix cristata*), the largest African rodent, a creature remarkable for its ferocity when attacked. The Asante believe that it can discharge its spines into an enemy like spears, while instantly growing new ones to replace them. Porcupine rings are thus a powerful political symbol, and are often worn on public occasions by senior Asante chiefs. Among the best-known proverbs relating to them are the following:

(1) *Kotɔkɔ a ne mpea gu n'aso soɔ, hwan na ɔbetumi ne ho adi asie.*
    The porcupine whose spears (quills) cover its back, who is able to conquer it?
    (A reference to the alleged invincibility of the Asante.)

(2) *Asante kotɔkɔ: kum apɛm a, apɛm bɛba.*
    The Asante porcupine: if a thousand are killed, a thousand more will come.
    (A royal appellation, again referring to the might of the Asante army.)

(3) *Obi mpopa ne to wɔ kotɔkɔ akye.*
    No one rubs bottoms with a porcupine.

This ring probably dates from about the second quarter of the 20th century.

Size: 6.8 cm
Weight: 57 gm

1033-78 **Plate 41**

151
Ghana
Akan: Asante

Gold finger-ring of a porcupine.

This ring probably dates from about the second quarter of the 20th century, shortly after the return from exile of the Asantehene Prempeh I.

Size: 4.3 cm
Weight: 41 gm. About 5 carats

1033-43 **Plate 41**

152
Ghana
Akan

Gold finger-ring of a hunter shooting a monkey that is eating a grasshopper.

The grasshopper is a favourite food of monkeys, a fact commented on both in drum music and proverbs:

(1) *Krakansenmpobi (Sakatimpobi) ne no, yɛɛko no na ɔsɔ mmɛbɛ.*
    That is the monkey, while we are hunting him he eats grasshoppers.

(2) *Wokum Sakatimpobi: na ɔsɔ mmɛbɛ.*
    You tell the monkey, but it is eating grasshoppers.
    (Said of someone who fears nothing.)

This ring is of fairly recent date, perhaps made around the mid-20th century.

Size: 4.6 cm
Weight: 41 gm. 10 carats

1033-17 **Plate 41**

153
Ghana
Akan

Gold finger-ring of two crocodiles with a single body.

The popular motif of the double crocodile (also well known as a goldweight) represents the following proverb:

Funtumfrafu- ne-dɛnkyɛmfrafu, yɛn nyeraa afunu korɔ nso sɛ yɛredidi a, na yɛrefom, efiri yɛse aduase yɛdi no mere mu twitwi.

Bellies joined, crocodiles joined; we all have one stomach but when we are eating we scramble because we say that we relish the food in our throats.

(A proverb stressing the need for unity in the family or state. Members should not quarrel or fight for selfish interests, for what each gains is for the benefit of all.)

Size: 6 cm
Weight: 25 gm. About 6 carats, alloyed with silver

1033-83 **Plate 41**

154
Ghana
Akan

Gold finger-ring of a scorpion.

This ring may depict either the large black scorpion or the smaller brown scorpion; most informants in Kumasi named it as the latter. Among the many proverbs are the following:

(1) *Ana-kɔnkɔnkyea, ɔka wo a gye sɛ anumerɛ na atɔwɔ ɔde ne to na ɛka.*
    The brown scorpion: when it stings you the pain goes on till nightfall.
    (If you incur the chief's displeasure you will feel it for a long time.)

(2) *Ana-kɔnkɔnkyea a ɔka nipa ma no to.*
    The brown scorpion which bites a man to death.
    (A royal appellation.)

(3) *Ana kɔnkɔnkyea anafia atworodo, ɔka ɔbaatan ba a, gye sɛ asomorofi adwo.*
    The brown scorpion, when it stings a good mother's child, the pain lasts until the hearth grows cold.

(4) *Yɛmfa nyanyankyerɛ nni mmɔfra-goro.*
We don't use the black scorpion to take part in a children's game.
(A warning to take something seriously and keep away from danger.)

This large and very heavy ring would have been worn by a chief of senior rank. It probably dates from the first half of the 20th century.

Size: 6.5 cm
Weight: 76 gm
1033-49 **Plate 41**

155

Ghana
Akan

Gold finger-ring of a frog.

This unusual royal symbol represents the proverb:

Aponkyerenɛ wu a, na yɛhunu ne tenten.

The length of the frog is known only after his death.

(A man's worth is not appreciated in his lifetime.)

This ring probably dates from the first half of the 20th century.

Size: 4 cm
Weight: 31.5 gm. About 8 carats
1033-29 **Plate 42**

156

Ghana
Akan

Gold finger-ring of a frog.
Proverb as for no. 155.

This ring has been slightly filed at the base. It may date from around the mid-20th century.

Size: 4.4 cm
Weight: 31 gm
1033-18 **Plate 42**

157

Ghana
Akan

Gold finger-ring of a mudfish.

The mudfish is a common symbol on Akan royal finger-rings. Its meaning is rather ambiguous and it may be interpreted in various ways, but it is often seen as subordinate to the crocodile, with whom it lives in close association. Proverbs such as the following are cited:

Opitire memene adeɛ a, ɔmemene ma owura.

If the mudfish swallows something of value it does so for its master (i. e. the crocodile).

This ring probably dates from the second or third quarter of the 20th century.
Gift of Emil Storrer in memory of Josef Müller

Size: 5.8 cm
Weight: 48 gm. About 5 carats, heavily alloyed with silver
1033-71 **Plate 42**

158

Ghana
Akan

Gold finger-ring of a mudfish.

Proverb as for no. 157.

This ring is said to have come from a Baule chief, but nevertheless appears to be Akan work from Ghana. It is well known that Ivoirian chiefs buy items of gold regalia from Ghana, and notably from Kumasi.

Circa mid-20th century.

Size: 7.5 cm
Weight: 75 gm
1033-85 **Plate 42**

159

Ghana
Akan

Gold finger-ring of a mudfish.

Proverb as for no. 157.

This ring is heavily alloyed with cuprous metal. It may date from around the mid-20th century or a little later.

Size: 7.5 cm
Weight: 79 gm
1033-23 **Plate 42**

160

Ghana
Akan

Pair of chief's ankle bands (*abirempon naaseɛ*), each consisting of a multicoloured silk cord from which are suspended twelve carved wooden ornaments covered with gold leaf.

According to some informants, only paramount chiefs may wear such ankle bands. The gold leaf ornaments are identified both as bells (*ɔdawuru*) and as amulets (*sɛbɛ*).

20th century.

Size: each about 22 cm
1009-59 A, B **Plate 34**

161

Ghana
Akan

Gold sandal ornament in the form of a palm beetle (*asomorɔdwe*).

The grub of this beetle is considered a great delicacy. The beetle itself is depicted (both among gold ornaments and brass weights) to represent the popular proverb:

Sɛ wowe asomorɔdwe na anyɛ wo dɛ na wo de wani ato akɔkono so.

If you don't like the taste of the palm beetle, console yourself with the thought of its grub.

(When hard times come, think of the better days ahead).

Size: 4.5 cm
Weight: 6 gm. About 13 carats
1034-167 **Plate 30**

162

Ghana
Akan

Two sandal ornaments of unidentified form. Perhaps gilded silver or brass.

Size: each 2.3 cm
Weight: each 7 gm
1034-211 A, B **Plate 30**

163

Ghana
Akan

Pair of chief's sandals (*mpaboa*) of blackened leather, with attached talismans (*nsɛbɛ*) of carved wood covered with gold leaf.

These may perhaps be a queen-mother's sandals (*ɔhenemaa mpaboa*) due to their small size.

Size: 22 cm
1009-66 A, B **Plate 43**

164

Ghana
Akan

Pair of chief's leather sandals (*mpaboa*), adorned with triangular amulets (*nsɛbɛ*) and a central bird (*anomaa*) of carved wood covered with gold leaf.

Size: 30 cm
1009-53 A, B **Plate 43**

165

Ghana
Akan

Pair of chief's leather sandals (*mpaboa*), each decorated with cast gold ornaments of cowry shells (*sidie*) and a bird (*anomaa*).

The cowries symbolise wealth. The bird may perhaps be the *asantrofie* or nightjar, representing the following proverb:

Asantrofie anomaa, wofa no a wafa mmusuo, wogyae no a wagyae sadeɛ.

As for the *asantrofie* bird, if you take it you take bad luck, and if you leave it you leave good luck.

This fine old pair of sandals has been much used. It may date from the first half of the 20th century.

Size: 30.5 cm
1009-129 A, B **Plate 43**

166

Ghana
Akan

White horse-tail whisk (*bodua*) with a strap of red, yellow and green silk, the handle with four rectangular amulets (*nsɛbɛ*) of carved wood covered with gold leaf.

Whisks with attached amulets are known as *sɛbɛ bodua*. On public occasions they are held or carried before the chief by his attendants. They are not used primarily as fly-whisks, but serve to drive evil spirits from the royal presence.

The white horse-tails used for these whisks are not of local origin, but were formerly imported from Europe.

Size: 48 cm
1009-34 **Plate 44**

167

Ghana
Akan

White horse-tail whisk, the leather handle covered with gold foil, and with two suspended amulets of leather and gold.

Size of handle: 19.7 cm
1009-85 **Plate 44**

168

Ghana
Akan: probably Asante

Sword ornament of a mudfish, cast in gold.

This casting falls into the broad class of ornaments known as *abosodeε*, and was attached to a state sword.

Proverb as for no. 157.

Size: 19 cm
Weight: 456 gm. 12–15 carats
1034-171 **Plate 45**

169

Ghana
Akan: northern Asante

Skink or monitor lizard of cast gold.

Asante informants gave two quite different interpretations for this sword *abosodeε*. The majority identified it as a skink (*ɔbɔmɔte*), a small reptile whose head resembles that of a snake. The skink is much feared by the Akan, for it is reputed (quite falsely) to have a poisonous bite. It is said that if the skink bites you, it will die if you can reach water before it does. But if it reaches water first, you will die. The symbolism indicates that a chief, like the skink, can be dangerous. He too can bite if people do not take care.

A few Asante on the other hand regarded this as a casting of a monitor lizard (*ɔmampam*). This large and fearsome-looking reptile is, paradoxically, regarded as the symbol of a peacemaker. It is not uncommon in Akan art for symbols to give rise, as in this case, to a variety of interpretations, which are sometimes diametrically opposed.

This casting may date from the late 19th or early 20th century. It comes from Berekum. Published in Kyerematen, 1964, p. 37

Size: 21.8 cm
Weight: 347 gm. About 9–10 carats
1009-63 **Plate 45**

170

Ghana
Akan: Asante

Crocodile of cast gold.

The crocodile is a popular motif among sword *abosodeε* from Asante. This large and ambitious example is finely modelled, the texture of the skin being rendered by tiny impressed circles and lines. The underside of the body and the suspension loop are well worn where they have rubbed against the accompanying state sword. This casting may date from the late 19th or early 20th century. Its quality suggests that it may be the product of an Asante royal workshop. It comes from Mampong.

The crocodile, like the chief whom it represents, was regarded as having a versatile character. Among the proverbs and royal appellations associated with it are the following:

(1) *Ɔdεnkyεm da nsuo mu, nso ɔhome.*
The crocodile lies in the water but it also breathes air.

(2) *Dεnkyεm niampa a εduru afeε a ɔmene boɔ.*
The great crocodile that swallows a stone every year.
(A royal appellation, for instance of the Omanhene of Mampong.)

This casting appears to have been made with the royal appellation in mind, for in the crocodile's mouth is a small spiral, representing a pebble. The Asante belief that crocodiles swallow a stone every year may have been based on natural observation – the finding of pebbles in their stomachs. Alternatively, it may have arisen from the fact that some crocodiles, shortly before the hatching of their eggs, dig these up and carry them in their mouth to a place of greater safety.
Published by Meyerowitz, 1951, pl. 22; Ross, 1977, pp. 21, 24; Cable, 1983, p. 108

Size: 33.5 cm
Weight: 636 gm. 14 carats
1009-69 **Plate 45**

171

Ghana
Akan: northern Asante

Lion of cast gold.

The lion (*gyata*) is a common motif among sword ornaments in the Asante chiefdoms. Is also occurs among royal finger-rings. Doran Ross has shown that the lion motif in Asante art derives from the European heraldic lion, with head turned sideways and tail curled over the back.

Most Asante depictions of the lion date from the colonial period. This casting, which comes from Berekum, may have been made about the 1920s or 1930s, when there was a revival in the casting of gold regalia following the return from exile of the Asantehene Prempeh I. Its style is characteristic of the work of this period, the lion's fur and name being rendered by incised lines and patterns rather than wax threadwork. The hind legs bear file marks, and in several places the gold is visibly alloyed with cuprous metal.

The lion represents the bravery of the chief. It is the subject of various proverbs and royal appellations, including the following:

(1) *Woboro gyata a, wo tiri na εpae wo.*
If you beat a lion, it is your own head that aches.
(If you are disrespectful of a chief you will suffer for it.)

(2) *Gyata tumfuɔ a, ɔte prεm, so.*
The powerful lion sits on a cannon.
(A royal appellation.)

For similar lion sword ornaments from Juaben, Nsuta and Mampong, see Ross, 1977, pp. 17, 23, 24. Published in Kyerematen, 1964, p. 37

Size: 14.5 cm
Weight: about 743 gm. 9–10 carats
1009-62 **Plate 46**

172

Ghana
Akan

Padlock (*krado*) of silver-gilt.

European padlocks were imported to the Akan region from the 16th or 17th century onwards. They were commonly used to secure large chests containing cloths and other valuables, as well as some of the smaller containers for gold-dust. The padlock had a particular fascination for the Akan. At least as early as the 17th century Akan goldsmiths were casting copies in brass, some of which were apparently intended to be functional.

In some of the richer chieftaincies padlocks such as this were cast in gold and silver. These were attached to the large, finely embroidered purses known as *kotokuo* (pl. *nkotokwaa*) that accompanied the chief when he was travelling. These bags contained the gold required for his daily expenses. They were made in pairs, one being secured by a padlock of gold and the other by a padlock of silver.

Size: 12.9 cm
Weight: 137 gm
1034-206 **Plate 29**

173

Ghana
Akan: probably Asante

Pellet bell (*dawa* or *εdon*) of cast gold.

Bells of this form, wrought in iron by the blacksmith, were once well known throughout the Akan region. They were used in many contexts. Some served as adornments for the equipment of a hunter or warrior; they were attached to cartridge belts, leather wallets, and the large rectangular shields that were in use up to the 18th century. Others were worn by dancers and fetish priests. Sometimes a bell of this kind was hung round a dog's neck, giving rise to the proverb:

Ɔkraman bεwe ade nhina a, ɔnwe ne kɔnmu dawa.

A dog will chew everything, but he can't chew the bell round his neck.

While serving as musical instruments, it is possible that these bells once had a deeper significance. When worn by a warrior, hunter or fetish priest they may have been intended to "summon the spirits" around the wearer, so that he would be protected from any misfortune.

The present example, cast in gold, is a copy of one of these iron bells. It presumably formed part of the regalia of a paramount chief, and may have served to adorn the equipment of one of his bodyguards.

Size: 6 cm
Weight: 34 gm. 9–10 carats
1034-207 **Plate 32**

174

Ghana
Akan

Gold cockle-shell (*adam*), used to adorn a warrior's cartridge belt or bandolier bag.

These castings are usually said to depict a kind of red sea-shell (Asante *adam*, Baule *ala*) which was often used for adornment by the Akan and Baule. These shells were highly prized, being sometimes worth their weight in gold, and for centuries they were imported from the Canary Islands.

Some Asante informants, however, identify these castings as a kind of water-beetle called *apirekyiwa*.

Size: 4 cm
Weight: 18.5 gm. About 7.5 carats, alloyed with silver

1034-168 **Plate 46**

175
Ghana
Akan

Pair of gold jawbones (*abogye*, pl. *mmogye*).

In former times when an important enemy was slain in battle, the victorious chief would cause the dead man's jawbones to be removed and attached to one of the royal drums or ivory horns. This was an effective way to insult and humiliate the dead man, for at festivals these instruments were used to sing the chief's praises. Since the jawbones were placed round the instrument, those praises were in effect sung "through the mouth" of the vanquished enemy.

Small jawbones cast in gold were sometimes used to decorated items of regalia. In 1817 Bowdich mentioned that he saw them on the belts of guards standing behind the Asantehene's chair. The present castings, made as a pair, may have been used in this way or alternatively as sandal ornaments.

Size: 5.3 and 5 cm
Weight: 29 and 32 gm. Each 10 carats

1034-208 A, B **Plate 33**

176
Ghana
Akan

Sword (*afena*) with an iron blade and a carved wooden pommel covered with gold leaf.

In Kumasi the distinctive ribbed pommel of this sword was named as *bobɔmfrada*; the design is said to derive from a seed of that name.

Swords have played an important role in Akan life since at least the 17th century. They function in a variety of ritual and ceremonial contexts. The most important are used in the installation of major chiefs, who hold a particular sword while taking the oath of office. Others are held by subchiefs when swearing allegiance. Swords were carried by royal messengers and ambassadors, and used in the rituals for purifying the chief's soul and the ancestral black stools. Paramount chiefs maintain a group of sword-bearers, each of whom carries one of the state swords on public occasions. But while swords are thus essential items of regalia, their use is symbolic: they have unsharpened blades and are not intended for use in warfare.

Size: 65.5 cm

1009-42 **Plate 47**

177
Ghana
Akan

Sword with an iron blade, the carved wooden pommel covered with gold leaf.

Size: 70.5 cm

1009-35 **Plate 47**

178
Ghana
Akan

Sword with an iron blade and a carved wooden pommel which is partly whitened and partly covered with gold leaf.

In Kumasi this sword was named as *akrafena*. The whitened pommel indicates that it is a sword used by the "soul-washer" (*ɔkra*) in the ritual for purifying the chief's soul.

Size: 72.5 cm

1009-36 **Plate 48**

179
Ghana
Akan

Sword with an iron blade and a carved wooden pommel covered with gold leaf.

Size: 70 cm

1009-17 **Plate 48**

180
Ghana
Akan

Umbrella finial (*kyinie akyi*) in the form of a hand holding an egg. Carved wood covered with gold leaf, the egg painted white.

This finial represents the well-known Akan proverb:

Kosua sɛ: Mete sɛ tumi, womia me a, mebɔ, wogyae me mu a, mebɔ fam.

The egg says: "I am like authority. If you hold me too hard I break, if you let me go I fall and break to pieces on the ground."

(A chief should be neither too severe nor too lenient; he must exercise his responsibilities with care and moderation.)

Size: 14.3 cm

1009-70 **Plate 49**

181
Ghana
Akan: Asante

Linguist staff finial (*poma tiri*) of a man seated on a stool and holding an egg. Carved wood covered in gold leaf.

This staff top was probably carved in the 1960s or 70s by Kojo Bonsu of Kumasi, a prolific carver who is still active today. He is a son of the famous Asante carver Osei Bonsu (1900–77).

This finial represents the same proverb as No. 180.

Size: 30.7 cm

1009-31 **Plate 49**

182
Ghana
Akan

Linguist staff top (*poma tiri*) of a bird with its head turned backwards. Carved wood covered with gold leaf.

The bird with its head turned back, called *sankɔfa*, is a common Akan motif. It represents the famous proverb:

To w'akyi a fa.

Pick it up if it falls behind you.

(Learn from the experience of the past.)

Size: 26.8 cm

1009-60 **Plate 49**

183
Ghana
Akan

Linguist staff (*poma*) with a finial showing one man eating food from a bowl while another man looks on. Carved wood covered with gold leaf.

This scene is commonly represented among linguist staffs. It represents the proverb:

Deɛ adeɛ wɔ no na odi, ɛnyɛ deɛ ɛkɔm de no.

The man who owns a thing eats it and not the man who is hungry.

(Only he who possesses the chieftaincy has the right to enjoy it.)

This is a warning to would-be claimants to the chieftaincy (represented on the staff by the bowl of food) that they should not cause trouble; they have no claim in the face of the rightful occupant.

Size: 163 cm (finial 22 cm)

1009-52 **Plate 50**

184
Ghana
Akan

Linguist staff (*poma*) with a finial showing a man scraping bark from a tree for use as medicine. Carved wood covered with gold leaf.

The finial, which may have been carved around the second quarter of this century, represents the following proverb:

Baako wɛre aduro a, ɛgu.

If one man alone scrapes bark, it falls.

(People should co-operate if they want to succeed. The whole community should co-operate if the state is to be prosperous).

Size: 179 cm (finial 32.5 cm)

1009-55 **Plate 50**

185
Ghana
Akan

Linguist staff top (*poma tiri*) of a bush-cow with three birds perching among its horns. Carved wood covered with gold leaf.

According to one proverb:

Kwaakwaadabi anhunu atoɔ anto no, na ɔkotoɔ ɛkɔɔ mmɛn mu.

The crow which did not know how to lay pro-perly, laid its eggs in the horns of a bushcow.

Some Asante interpret this as a warning that improvidence can lead to foolish actions (the bush-cow being one of the most dangerous animals in the forest). Others give a contrary interpretation, suggesting that the bird, in attempting a highly difficult task, exemplifies the unusual patience of the chief. Yet other informants liken the bush-cow to the chief: he will remain patient unless irritated by fools. Evidently this staff top is open to multiple interpretations, though it relates in some way to the patience of a chief.

The carver of this staff may not have seen a bush-cow, for he has given it a reindeer's antlers.

Size: 31.8 cm

1009-65   **Plate 50**

186
Ghana
Akan

Linguist staff (*poma*) with a finial showing an elephant and a bush-cow standing side by side. Carved wood covered with gold leaf.

The bush-cow (*ɛkoɔ*) is one of the biggest animals in the forest, but the elephant (*ɛsono*) is even larger and stronger. Hence the proverb:

Ɛkoɔ sɛ: ɛsono nni man mu a, anka ɔyɛ bɔpɔn.

The bushcow says that if the elephant is not around, he is the mountain.

(When a more important person is absent, the lesser thinks himself great.)

There is a variant of this proverb: *Ɛsono nni wuram a, anka ɛkoɔ yɛ hene* (if the elephant were not in the bush, the bush-cow would be king).

Size: 153 cm

1009-56   **Plate 51**

187
Ghana
Akan

Linguist staff (*poma*) representing birds pecking at the trunk of a tree. The finial is in the form of a larger bird. Carved wood covered with gold leaf.

This staff refers to a well-known saying: The woodpeckers hope the silk-cotton tree will die.

This is probably an early 20th century carving, the gold leaf being fixed with tiny staples rather than glued as in more recent examples.

Total height: 141 cm

1009-128   **Plate 51**

188
Côte d'Ivoire
South-eastern region

Downward-pointing crescent moon of alloyed gold.

The crescent moon occurs frequently in metalwork from Burkina Faso, Ghana and Côte d'Ivoire. In the savanna such crescents are cast in brass or cut from sheet iron, and worn by children as a form of magical protection against eye and skin ailments. In Ghana, at least in Asante, they were made of hammered silver or

gold, and worn round the neck by priests of Tano. In south-eastern Côte d'Ivoire they were cast in gold, and used as hair ornaments and in public displays of wealth.

It is difficult to determine the provenance of most Ivoirian gold crescent castings. They were well known to the coastal peoples around the lagoons of the south-east, but whether they were also made further afield, for instance by the Anyi and Baule, remains uncertain. Some Baule goldsmiths claim that this form exists in their country. They call it *anglo*, "moon", and cite for it the proverb:

Anglo fi ɔ fia man.

When the moon comes out, all can see it.

(Secrets will one day be revealed, so it is better to be open in your behaviour).

The present casting was acquired from a European dealer who stated in writing that it had been given in about 1880 to Captain Binger, the founder of Bingerville in south-eastern Côte d'Ivoire. This information is unverified and

must be regarded with caution; even if it were based on fact it is inaccurate. Binger did not enter Côte d'Ivoire until 1888, when on a mission of exploration. He was made Governor of Côte d'Ivoire in 1893, and revisited the country in the 1930s, a few years before his death. If he was indeed given the pendant, this is most likely to have occurred in the 1890s or 1930s, at Grand Bassam or one of the other coastal towns.

The pendant was constructed from wax threads with openwork designs, and decorative ringlets and suspension loops are attached. It is a fairly old and finely worked piece, which could date from the late 19th or early 20th century.

Size: 7.7 cm
Weight: about 25 gm

1034-78   **Plate 52**

189
Côte d'Ivoire
South-eastern region

Downward-pointing crescent moon of alloyed gold.

This pendant was modelled in wax threads with openwork designs formed by bisected spirals. Two triangular apertures were cut into the model. There are two suspension rings, and around them the remains of six large casting sprues which have been unskilfully removed.

In style this crescent is similar to three of the pendant gold heads, nos. 221, 223 and 224 with cut-out triangles and numerous casting sprues. Such castings come from the south or south-east and may well be Ebrie work, perhaps from around Bingerville. This crescent may date from the first half of the 20th century.

Ex coll. R. Bédiat

Size: 8.3 cm
Weight: 14 gm

1034-36   **Plate 52**

190
Côte d'Ivoire
South-eastern region

Downward-pointing crescent moon of alloyed gold or gilded brass.

This crescent is similar in style to the last, with cut-out triangles and the remains of six crudely removed casting sprues. It comes from the same region and perhaps from the same workshop. The casting was imperfect, leaving a large hole in the upper part of the pendant that has been filled by a cut-out rectangle of metal, inexpertly soldered on.

This casting is fairly recent. It may date from the second or third quarter of the 20th century.

Size: 8.2 cm
Weight: 32 gm

1034-25   **Plate 52**

191
Côte d'Ivoire
Lagoons area

Hair ornament in the form of a modified crescent. Cast gold.

This jewel was made in December 1987 by Akesse Raphael, aged about 40, one of the last Ebrie goldsmiths in the village of Anna near Bingerville. It was a commission for a client. The form was modelled in wax threads laid over a charcoal core. The four triangular apertures cut into the design are a common feature of Ebrie goldwork.

This is a traditional casting which the Ebrie call *kontro sɛ*, "male crab".

Size: 8.4 cm
Weight: 14 gm

1034-267   **Plate 52**

192
Côte d'Ivoire
South-eastern region

Downward-pointing crescent moon of alloyed gold.

This crescent has been skilfully constructed from wax threads laid vertically and diagonally. The vertical threads have been double-looped and their ends, symmetrically arranged, overlap the diagonal threads. There are three suspension loops (two damaged) and remains of three widely spaced casting sprues.

This casting has an exceptionally smooth inner surface, which indicates that the goldsmith used a very finely pulverized charcoal for the core.

There are signs of wear and damage on this finely worked pendant, which may date from the 19th or early 20th century. A virtually identical example, evidently by the same artist, has been published by Kamer (1979).

Size: 9.1 cm
Weight: 34 gm

1034-24   **Plate 52**

193
Côte d'Ivoire
South-eastern region

Downward-pointing crescent moon with a rudimentary human face. Alloyed gold.

This crescent was probably made by the same goldsmith as the last. It is constructed in the same way, from double-looped threads laid vertically and diagonally. It has the same remarkably smooth inner surface, and remains of three widely spaced casting sprues. The design differs, however, in several respects. In the centre of the crescent is a rudimentary human face consisting of a nose and two cross-shaped scarification marks. At each side is a rectangular openwork grill.

The crescent with human face may be an old form. Two examples were presented to the Musée de l'Homme by M. Bricard in 1892 (Ratton, 1951, p. 141). The present casting may date from the 19th or early 20th century. It probably came from a lagoons workshop, though its exact provenance is unknown. In the lagoons village of Anna, near Bingerville, the Ebrie goldsmith Akesse Raphael still casts such pendants adorned with a human face. He calls them *pɛ*, "moon".

Size: 10 cm
Weight: 45 gm

1034-22 **Plate 52**

194
Côte d'Ivoire
South-eastern region

Downward-pointing crescent moon with a human face.

This ornament is not stylistically close to the usual products of the lagoons region, but may perhaps have been made in the southern Baule or Atie region. The casting is crisp and perfect. Bisected spirals have been used for the ears, suggesting Baule influence.

This casting is considerably smaller than recent examples of the type, and the gold is purer (14–15 carats). It is likely to date from the nineteenth century.

Size: 6.5 cm
Weight: 16 gm

1034-230 **Plate 52**

195
Côte d'Ivoire
Lagoons area

Downward-pointing crescent moon with a human face. Alloyed gold.

This pendant is in a degenerate lagoons style, perhaps Ebrie. It has been modelled from wax threads, with eight crudely cut openwork triangles on one side of the head and nine on the other. There are remains of eight large casting sprues. The standard of workmanship is low, and the general effect unpleasing.

This casting may date from the 1920s or 1930s. Acquired by J. Müller from E. Ascher in January 1939

Size: 11.2 cm
Weight: 58 gm

1034-1 **Plate 53**

196
Côte d'Ivoire
South-eastern region

Downward-pointing crescent moon with a human face. Alloyed gold.

This pendant comes from the lagoons region and is perhaps Ebrie work. It is modelled from wax threads, with a border of six small cut-out triangles at each side of the face. The face is rudimentary, without hair, ears or beard. Each point of the crescent terminates in a tiny bisected spiral. There are three suspension loops, surrounded by remains of five casting sprues.

An Ebrie man interpreted this casting to mean: "When you shine all people can see you." In Baule country the proverb was given as follows: *Sɛ be nyoru ti kɛ anglo sa, sran kloua-kloua kloua oun yi.*

If a man's face was like the moon, all the world would see it.

(You can't see a man's thoughts).

Ratton published this pendant in 1951 (p. 148 and fig. 67). He named it as *sarai*, "moon", apparently in error. This would appear to be the Baule word *sran*, "a person", referring not to the crescent shape but to the face.

The pendant may date from the early 20th century.
Acquired by J. Müller from E. Ascher in October 1938

Size: 9 cm
Weight: 50 gm

1034-3 **Plate 53**

197
Côte d'Ivoire
Lagoons area

Lozenge-shaped ornament of gilded white metal, perhaps silver. Modelled from loops and bands of wax threads, with five casting sprues.

This is a traditional Ebrie design named as *kontro bie*, "female crab". Similar castings are still made in the Ebrie village of Anna. In a photograph taken by Himmelheber in 1934 such ornaments can be seen among a group of gold castings from the lagoons region. These were shown in Abidjan at a colonial exhibition (Fischer, Himmelheber and Fröhlich, 1981, fig. 47).

This ornament may date from the first half of the 20th century.

Size: 11.3 cm
Weight: 41 gm

1034-27 **Plate 53**

198
Côte d'Ivoire
Lagoons area

Lozenge-shaped ornament of gilded white metal, perhaps silver.

This is another example of the design called by the Ebrie *kontro bie*, "female crab". Like the last it has been modelled from wax threads with a design of openwork loops. Four circular holes have been made at each end of the lozenge. There were originally two suspension loops

(one now missing), and around them are the remains of six crudely removed casting sprues.

This work is typical of products from the lagoons area. It may date from the first half of the 20th century.

Size: 9.4 cm
Weight: 31 gm

1034-26 **Plate 53**

199
Côte d'Ivoire
Lagoons area

Human face on a stylised ram's head with downward-curving horns.

This ornament has been painstakingly modelled from wax threads, those forming the face being smoothed over. The face is not in Baule style, but has a broad nose, a ropework moustache and beard, crudely rendered eyes, and open triangular nostrils. There are remains of four casting sprues on the head and three around the suspension loops.

Ram's head castings with a superimposed human face are still made by the Ebrie goldsmiths at Anna. This example is characteristic of lagoons style. Baule goldsmiths interviewed in 1986 attributed this casting to the south, as did a Nzima goldsmith at Grand Bassam. The Nzima smith interpreted it as a "horned fetish figure for adoring".

Other examples of this combined human face and ram's horns are known: see for instance Bardon, 1948, plate 15, and Fischer, Himmelheber and Fröhlich, 1981, fig. 47. Both of these pieces are likely to be from the lagoons area; one came from the Géraudel collection and the other was exhibited at Abidjan in 1934.

The present casting may date from the late 19th or early 20th century.
Acquired by J. Müller from E. Ascher in January 1939

Size: 12.5 cm
Weight: 77 gm

1034-40 **Plate 53**

200
Côte d'Ivoire
Lagoons area

Stylised ram's head with horns pointing downwards.

A slightly asymmetrical casting, modelled in wax threads, with four crudely cut triangular apertures. Remains of three casting sprues can be seen around the suspension loops.

Stylistically this piece is inferior to Baule work, but resembles other castings with cut-out triangles from south-eastern Côte d'Ivoire. The design remains popular among Ebrie goldsmiths, who call it *gose*, "male sheep, ram". Though not made by Baule goldsmiths, the form is familiar to them; they name it as *bwa trɛ* (ram's head) or *bwa wue* (ram's horns), and cite the proverb: *Mi umien wo mi wue nu*, "My strength is in my horns." Here the ram signifies the chief, for it is powerful, intelligent and wise. A similar explanation was given in the lagoons area.

Charles Ratton, writing about 1950, noted that most of the ram's head ornaments known to him had entered European collections in the previous twenty years (1930–50), although a few were older. He cited several examples from the lagoons area: one, in the Géraudel collection, from the Adiukru village of Cofrou, and four others that came from the chief of Jackville (an Alladian village west of Abidjan). However Géraudel, who lived in the region for some years, believed that most gold ornaments of the Alladians were made by Baule goldsmiths (Ratton, 1951, pp. 143, 148).

This casting is likely to date from the first half of the 20th century. It was formerly in the collection of R. Bédiat, who went to Côte d'Ivoire about 1928, and died about 1962.
Ex coll. R. Bédiat

Size: 9.7 cm
Weight: 50 gm
1034-20   **Plate 53**

201
Côte d'Ivoire
Lagoons area (?)
Elephant.

Modelled from wax threads, with openwork panels of lattice and bisected spirals. The ears are modelled from plain wax sheet. No suspension rings. Remains of 22 casting sprues on the lower parts of the head, body, feet and tail.

A number of related elephant castings exist, both in gold and brass. In an American collection there is one of very similar appearance in gold, that differs only in having bisected spiral ears and a trunk that points downwards instead of outwards (Ratton, 1975, p. 44). Another openwork elephant in brass, of larger size and finer workmanship, is in an Abidjan private collection; it appears to be older and has a rich dark patina.

In Abidjan, several local *antiquaires* attributed the present casting to the Baule. This was, however, denied by Baule goldsmiths, who regarded it as a southern casting, possibly from the Anyi or Atie region. The southern origin seems more probable; it may even have come from an Ebrie workshop.

In both the Baule and lagoons area the elephant was seen as representing the invincible power of the chief. A Nzima goldsmith of Grand Bassam remarked that "a trap cannot catch the elephant. As it is king it will just walk over the trap and break it." The same idea was expressed by a Baule goldsmith with the proverb:

Sui tia aya su ɔ kloua fandi man.

If the elephant walks on a trap it does not close.

(The chief is too powerful to be caught).

This casting may date from about the second quarter of the 20th century. It was formerly in the collection of Roger Bédiat, and may have been acquired by him directly from the maker's workshop, in the 1930s or 1940s.
Ex coll. R. Bédiat

Size: 8.8 cm
Weight: 66 gm
1007-73   **Plate 54**

202
Côte d'Ivoire
Lagoons area (?)
Stylised leopard.

The head and tail are modelled from wax threads, and the body built up from 57 spirals arranged in rows. There are remains of six casting sprues to the rear. The casting stands on a rectangular base, and there are no suspension rings.

Baule goldsmiths thought this might be an Anyi or Abron casting, but a lagoons origin seems more likely: the presence of a stand and the absence of suspension loops suggest that this casting was not worn but intended for display in a public exhibition of wealth. Such displays are characteristic of the lagoons region.

For other gold leopards cast in openwork spirals, see Ratton, 1975, p. 63 (identified only as an "animal"), and Kamer, 1979, no. 23 (described as a "stylised reptile").

According to one Ebrie man, the leopard shows the ingratitude of false friends. He gave the following story: "The leopard and the cat were once great friends, but the leopard didn't know how to hunt. So the cat taught him how to use his right hand in hunting for food. One day the leopard tried to catch the cat with his right hand. The cat said: Why did you try to catch me? I didn't want to teach you to hunt with the left hand. So the cat became annoyed and went to live in the town."

This casting may date from around the first three decades of the 20th century.
Acquired by J. Müller from Charles Ratton in July 1939

Size: 8 cm
Weight: 58 gm
1034-5   **Plate 54**

203
Côte d'Ivoire
Lagoons area
Cow.

Modelled from wax threads, with open lattice forming the body. A triangular aperture has been cut below each ear (similar to the apertures on the ram's head, no. 200, and the terrapin, no. 209 – both lagoons area pieces). There is an extraordinary number of casting sprues: remains of about 25 can be seen on the lower parts of the head, body, feet and tail.

There are no loops for suspension, suggesting that this casting may not have been intended to be worn. It was probably made to be exhibited on a table at one of the public displays of wealth popular in the lagoons area.

For a bovine of similar appearance, with lattice panels for the body but with upward-curving horns, see Kamer, 1979, no. 28. Other animals such as hens and a snail are known in the same style, perhaps from the same workshop (*ibid.*, nos. 22, 24). Kamer attributes the snail to the Adiukru.

The present casting is also in very similar style to nos. 201 (elephant) and 207 (catfish) in this catalogue. The workshop or workshops concerned may have specialised in animal

representations. One distinctive feature of the style is the rendering of small parts such as ears (on the cow and elephant) and pelvic fins and tail (on the fish) from plain undecorated sheets of wax. (In contrast, a Baule caster would probably have used spirals or bisected spirals for these details). The use of lattice panels is also a striking feature of the style.

Baule goldsmiths regarded this cow as a "foreign" casting, and a lagoons origin seems likely. Ebrie and Nzima informants identified it as a bush cow (despite the horns, which resemble those of a domestic cow). One interpreted it as meaning: "Always persevere; don't withdraw before any obstacle."

This casting may date from around the second quarter of the 20th century. It was formerly in the collection of Roger Bédiat, and may have been new when acquired by him.
Ex coll. R. Bédiat

Size: 11.2 cm
Weight: 83 gm
1007-72   **Plate 54**

204
Côte d'Ivoire
South-eastern region
Pangolin.

This animal's body has been modelled in wax threads, over which the scales have been placed in rows. There are no suspension rings. Along the lower parts of the body are the remains of about 18 casting sprues.

This is a superbly modelled casting that probably represents the Giant Ground Pangolin (*Manis gigantea*). Growing up to six feet long, this pangolin is powerful enough to kill most attacking animals with its tail and claws. It has even been known to kill an attacking leopard. It is found in both forest and savanna.

Informants saw this casting as representing a chief: "Just as the pangolin is a very fearsome animal, so everyone should fear the chief."

This casting differs greatly in style form lagoons goldwork, and one may be correct in attributing it to one of the Akan kingdoms close to the Ghana frontier – Anyi or Abron. By reason of its fine workmanship and unusual weight it may have come from the "treasure" of an Akan king. It was collected by Roger Bédiat in the Côte d'Ivoire, probably in the 1930s or 1940s, and may date from the late 19th or early 20th century.
Ex coll. R. Bédiat

Size: 13.4 cm
Weight: 130 gm
1007-71   **Plate 54**

205
Côte d'Ivoire
Probably lagoons area
Chicken.

Modelled from wax threads. Remains of five casting sprues.

Goldsmiths in Bouake regarded this as a Baule work, and one man cited for it the following proverb:

Akɔwa n'ga ɔ mɛtɛn i ni yo di klanna sɔwa.

It is the chick that stays close to its mother that eats the cricket's leg.

(If you stay near a wise man, you benefit from his advice).

In style, however, this ornament seems more likely to be a lagoons casting. It may date from the first half of the 20th century. It was published by Charles Ratton in 1951, when in the collection of Pierre Matisse.

Ex coll. Pierre Matisse, New York

Size: 9 cm
Weight: 39 gm
1034-57 **Plate 55**

206

Côte d'Ivoire
Lagoons area

Chicken holding a seed in its beak.

This casting was modelled in wax thread with openwork designs. There are two square apertures in the neck (similar to those on the convex disc, no. 210), and circular holes in the neck and tail (similar to those on the lozenge-shaped ornament, no. 198). It is probably from a lagoons workshop, dating perhaps from the 1920s or 30s.

A very similar casting of a chicken, perhaps from the same workshop, was published in 1955 (*Les Arts Africains*, Cercle Volney, Paris, 1955, no.143).

Acquired by J. Müller before 1939

Size: 8 cm
Weight: 41 gm
1034-139 **Plate 55**

207

Côte d'Ivoire
Lagoons area

Catfish of base metal, perhaps gilded brass.

This has been modelled from wax threads that have been subsequently smoothed. A section of open lattice forms the centre of the body. The pelvic fin and tail are modelled from wax sheet; dorsal and pectoral fins are indicated by lengths of casting sprue. There are remains of five sprues around the suspension loops.

Baule goldsmiths attributed this casting to the lagoons people. They offered the proverb:

Jue ble be goua akpa su, kun bu mɛn i mangu lwa di man.

The fish on the griddle cannot eat each other's tails.

(All are now equal; none is stronger than the other.)

At Grand Bassam it was said that "the catfish always hides and doesn't show itself since it is very intelligent. Even when it is killed and put in the pot it wants to see the bottom of the pot." An Ebrie man interpreted it as meaning: "When you fish some people say you fish for nothing, but one day you will make a catch."

This casting may date from the first half of the 20th century.

Size: 9 cm
Weight: 41 gm
1034-21 **Plate 55**

208

Côte d'Ivoire
Lagoons area

Tortoise.

This casting has been finely modelled from wax threads, with an openwork design formed by rows of bisected spirals. There are remains of eleven casting sprues.

Baule casters interviewed in 1986 attributed this ornament to the south. A Nzima goldsmith of Grand Bassam saw it as representing foresight: "The tortoise is very proud of itself because it is already in its coffin. The day it dies it doesn't need a coffin." (This interpretation is a paraphrase of an Akan proverb).

The casting may date from the 1920s or 1930s.
Acquired by J. Müller in 1942

Size: 9.5 cm
Weight: 51 gm
1034-4 **Plate 55**

209

Côte d'Ivoire
Lagoons area

Tortoise, freshwater terrapin or turtle.

This casting resembles a flat-bodied terrapin, but the form is stylised and it may equally be intended as a tortoise or turtle. The modelling is in wax threads, with four squares of open lattice and two rows of openwork triangles.

This ornament is typical of lagoons style. The Ebrie call it *guprɛ*, "tortoise". An Ebrie from the lagoons village of Petit Cocody saw it as representing a well-known Akan proverb: "Like the tortoise within its shell, a man's thoughts are hidden inside him." At Grand Bassam a Nzima goldsmith said it would be worn by a third or an eighth son, or by twins, to show their special position in the family.

This casting may date from the 1920s or 30s.
Acquired by J. Müller from E. Ascher in January 1939

Size: 10.6 cm
Weight: 54 gm
1034-37 **Plate 56**

210

Côte d'Ivoire
Lagoons area

Convex disc.

This casting has been built up from wax threads, and has four irregularly placed square apertures. Two suspension loops are placed on the rim and one at the highest point of the dome. There are remains of seven casting sprues, one still present to a length of 3 mm.

Informants could give no name for this object, which comes from a lagoons workshop. The modelling is inferior to Baule work.

This casting may date from the first half of the 20th century. It was sold by Christie's in 1973.

Size: 8.8 cm
Weight: 52 gm
1034-56 **Plate 56**

211

Côte d'Ivoire
Lagoons area

Human face in the centre of an open hand.

This may be a relatively early piece, on which the goldsmith has expended considerable care and effort. It is elaborately modelled from wax threads, and (as with no. 199), those forming the face have been smoothed over. The surface of the hand is profusely ornamented with bisected spirals, triangles and latticework, and there is a row of seven openwork triangles along each side of the hand. The original casting was defective as the lower part of four fingers are missing; this has been made good by a skillful burnt-in repair, using four sprues. Elsewhere there are remains of eight crudely removed casting sprues.

Despite the care lavished on this piece, the metal is of poor quality, being little more than gold-washed brass.

In style this casting does not resemble Baule work, but comes without doubt from the lagoons region, where the superimposed human face is a common Ebrie motif. Baule goldsmiths suggest that this ornament might represent the following proverb:

Be kloua fa be sa kungba be bo man ndɛ.

You can't use only a single hand to clap.

(Co-operation is necessary; you need the help of others in life.)

Ebrie and Nzima informants gave rather different interpretations. To one man it indicated that "gold" (money) comes to those who work: "My hand brings me wealth." According to a Nzima smith: "The face means a person's intelligence. Even though you may try to cheat me I still have my intelligence, and I can always succeed by my own efforts. I worked for you but you did not pay me. But my hands are not cut off and I can still work to live."

This casting may date from the late 19th century.
Acquired by J. Müller from E. Ascher in July 1939

Size: 13.1 cm
Weight: 110 gm
1034-2 **Plate 56**

212

Côte d'Ivoire
Unknown provenance

Pendant of a human head. Gold heavily alloyed with cuprous metal.

This and the following head are in a curious style whose provenance has not yet been determined. They do not resemble traditional Baule castings, nor those from the south-east (though present Baule goldsmiths attributed them to the lagoons area). It is not impossible that they were produced for the French tourist market in the 1920s or 30s, perhaps in the vicinity of Grand Bassam or Abidjan, but the question of their origin remains open. They are competently cast, but the poor alloy makes it unlikely that they were intended for use as gold display pieces in a traditional context.

The present head is elongated, with a broad bun-shaped hairstyle. There are no ears or beard. The mouth is circular and protruding, with a large ring set vertically over it. Scarification consists of large cat's whiskers on the cheeks, and small pellets on cheeks and eyebrows. There are two small suspension loops at the top of the head, with the remains of five casting sprues around them.

The ring over the mouth is a unique feature which suggests that the casting was intended to be hung upside down, perhaps under a stool in the manner of a trophy head. (There are, however, no signs of wear on the inner surface of the ring to suggest that it has actually been used in this way.) A Nzima goldsmith at Grand Bassam interpreted this feature as showing that the head represented a slave: "When his mouth is closed he can say nothing. He doesn't have the right to open his mouth to speak."
Acquired by J. Müller before 1940
Size: 13.4 cm
Weight: 120 gm
1034-10   **Plate 56**

213
Côte d'Ivoire
Unknown provenance

Pendant of a human head. Gold heavily alloyed with cuprous metal.

In style this piece is very similar to the last. The fabric of the two castings is almost identical, and they may well be from the same hand.

This casting has been modelled in wax threads laid over an irregular core shape, the threads being subsequently smoothed. The hairstyle consists of five pellets. There are no ears or beard. The nose is broad and bulbous, and the mouth crudely rendered by a horizontal depression. Scarification consists of large cat's whiskers radiating from each corner of the mouth, diagonal lines from nose to jaw, and various pellets. There are two suspension loops at the top of the head with remains of three casting sprues around them.

Both Ebrie and Nzima informants interpreted this as a portrait of a king: "He must always be obeyed and his orders are always carried out." However, the absence of a beard makes it unlikely that this is a royal portrait. The diagonal scarifications on the cheek suggest that it may rather be intended as a foreigner from the savanna of northern Ghana or Burkina Faso, where such marks are common. Like the last casting it may perhaps be intended to represent a slave.
Acquired by J. Müller before 1940
Size: 10 cm
Weight: 110 gm
1034-11   **Plate 56**

214
Côte d'Ivoire/Ghana border region
Perhaps Anyi or Abron

Human head of gold alloyed with cuprous metal, heavily tarnished.

In style this head resembles neither Baule nor lagoons work, but gives the impression of being

an Akan casting. It appears to come from the Côte d'Ivoire/Ghana border region.

The head is modelled from wax sheet spread over an elongated egg-shaped core. Eyes, nose and lips are rendered naturalistically, the forehead is domed, and the hairstyle consists of fifteen corkscrew tufts and two large bisected spirals set diagonally. There is no beard or moustache. Ears are indicated only by small curved lines of applied wax thread. The facial scarification, however, is elaborate: small cat's whiskers at the side of the mouth, three short vertical lines on the nose, two short diagonal lines and a raised central keloid on the forehead, and two long diagonal lines running from the nose to the jaw.

The casting of this head was imperfect. There are several large holes around the eyes and mouth, and a large burnt-in repair on the left temple. A single casting sprue was placed below the chin, and another at the site of the burnt-in repair. There is no suspension loop.

This casting shows appreciable signs of wear, and may well date from the 19th century. It was acquired in 1969 from a European seller who claimed that it had been "found in a tomb in Baule country, near Bouake, by a French colonial officer." This supposed provenance need not be believed.

While it is difficult to interpret scarification marks, it may be noted that the cat's whiskers and central keloid on this head also occur on an early brass shrine figure from the Brong (Abron) region of Ghana (see Ross and Garrard, 1983, p. 47). On the other hand the diagonal lines from nose to jaw are not used by the Akan; instead they are common in the savanna of northern Ghana and Burkina Faso. This suggests that the head represents a non-Akan person, and presumably not a chief since he is unbearded. The casting may therefore be an Akan trophy head, representing either a slave or a foreign enemy killed in battle.
Size: 8.5 cm
Weight: about 75 gm
1034-38   **Plate 57 and cover**

215
Côte d'Ivoire
Baule

Gold pendant of a human head (*sran trɛ*).

Goldsmiths in and around Bouake identify this head as a casting in Baule style. It is one of the smallest examples known. The basic form was modelled from wax threads laid over an egg-shaped core. The mouth, as usual in Baule art, is set very low down on the face, and there is a projecting spike (representing a moustache) at each corner. The ears are formed from tiny bisected spirals, and a beard is indicated by vertical incised lines. Below each eye is a cross-shaped scarification mark. The original loops for suspension, which would have been present at the top of the head, have been removed.

This casting is likely to date from the 19th century. The gold is about 9–10 carats.
Size: 2.9 cm
Weight: 6 gm
1034-41   **Plate 57**

216
Côte d'Ivoire
Baule

Gold pendant of a human head.

Baule goldsmiths to whom a photograph of this head was shown in 1986 (at Bouake and N'gata Dolikro) expressed great admiration for it. They declared that it was in true Baule style, and commented on the quality of the modelling and casting.

The head is clearly from the same workshop as the following one (no. 217), which is said to have come from Sakassou, about 42 kilometres south-west of Bouake.

The basic form has been modelled in wax over an egg-shaped core. The mouth is set at the bottom of the face, with a projecting spike at each corner. The nose is long and narrow. Ears and beard are formed from tiny bisected spirals. The hairstyle consists of 27 corkscrew spiral tufts arranged in three parallel rows, while other facial hair is rendered by applied surface ornament. There is no facial scarification.

This head exhibits the fine, delicate workmanship of a Baule master goldsmith. It dates probably from the 19th century, and was in Europe by the 1930s. In 1951 it was published by Ratton (fig. 70). At that time a suspension loop was present at the top of the head; this has since been removed.

Another fine head possibly by the same goldsmith is in the collection of the Institut Fondamental d'Afrique Noire (see Bardon, 1948, plate XI, no. B.47.2017).
Acquired by J. Müller from E. Ascher in January 1939
Size: 4.3 cm
Weight: 20 gm
1034-140   **Plate 57**

217
Côte d'Ivoire
Baule

Gold pendant of a human head.

This casting is clearly by the same hand as the preceding one, though differing from it in detail. It is said to have come from Sakassou, south-west of Bouake, where a family of goldsmiths is still active.

The basic form is modelled over an egg-shaped core. A small raised keloid is present at the centre of the forehead, but there is otherwise no facial scarification. Ears and beard are rendered by small bisected spirals, and a small braid of hair descends to the right ear. The original suspension loop is present.

Like the last, this head probably dates from the 19th century.
Size: 4 cm
Weight: 14 gm
1034-184   **Plate 57**

218
Côte d'Ivoire
Baule

Gold pendant of a human head.

This head is thought to have been made south

of Bouake, perhaps in the region of Tiebissou or Sakassou.

It is modelled over an egg-shaped core. The mouth is set low down on the face, with a projecting spike at each corner. The ears are bisected spirals, while a beard is indicated by five pinched wax threads. The hairstyle is formed from 21 spiral tufts set in a row. There is no facial scarification. A small casting flaw on the forehead has been made good with a burnt-in repair. One suspension loop is present at the top of the head.

This fine casting is likely to date from the 19th century.

Acquired by J. Müller from E. Ascher in July 1939

Size: 6 cm

Weight: 31 gm

1034-6   **Plate 58**

219
Côte d'Ivoire
Baule

Gold pendant of a human head, perhaps alloyed with cuprous metal.

This head, like the preceding examples, has been modelled over an egg-shaped core. The model was formed from wax threads laid horizontally and then smoothed with a spatula. The nose is long and narrow, and the mouth set at the bottom of the head, with a projecting spike at each corner. There are bisected spiral ears and a short plaited beard. The hairstyle consists of five spiral tufts on each side of the head. There is no facial scarification. Three suspension rings were once present, but one is now missing and the others are blocked by surplus metal.

The casting is thin, and was not entirely perfect. Several small holes remain in the forehead, and other casting flaws have been made good by burnt-in repairs to both cheeks. These repairs illustrate the great care that the goldsmith took to produce a visually acceptable casting.

Present Baule goldsmiths regard this as a work in characteristic Baule style, but its exact place of origin is not known. It probably dates from the 19th century, and was in the collection of Olivier Le Corneur by the 1950s.
Ex coll. Olivier Le Corneur, Paris

Size: 7.8 cm

Weight: 34 gm

1034-18   **Plate 58**

220
Côte d'Ivoire
South-eastern region

Gold pendant of a human head.

This remarkable head was not recognised as Baule by any of the goldsmiths interviewed in 1986. Baule smiths attributed it to the south, but it may equally have come from the east, towards the Ghana frontier. Its precise place of origin is unknown. Ebrie and Nzima elders claimed that it was the portrait of an ancestor king.

The basic form has been built up from wax threads, which, as in many works from south-eastern Côte d'Ivoire, have been left unsmoothed to provide a ridged surface. This surface has been elaborately ornamented with applied wax threads: seven vertical double lines on the forehead, and zigzags above them; a seven-rayed circle on each cheek; a band of decoration down the nose and across the nostrils; and two diagonal lines between nose and mouth. There are six suspension rings at the top of the head, and around them, clearly visible, the remains of five casting sprues. On gold from southern Côte d'Ivoire it is common to find remains of multiple casting sprues, often crudely removed, whereas on good Baule work these are rarely visible and never obtrusive.

But although in overall appearance and technique this head is far removed from Baule style, it has features suggestive of Baule influence. The original core was egg-shaped, although more elongated than on Baule heads. The ears are formed from bisected spirals. The mouth is set low down, with a projecting spike at each corner. Hair and beard are rendered by small spiral tufts. One might hazard a guess that the maker, though himself probably not a Baule, had some familiarity with Baule style.

In the 1950s this head was in the collection of Olivier Le Corneur. It presumably dates from the 19th or early 20th century.
Ex coll. Olivier Le Corneur, Paris

Size: 9.1 cm

Weight: 85 gm

1034-17   **Plate 59**

221
Côte d'Ivoire
South-eastern region

Gold pendant of a human head.

This very fine head differs considerably both from the preceding example and from Baule work. The only features suggestive of Baule influence are the ovoid core shape, the bisected spiral ears, and perhaps the carefully modelled circular nostrils.

The basic form has been constructed from wax threads, which have been left unsmoothed. The nose is narrow, but with broad nostrils. No mouth is shown. A triangular aperture has been cut in each cheek. Facial scarifications include two vertical lines under each eye, and a grid of small marks beside each ear. There are two suspension loops and around them the remains of six casting sprues.

A number of these features suggest a south-eastern origin, notably the wax threadwork, triangular apertures and visible multiple sprues. The Baule caster Kouassi Kouassi of N'gata Dolikro attributed it to the lagoons area of the south-east, saying that it was certainly not of Baule origin. It has been published both as Baule (Soupault, 1957, p. 68) and as an Ebrie work from Ouelle (Allemand, 1956, p. 16 and fig. 54). The latter provenance appears confused, for the Ebrie live in the vicinity of Abidjan, whereas the small town of Ouelle lies 220 kilometres further north, in the territory of the eastern Baule. It is of course possible that this head is an Ebrie work that somehow found its way to Ouelle, but in the absence of clear documentation its true origin remains unknown.

This head may date from the 19th or early 20th century. It was in the collection of Le Corneur-Roudillon by the 1950s.
Acquired by Gertrud Dübi-Müller in the 1950s

Size: 6.4 cm

Weight: 25 gm

1034-8   **Plate 58**

222
Côte d'Ivoire
South-eastern region

Gold pendant of a human head.

This highly stylised head has been modelled with wax threads over a shallow ovoid core. The eyes and long nose are prominently modelled in relief, while the mouth has been reduced to a small hole. Ears and hair tufts have been omitted, greatly increasing the dramatic impact. Facial scarification consists of three short parallel lines beside each eye, and a "cat's whisker" mark on each cheek. There are two suspension loops, and the remains of ten crudely removed casting sprues around them.

The "cat's whisker" marks probably do not denote a specific ethnic group. They are used by several Ivoirian peoples. Among the Baule they are said to be placed on a third-born child whose elder siblings have died.

Diby Koffi, a well-known brass-caster and goldsmith at Bouake, declared that this head was not Baule work. He attributed it to the Ebrie or Adiukru in the south. An almost identical head in the IFAN collection, probably by the same hand, has been published by Bardon (1948, plate VI, no. B.47.1987).

This head was probably made between 1900 and the 1930s.
Acquired by J. Müller before 1940

Size: 8.5 cm

Weight: 55 gm

1034-7   **Plate 59**

223
Côte d'Ivoire
South-eastern region

Gold pendant of a human head.

This head is stylistically related to the last, but of more abstract form. The model was made from wax threads laid over a shallow ovoid core. Basic features have been reduced to eyes and a nose. There is no further detail other than six triangular apertures cut into the model. At the top of the head are the remains of six casting sprues around the suspension loops.

Baule goldsmiths attributed this head to the south-east, and it may well be Ebrie work from the lagoons region, made around the 1930s. Until recently Ebrie goldsmiths at Anna near Bingerville were still casting heads in this style.
Acquired by J. Müller before 1939

Size: 6.9 cm

Weight: 28 gm

1034-9   **Plate 58**

224
Côte d'Ivoire
South-eastern region
Gold pendant of a human head.
This head is almost identical to the last apart from its larger size. It appears to be considerably alloyed with cuprous metal. Probably circa mid-20th century.
Size: 8.8 cm
Weight: 41 gm
1034-16   **Plate 58**

225
Côte d'Ivoire
Western lagoons area (?)
Gilded pendant of a human head.
This unusual abstract head is modelled in wax threads, and consists merely of eyes and a nose with four large panels of open mesh. The gilding has worn away from the high points of the nose to reveal a whitish metal.
This casting entered the collection of Sadruddin Aga Khan in the 1960s or 70s, and his sale catalogue describes it as an Atie work from Dabou. This attribution is confused. Dabou does not lie in Atie territory, but is an Adiukru village on the northern shore of the long coastal lagoon, about 50 kilometres west of Abidjan. Given the extreme stylisation of this pendant head, an Adiukru provenance would seem not implausible.
There is said to have been a local goldsmith in Dabou who worked up to the 1940s, and who made gold ornaments to be worn at festivals. This casting presumably dates from before that time.
Size: 10.2 cm
Weight: 43 gm
1034-58   **Plate 59**

226
Côte d'Ivoire
South-eastern region (?)
Pendant of a human head on an elongated oval plaque. Cuprous metal lightly alloyed with gold.
This casting has several Baule-style features. It has been modelled on an egg-shaped core. The ears are formed from bisected spirals. The mouth is set low down, with projecting moustaches at each corner, and the plaited goatee beard also occurs in Baule casting. The hairstyle consists of five corkscrew tufts arranged in a circle, surmounted by a plaited ring.
Despite these points of resemblance, this head mystified every Baule goldsmith to whom a photo was shown (1986). They were disturbed by the oval plaque, which they declared to be a non-Baule feature. In the Rietberg-Museum in Zurich there are two gold heads of similar style but without plaques (Rietberg nos. RAF 578 and 579). Baule goldsmiths were equally perplexed by photographs of these. They agreed that the ears, mouth and beard were in Baule style, but pointed out that details of the coiffures appeared non-Baule.

These observations suggest that the heads on plaques were made further south, perhaps in the coastal lagoons region. Some are clearly lagoons work; others such as this head could have been made by an immigrant Baule caster in one of the coastal towns.
The mysterious plaque form would seem to be of European inspiration (see Chapter 4).
This head may date from the early 20th century. When purchased by Josef Müller in 1939 it was thought to be a Baule goldweight. Acquired by J. Müller from Roudillon senior in July 1939
Size: head 7.4 cm, plaque 13.2 cm
Weight: 99 gm
1034-12   **Plate 59**

227
Côte d'Ivoire
Baule
Pendant of a human face on an openwork medallion.
This pendant is said to come from the region of Botro, a Baule village north-west of Bouake. It has seen some use, and may date from the first half of the 20th century. Its style is characteristic of work from the Baule region.
Size: 5.1 cm
Weight: 30 gm
1034-220   **Plate 60**

228
Côte d'Ivoire
Baule
Flat disc-shaped bead of openwork design, incorporating a human face.
This unusual casting represents a combination of bead and pendant forms. It was probably intended to be worn as a central medallion in a necklace.
The openwork design includes an outer row of triangular apertures, which at first sight call to mind the triangular apertures found on many gold castings from the lagoons region. There is, however, a significant difference of technique. Those on lagoons goldwork are usually no more than holes crudely cut in the wax model. On this bead, in contrast, carefully made triangular segments have been added to the wax model to create the openwork effect. Goldsmiths in Bouake insist that this bead is of Baule rather than lagoons origin. Their claim is borne out not only by the difference in the technique used to create the openwork effect (additive rather than subtractive), but by the style of modelling of the face, and by the higher standard of workmanship in general.
Size: 5.1 cm
Weight: 30 gm
1034-222   **Plate 60**

229
Côte d'Ivoire
Baule
Large tubular bead.
This unusually massive bead has been built up from wax threads, and bisected spiral ornament

has been added on one face. It is not a recent casting, and may date from the first half of the 20th century if not earlier.
Size: 5.7 cm
Weight: 24 gm
1034-221   **Plate 60**

230
Côte d'Ivoire
Baule
Necklace of 27 cast gold beads.
The largest rectangular bead is a particularly splendid example of Baule openwork casting. There are also two perfect examples of smaller disc-beads with a pellet border. The smallest beads, all of very fine quality, include several unusual forms such as a lion's claw.
Total length: 37 cm
Weight: 160 gm
1034-223   **Plate 60**

231
Côte d'Ivoire
Baule
Necklace of 23 cast gold beads, mostly discs and rectangles.
The rectangular beads are called *srala* ("bamboo door") or *boloa atrε*. The bamboo door is said to symbolise the chief; it sees what is happening both inside and outside the house, just as the chief knows all that is happening both in his village and outside. Large gold beads of this form are sometimes hung in front of a chief on public occasions, suspended from a string. Smaller examples were cast both in gold and brass, and a few are known in silver.
The disc-shaped spiral beads are called *sεnzε* ("setting sun") or *taliε*. The basic form is obtained from a tightly coiled thread of beeswax. Older examples such as these often have threads of incredible fineness, exhibiting the Baule goldsmith's greatest skill. The finest castings are thin and brittle, and have a tendency to crack if not handled with care. Beads of this form have long been popular among the Baule and they are still made today, notably in the village of N'gata Dolikro south of Bouake. These modern products are relatively coarse, the wax threads being thicker and the workmanship less skilful.
Total length: 75 cm
Weight: 160 gm
1034-232   **Plate 61**

232
Côte d'Ivoire
Baule
Necklace of 23 cast gold beads and a small gold pellet bell. The beads include discs, rectangles and tubular forms.
Total length: 75 cm
Weight: 152 gm
1034-235   **Plate 62**

233
Côte d'Ivoire
Baule
Necklace of 24 cast gold beads comprising discs, rectangles and tubular forms.
Total lenght: 78 cm
Weight: 166 gm
1034-233 **Plate 63**

234
Côte d'Ivoire
Baule
Necklace of 23 gold and 3 silver beads, including a variety of characteristic Baule bead forms. There are 11 rectangles, 10 discs, 2 tapered tubular beads, a horn and two beads formed from bisected spirals.

The small tusk-shaped bead is called *awɛ*, a horn, while the tubular and elongated beads are *ayɛkpɛ*.

The three silver beads on this necklace are considerably rarer than those in gold. Two are in the form of discs with openwork spiral designs resembling the "back of the tortoise" design (*akyekyedeɛ akyi*) made by the Akan of Ghana.
Size of central rectangular bead: 6.1 cm
Total length: 83 cm
Weight: 150 gm
1034-191 **Plate 64**

235
Côte d'Ivoire
Baule
Necklace of 21 gold beads. This necklace is composed of 17 alternating discs and rectangles with 4 tapering tubular beads.
Size of central rectangle: 7.4 cm
Total length: 76.5 cm
Weight: 198 gm
1034-192 **Plate 66**

236
Côte d'Ivoire
Baule
Necklace of 21 gold beads.
On this necklace 19 discs and rectangles alternate, and there are also 2 tubular beads (one with openwork designs).
Size of central disc bead: 6.7 cm
Total length: 84 cm
Weight: 252 gm
1034-193 **Plate 65**

237
Côte d'Ivoire
Baule
Necklace of 19 cast gold beads.
Total length: 62.2 cm
Weight: 142 gm
1034-218 **Plate 67**

238
Côte d'Ivoire
Baule
Disc-shaped spiral bead of cast gold. This is another large bead of exceptionally fine workmanship.
Size: 7.6 cm
Weight: 34 gm
1034-172 **Plate 68**

239
Côte d'Ivoire
Baule
Disc-shaped spiral bead of cast gold, with an openwork design forming a central sun motif.

This very large bead may have formed the central pendant for a woman's necklace, or part of a chief's regalia. It has a finely plaited border and bisected spiral ornaments on the central shaft. The threads are coiled at 21 to the centimetre. The central sun motif identifies the bead as *sɛnzɛ*.
19th or early 20th century.
Acquired by J. Müller before 1942
Size: 7.6 cm
Weight: 58 gm
1034-39 **Plate 68**

240
Côte d'Ivoire
Baule
Disc-shaped spiral bead of cast gold, with designs of bisected spirals.
Size: 4.9 cm
Weight: 18 gm
1034-225 **Plate 68**

241
Côte d'Ivoire
Baule
Disc-bead with central motif of a crocodile (*ɛlɛngɛ*).

This is an old and well used bead with distinct signs of wear. It is rare to find animal motifs on such older Baule beads; they have become common only in recent times. This bead can clearly be distinguished from modern work by the much finer wax threads used for making the disc and the plaited border.
Size: 5.8 cm
Weight: 18 gm
1034-298 **Plate 68**

242
Côte d'Ivoire
Baule
Small gold pellet bell (*glin*) from a necklace.
Pellet bells served many purposes. Some were worn by dancers, spirit mediums and small children, occasionally even by dogs. Others were used to adorn wooden statuettes.
Most are of brass; but a few, cast in gold, are found on Baule necklaces.
Size: 1.5 cm
Weight: 4 gm
1034-299 **Plate 68**

243
Côte d'Ivoire
Baule (?)
Gold pendant in the form of a bellows.
The origin of this finely cast pendant is uncertain, but it may be an example of 19th century Baule goldsmith's work. For an "animal mask" pendant of similar style, attributed to the Baule, see Soupault, 1957, p. 69.

According to one Baule man this bellows (*fa*) represents the wind. He cited the following proverb:
Ahamwan nga ɔ utu sanmlen yo jo baka nio.
The wind that scatters the flour also cools the soup.
(Nothing is entirely bad; some good may come of it. You may think work disagreeable but the result may be worthwhile).
Ex coll. R. Bédiat
Size: 7 cm
Weight: 18 gm
1034-19 **Plate 68**

244
Côte d'Ivoire
Lagoons area (?)
Triangular hair ornament of cast gold.
This small jewel had three suspension loops (one now missing) by which it could be attached to the hair. It was at first thought to be a Baule casting, but goldsmiths at Bouake pointed to the presence of three cut-out triangular apertures in the design, which they say is a non-Baule feature. Instead they suggested that it came from an Ebrie or Adiukru workshop.
Size: 3 cm
Weight: 8 gm
1034-269 **Plate 68**

245
Côte d'Ivoire
Baule
Three rectangular gold beads (*srala* or *boloa atrɛ*) and two tusk-shaped gold beads (*kangale je*) incorporated into a European necklace.

Baule informants named the tusk-shaped beads as *kangale je*, "leopard's tooth". Leopard's teeth are said to symbolise the chief, for this animal like the chief is proud and powerful. Unlike the hyena and other scavengers the leopard only eats meat that it kills itself.
These beads date from the 19th or early 20th century.
Acquired by J. Müller from E. Ascher in 1939
Sizes: 1.9, 2, 3.6, 4.1 and 4.4 cm
Weight: 42 gm
1034-13 **Plate 69**

246
Côte d'Ivoire
Baule
Finger-ring (*samma nga*) with a motif of two small birds.

Baule goldsmiths almost never make finger-rings. The chiefs of this ethnic group wear rings purchased from the Akan, usually from Asante. This ring of local manufacture is therefore a rarity, although not of great aesthetic quality. It seems to be inspired by an Akan model.

The ring was acquired in Bouake.

Size: 3 cm
Weight: 10 gm
1033-94   **Plate 69**

247
Côte d'Ivoire
South-eastern region

Finger-ring with a high dome-shaped bezel divided into six lobes, of which three are decorated with a crocodile, a snake and an unidentified object.

Gold finger-rings of local manufacture are almost unknown among the Baule and lagoons peoples. This ring was not recognised by Baule goldsmiths (despite the fact that Josef Müller acquired it from Charles Ratton in 1939 as a "Baule mushroom ring"). Nor is anything like it at present known from the lagoons region, or from the Akan of Ghana. The most likely provenance may be one of the Akan border kingdoms such as Abron or Anyi.

This splendid ring was presumably made for an important Akan chief. The significance of its dome-shaped motif is not known, though Ross (1986) interprets it as a chief's hat or crown. The ring may date from the late 19th or early 20th century.
Acquired by J. Müller in 1939

Size: 5.1 cm
Weight: 85 gm
1033-3   **Plate 69**

248
Côte d'Ivoire
Baule

Rectangular amulet (*sɛbɛ blawa*) of carved wood covered in gold leaf, suspended from a twine thread.

This may be an imitation of a leather amulet. It is carved with motifs of a crescent moon (*anglo*) and two rectangular beads (*boloa atrɛ*).

Size: 5.4 cm
1034-182   **Plate 70**

249
Côte d'Ivoire
Baule

Hairpin (*kona*) of carved wood covered with gold leaf.

It is said that such hairpins, which generally have two prongs, were worn by men on one side of the head.
20th century.

Size: 13.2 cm
1007-102   **Plate 70**

250
Côte d'Ivoire
Baule

Small comb (*saka* or *kwɛkwɛ*) of carved wood covered with gold leaf.

This is a fairly recent carving in traditional style, probably from the region of Assabonou. The two birds delicately perched on top of the comb are typical of the Baule love for fine ornament.

Size: 16 cm
1007-183   **Plate 70**

251
Côte d'Ivoire
Baule

Comb (*saka* or *kwɛkwɛ*) of carved wood covered with gold leaf. Early 20th century.

The handle is carved with a face and two imitation brass tacks. There are six tines, bound with brown and black threads.

Gold leaf has been applied in two separate sheets, in front and behind. These are joined and secured at the edges of the comb by tiny staples.

Size: 13 cm
1007-178   **Plate 70**

252
Côte d'Ivoire
Baule

Two knives with gold-leafed handles in a double sheath.

These gold-leafed knives, called *laliɛ blawa*, form part of a chief's accoutrements. A similar pair is illustrated in Ratton, 1951, fig. 109. They represent the Baule proverb:

Laliɛ kungba gbe kla fa se men i bɔbɔ i waka.

The blade of a knife cannot carve its own handle.

(A second knife is necessary to carve a handle for the first. What you cannot do alone, you can achieve through co-operation.)

The blades of these knives are of iron, the sheath of antelope skin with triangular panels of tin (?) and red cloth. Gold leaf is attached to the handles by tiny wire staples, a technique that was abandoned early in this century in favour of glue. These knives may therefore date from the late 19th or early 20th century.

Size: 25.3 cm
1007-169   **Plate 71**

253
Côte d'Ivoire
Baule

Fly-whisk handle surmounted by a parrot, and having at its base two faces and two birds with heads turned backwards. Carved wood covered with gold leaf.

This whisk was acquired in 1959. It dates from about the second quarter of the 20th century, and was probably made in Assabonou. Informants named the main motif as *anyi ako*, "talking parrot", explaining that the parrot, like the chief, knows everything and says whatever he likes. One of the secondary motifs, that of birds with heads turned backwards, is widely known among the Akan of Ghana, where it indicates that one should learn from the wisdom of the past (see no. 182).

Size: 28 cm
1007-15   **Plate 72**

254
Côte d'Ivoire
Baule

Horse-tail fly-whisk, the carved wooden handle covered with gold leaf.

Whisks (*nandwa*) form part of the regalia of chiefs and notables. They are owned in remarkable numbers. Even a minor village notable may have a dozen or more, which are set in front of him on public occasions, piled up in a basin. A Baule chief may himself hold a fly-whisk, unlike the Akan chiefs of Ghana whose whisks are always carried by attendants.

Whisks covered with gold leaf are called *nandwa blawa* in Baule. In this century the main centre for the gold-leafing of carved wooden objects has been the village of Assabonou, south of Bouake, where the technique is still practised. The present whisk was probably made in or near Assabonou, and may date from the third quarter of the 20th century. It is carved with a series of stock motifs: a Baule face, a crescent moon and a rectangular bead.

Informants cited the following proverb in relation to fly-whisks:

Sika tikɛ nandwa sran kungba tra man mu.

Money (gold) is like a fly-whisk, a single person cannot catch it.

(Today you may have money, but tomorrow you will be poor again.)

Many fly-whisks made by the Baule have been purchased by notables in the lagoons region and elsewhere.

Size of handle: 15 cm
1007-100   **Plate 72**

Bibliography

Allemand, M.: *L'Art de l'Afrique noire et "l'Epoque Nègre" de Quelques Artistes Contemporains.* St. Etienne, 1956.

Almada, A.A. de: *Tratado Breve dos Rios de Guiné e Cabo Verde até os Baixos de Santa Ana,* reprinted in A. Brasio, *Monumenta Missionaria Africana,* 2nd series. Lisbon, 1964, vol. 3.

Barbot, J.: *Journal d'un Voyage de Traite en Guinée, à Cayenne et aux Antilles fait par Jean Barbot en 1678–1679,* ed. G. Debien, M. Delafosse and G. Thilmans. Dakar, 1979.

– *Description des Côtes d'Afrique,* ms, 2 vols, Public Record Office. London, 1688.

– *A description of the Coasts of North and South Guinea.* London, 1732.

Bardon, P.: *Collection des Masques d'or baoulé de l'IFAN.* Dakar, 1948.

Bellefond, V. de: *Relation des Costes d'Afrique, appellées Guinea, 1666–7.* Paris, 1669.

Blake, J.W.: *Europeans in West Africa, 1450–1560,* 2 vols. London, 1942.

Boizot, A.: *Bijoux de l'Afrique Noire.* Paris, 1980.

Bosman, W.: *A New and Accurate Description of the Coast of Guinea.* London, 1705.

Bowdich, T.E.: *Mission from Cape Coast Castle to Ashantee.* London, 1819.

Brackenbury, H.: *The Ashanti War: A Narrative,* 2 vols. London, 1874.

Burton, R.F., and Cameron, V.L.: *To the Gold Coast for Gold,* 2 vols. London, 1883.

Cable, M.: *The African Kings.* Chicago, 1983.

Cercle Volney: *Les Arts Africains.* Paris, 1955.

Christensen, J.B.: "The Adaptive Functions of Fanti Priesthood", in *Continuity and Change in African Culture,* ed. W.R. Bascom and M.J. Herskovitz, University of Chicago. Chicago, 1959.

Cole, H.M., and Ross, D.H.: *The Arts of Ghana.* Los Angeles, 1977.

Daniell, W.F.: "On the Ethnography of Akkrah and Adampe, Gold Coast, Western Africa," *Journal of the Ethnological Society,* iv. London, 1852.

Dieterlen, G. and Ligers, Z.: "Contribution à l'Etude des Bijoux Touareg", *Journal de la Société des Africanistes, xlii. 1972.*

Donne, J.B.: "West African Goldwork", *Connoisseur,*194. Feb. 1977, pp.100–106.

Dupuis, J.: *Journal of a Residence in Ashantee.* London, 1824.

Dupuis-Yakouba: *Industries et principales professions des habitants de la région de Tombouctou.* Paris, 1921.

Ehrlich, M.: *A Catalogue of Ashanti art taken from Kumasi in the Anglo-Ashanti war of 1874.* Ph. D. dissertation, Indiana University, 2 vols. 1976.

Elisofon, E.: "Africa's ancient splendor still gleams in the Akan people's golden art", *Smithsonian Magazine.* Jan. 1973, pp. 20–28.

Eudel, P.: *L'Orfèvrerie Algérienne et Tunisienne.* Algiers, 1902.

Fagg, W.: "Ashanti Gold", *Connoisseur,* 185, 743. Jan. 1974, pp. 41–48.

Fischer, E. and Himmelheber, H.: "Das Gold in der Kunst Westafrikas", *Du.* Dec. 1975, pp. 36–49.

– *Das Gold in der Kunst Westafrikas,* Museum Rietberg. Zurich, 1975.

Fischer, A.: *Fastueuse Afrique.* Paris, 1984.

Fleuriot de Langle: "Croisières de la Côte d'Ivoire", *Le Tour du Monde.* 1873(2), pp. 353–400.

Freeman, T.B.: *Journal of two visits to the Kingdom of Ashanti.* London, 1843.

Gabus, J.: *Au Sahara, Arts et Symboles.* Neuchâtel, 1958.

– *Sahara, Bijoux et Techniques.* Boudry, 1984.

– "Contribution à l'étude des bijoux touaregs", *Musée d'Ethnographie.* Neuchâtel, 1971.

Gardi, R.: *African Crafts and Craftsmen.* Berne, 1969.

Garrard, T.F.: *Akan Weights and the Gold Trade.* London, 1980.

Johnson, M.A.: *Black Gold: Goldsmiths, Jewelry and Women in Senegal.* Ph. D. dissertation, Stanford University. 1980.

Kamer, D. and H.: *Akkan Fetish Gold.* Paris, 1979.

Kiethega, J.B.: *L'Or de la Volta Noire.* Paris, 1983.

Kyerematen, A.A.Y.: *Panoply of Ghana.* London, 1964.

Labat, J.B.: *Nouvelle Relation de l'Afrique Occidentale,* 5 vols. Paris, 1728.

Lee, R. (Mrs. Bowdich): *Stories of Strange Lands; and Fragments from the Notes of a Traveller.* London, 1835.

Leuzinger, E.: *African Sculpture.* Zurich, 1963.

Loyer, G.: *Relation du Voyage du Royaume d'Issyny.* Paris, 1714.

Marees, P. de: *Beschryvinghe ende Historische Verhael van het Gout Koninckrijk van Gunea.* Amsterdam, 1602.

Maurice, Sir J.P. (anon.): *The Ashantee War: A Popular Narrative.* London, 1874.

McLeod, M.D.: *The Asante.* London, 1981.

Meyerowitz, E.L.R.: "Some Gold, Bronze and Brass Objects from Ashanti", *Burlington Magazine,* 139:526. London, Jan. 1947, pp. 18–21.

– "Concepts of the soul among the Akan of the Gold Coast", *Africa,* 21(1). Jan. 1951, pp. 24–31.

– *The Sacred State of the Akan.* London, 1951.

Mickelsen, N.R.: "Tuareg Jewelry", *African Arts,* 9(2). 1976, pp. 16–19, 80.

Mille, P., Delafosse, Dandy and Gentil: *Catalogue Raisonné de l'Exposition de la Côte d'Ivoire,* Exposition Universelle. Paris, 1900.

Mollien, G.: *Travels in the Interior of Africa, to the Sources of the Senegal and Gambia.* London, 1820.

Monteil, C.: *Monographie de Djenné.* Tulle, 1903.

Mueller, W.J.: *Die Africanische auf der Guineischen Gold-Cust gelegene Landschafft Fetu.* Hamburg, 1673.

Niangoran-Bouah, G.: *L'Univers Akan des Poids à Peser l'Or,* 3 vols. Abidjan, 1984–1987.

Noll, C., and N'Diaye, F.: *Esprits et Dieux d'Afrique.* Paris, 1980.

Paris, E.: "Bijoux de paille et poupées de cire Sonrai de Tombouctou", *Notes Africaines,* 51. July 1951, pp. 84–88.

Park, M.: *Travels in the Interior Districts of Africa.* London, 1799.

Ratton, C.: "L'Or Fétiche", *L'Art Nègre: Présence Africaine,* 10–11. 1951, pp. 136–155.

– *Fetish Gold,* University Museum, Philadelphia, and the Anko Foundation. Philadelphia, 1975.

Rattray, R.S.: *Religion and Art in Ashanti.* Oxford, 1927.

Reindorf, C.C.: *History of the Gold Coast and Asante.* Basel, 1895.

Robertson, G.A.: *Notes on Africa, particularly those parts which are situated between Cape Verd and the River Congo.* London, 1819.

Ross, D.H.: "The Iconography of Asante Sword Ornaments", *African Arts,* 9(1). 1977, pp. 16–25, 90–91.

– "The Verbal Art of Akan Linguist Staffs", *African Arts,* 16(1). 1982, pp. 56–67.

– "Cast Gold Rings of the Akan", Bulletin No. 30, Musée Barbier-Mueller. Geneva, 1986.

Ross, D.H., and Garrard, T.F.: *Akan Transformations.* Los Angeles, 1983.

Soupault, P.: "Magie des bijoux noirs", *Connaissance des Arts,* 62. April 1957, pp. 68–71.

Zeltner, F. de: "La Bijouterie Indigène en Afrique Occidentale", *Journal de la Société des Africanistes,* 1(1). 1931, pp. 43–49.

Index of Tribes and Places